Salem Church

HISTORY OF WACHOVIA
IN NORTH CAROLINA

HISTORY of WACHOVIA in NORTH CAROLINA

THE UNITAS FRATRUM OR MORAVIAN CHURCH
IN NORTH CAROLINA DURING A
CENTURY AND A HALF...
1752–1902

*From the Original German and English Manuscripts
and Records in the Wachovia Archives,
Salem, North Carolina*

John Henry Clewell, Ph.D.

HERITAGE BOOKS
2012

HERITAGE BOOKS
AN IMPRINT OF HERITAGE BOOKS, INC.

Books, CDs, and more—Worldwide

For our listing of thousands of titles see our website
at
www.HeritageBooks.com

A Facsimile Reprint
Published 2012 by
HERITAGE BOOKS, INC.
Publishing Division
100 Railroad Ave. #104
Westminster, Maryland 21157

Copyright © 1902 Doubleday, Page & Company

— Publisher's Notice —
In reprints such as this, it is often not possible to remove blemishes from the original. We feel the contents of this book warrant its reissue despite these blemishes and hope you will agree and read it with pleasure.

International Standard Book Numbers
Paperbound: 978-1-55613-387-9
Clothbound: 978-0-7884-9190-0

TO MY WIFE
Alice Wolle Clewell
THIS VOLUME
IS AFFECTIONATELY DEDICATED

PREFACE

THIS history is based chiefly on the original manuscripts and records of the Wachovia Archives, deposited in the building of the Historical Society, Salem, North Carolina. The manuscripts from 1752 to 1854 were written in the German language, and from 1855 to the present time in the English language. There is an unbroken file from the first year, and the value of these documents as a part of the general history of North Carolina and the special history of the Moravian Church in Wachovia cannot be overestimated.

The chapters which follow do not attempt to give a full résumé of the contents of these valuable papers. The future student of the history of Wachovia will find matter to fill a number of volumes; biography, religion, education, adventure, finances, industries, are all treated in the Archive records, and we trust that this book may act as an influence to stimulate further research into the story of Wachovia, which is so rich in historical lore, but which has thus far not been given its proper place in the literature of the State and Church.

The task of examining these records was beset with many difficulties. In fact, the writer could not have accomplished the work of translation had it not been for the interested, able, and tireless assistance of Mrs. Josephine Wurreschke, who has during the past four or five years given much time and effort to deciphering the papers, yellow with age and often in broken fragments. Mrs. Wurreschke's labour was not only that of a scholar and expert, but she was also influenced by the motive which comes from the good which she felt she was doing for the church.

Additional sources of information are the following: —
"Moravians in North Carolina." Reichel. 1857.
"Forsyth County." Fries. 1898.
"History of the Moravian Church." Hamilton. 1900.

From Mr. James T. Leinback, Treasurer of the Wachovia Land Office, were received various documents and maps. Articles and tables have been furnished by Bishop Rondthaler, Miss Emma Lehman, Miss Adelaide Fries, Miss L. C. Shaffner, Mr. C. B. Pfohl. Valuable assistance in connection with the preparation and publication of the work has been given by Mr. H. E. Fries, Dr. H. T. Bahnson, Mr. W. S. Pfohl, Dr. J. F. Shaffner, Sr., Mr. J. W. Fries, Mr. Walter H. Page, and other friends, and their interest is thankfully acknowledged.

This book has been written with the hope that church and community may be benefited by a study of our early and more recent history, and that it may in an humble way be instrumental in promoting the cause of Christ.

J. H. C.

WINSTON-SALEM, N.C., 1902.

TABLE OF CONTENTS

CHAPTER I
CAUSES WHICH LED TO THE FOUNDING OF THE MORAVIAN CHURCH IN NORTH CAROLINA 1

CHAPTER II
SPANGENBERG'S EXPLORATION AND SURVEYING TOUR . . 4

CHAPTER III
JOURNEY OF THE FIRST INHABITANTS OF WACHOVIA FROM PENNSYLVANIA TO NORTH CAROLINA 13

CHAPTER IV
THE FIRST YEAR IN WACHOVIA 20

CHAPTER V
INDIAN TROUBLES THREATEN WACHOVIA, AND THE BETHABARA FORT ERECTED 32

CHAPTER VI
WACHOVIA DURING THE FRENCH AND INDIAN WAR . . 44

CHAPTER VII
THE FOUNDING OF BETHANIA AND A TIME OF SORROW . . 53

CHAPTER VIII
BETWEEN THE INDIAN WAR AND THE AMERICAN REVOLUTION 72

CHAPTER IX
SALEM FOUNDED 84

CHAPTER X
TRYON, THE ROYAL GOVERNOR, MAKES TWO MEMORABLE VISITS TO WACHOVIA 95

CHAPTER XI
WACHOVIA DURING THE REVOLUTION 121

CHAPTER XII
FRIEND AND FOE 125

CHAPTER XIII
WITH THE LEGISLATURE 133

CHAPTER XIV
"IN THE VERY THEATRE OF THE WAR" 161

CHAPTER XV
PROVINCIAL AFFAIRS 172

CHAPTER XVI
THE CLOSE OF THE CENTURY 176

CHAPTER XVII
SALEM CHURCH BUILT 186

CHAPTER XVIII
SALEM FEMALE ACADEMY 191

CHAPTER XIX
HALF A CENTURY 198

TABLE OF CONTENTS

CHAPTER XX
MISSION WORK AMONG THE CHEROKEE INDIANS . . . 200

CHAPTER XXI
HOME MISSION WORK 204

CHAPTER XXII
WINSTON FOUNDED 209

CHAPTER XXIII
TRANSITION PERIOD 216

CHAPTER XXIV
SALEM FEMALE ACADEMY AFTER FIFTY YEARS . . . 220

CHAPTER XXV
THE TIME OF THE CIVIL WAR 235

CHAPTER XXVI
THE DECADE FOLLOWING THE CIVIL WAR 256

CHAPTER XXVII
A NEW ERA 259

CHAPTER XXVIII
HISTORY OF THE WATER SUPPLY AND FIRE PROTECTION . 262

CHAPTER XXIX
GROWTH OF THE TWIN CITY 274

TABLE OF CONTENTS

CHAPTER XXX

	PAGE
SUNDAY-SCHOOL ACTIVITY	278

CHAPTER XXXI

ENLARGED CHURCH WORK 283

CHAPTER XXXII

TWO CENTENNIALS 290

CHAPTER XXXIII

THE MORAVIAN CHURCH IN WACHOVIA AS IT IS TO-DAY . 296

PART TWO

THE DOCTRINAL POSITION OF THE MORAVIAN CHURCH . . 301
HISTORICAL SKETCH OF THE MORAVIAN CHURCH . . . 308
BIOGRAPHICAL SKETCH OF THE PRINCIPALS OF THE SALEM
    FEMALE ACADEMY 317
LISTS AND STATISTICS 336

MAPS AND ILLUSTRATIONS

SALEM CHURCH		*Frontispiece*
		PAGE
AUGUSTUS GOTTLIEB SPANGENBERG	*Facing*	4
MAP OF WACHOVIA		11
THE FIRST BUILDINGS IN WACHOVIA		19
HORTUS MEDICUS		22
MAP OF BETHABARA AND PLAN OF FORT		39
FREDERICK WILLIAM DE MARSHALL	*Facing*	86
CONGREGATION HOUSE, SALEM, 1771	*Facing*	90
PROPOSED PLAN FOR SALEM		94
SALEM GRAVEYARD	*Facing*	120
CEDAR AVENUE, SALEM	*Facing*	158
BETHABARA CHURCH, 1788	*Facing*	180
FIRST BUILDING OF SALEM FEMALE ACADEMY, 1805	*Facing*	196
EVOLUTION OF WINSTON AND SALEM CORPORATIONS.	MAP	210
FIRST FORSYTH COUNTY COURT-HOUSE, WINSTON		212
SECOND FORSYTH COUNTY COURT-HOUSE, WINSTON	*Facing*	214
IN THE PARK, SALEM ACADEMY AND COLLEGE	*Facing*	218
MAIN HALL		221
THE DELL		223
A FAVOURITE RETREAT		225
THE SPRING		227
ON THE HILLSIDE		229
A PEACEFUL SPOT		230

		PAGE
A GRADUATE		232
A CORNER IN SALEM SQUARE		234
GEORGE FREDERICK BAHNSON	Facing	238
ROBERT WILLIAM DE SCHWEINITZ	Facing	250
EMIL ADOLPHUS DE SCHWEINITZ	Facing	260
EDWARD RONDTHALER	Facing	284
SALEM ACADEMY AND COLLEGE	Facing	294

HISTORY OF WACHOVIA

CHAPTER I

CAUSES WHICH LED TO THE FOUNDING OF THE MORAVIAN CHURCH IN NORTH CAROLINA [1]

WHEN the Moravians came to America they were influenced by two motives. The one was to preach the gospel to the inhabitants of Pennsylvania and other colonies, somewhat in the same manner that the Diaspora work was and is now carried on in Europe. The Diaspora work is spiritual work done within the State Church, but without causing a separation from the State Church. Tens of thousands of members of the Lutheran Church in Germany are ministered to in this way by Moravian pastors. A century and a half ago, when the Moravians came to America, the condition of affairs was pitiful. The various little sects were without pastoral oversight, and what was worse, were engaged in bitter struggles with each other. The first object of the Moravians was to preach the pure gospel of love to these neglected and contentious inhabitants, and if possible to introduce friendship and harmony into their midst.

The second object was missionary work among the Indians.

Neither of these objects was fully realized, but the

[1] For a brief historical sketch of the Unitas Fratrum or Moravian Church, and also its doctrine, see Part II.

second, viz. mission work among the Indians, was actively prosecuted both during and after the Indian War.

A secondary result of the work in the northern portion of the American colonies was the founding of a number of towns, such as Bethlehem, Nazareth, and Lititz, in Pennsylvania, as distinctive Moravian towns, and these grew and flourished, becoming centres in the further history of the Moravian Church in America.

In the meantime certain causes were at work in the Moravian Church in Europe, which tended to bring about the purchase of the large tract of land in North Carolina, later known as "Wachovia." The foreign mission work was growing in importance and called for an outlay of money far beyond the ability of the church to provide, without the aid of friends. Some of their undertakings were not successful, and this occasioned great loss. Then, too, as a result of persecution, misfortune fell to their lot, and notwithstanding liberal gifts on the part of members and friends, the financial troubles about the middle of the eighteenth century were very great.

A business enterprise which is temporarily embarrassed is sometimes rescued by placing into the business more capital. So it was deemed advisable to make an effort to enter upon new and enlarged work in the mission fields, and begin a settlement in some section, later to be selected, which by its size and magnitude would strengthen the church, and restore full confidence in the Moravians.

This was at a time when noblemen had been given large grants of land in America. These noblemen desired worthy settlers for their possessions. It was hoped that mines would be discovered, the land cultivated, and towns and cities built. The Moravians were well known for their thrift and industry, and Lord Granville made them

FOUNDING OF MORAVIAN CHURCH

a liberal offer in connection with his North Carolina estates. This offer was carefully considered and later accepted.

The general plan of the authorities was to secure a tract of land sufficient in size to permit the building of a central town in which to locate the administration offices, where trades and industries could be established, educational institutions founded, and which would be a centre for conducting missionary work. Furthermore, it was the original plan of the church authorities, long before the selection of the Wachovia tract, to sell the land round about the central town to members of the church for farming purposes. Thus the new colony would differ from other Moravian settlements, because they would not only control the town, but also the surrounding neighbourhood for a distance of five to ten miles.

Another cause which led to the founding of the Moravian Church in North Carolina was the desire for religious liberty. This feature of the pilgrims to Carolina has not been emphasized in the same manner as in the case of the pilgrims to New England. A careful study of the situation in Europe shows that during the preceding twenty-five years Bohemia and Moravia had witnessed persecutions in the church even unto the death. In Germany bitter and hostile decisions were made by narrow-minded officials, and a good and noble man like Count Zinzendorf was heartlessly banished from his home and estates. Leases and contracts were cancelled on some technicality and caused heavy financial losses. From all these things the Moravians turned and said in effect, "Let us seek an estate where we can worship God without restraint, and where we will be able to use our lives and our means to promote his glory."

CHAPTER II

SPANGENBERG'S EXPLORATION AND SURVEYING TOUR

RECEIVING the grant of land from Lord Granville did not remove all the difficulties in connection with the founding of the proposed Moravian settlement. Little was known of North Carolina by the average inhabitant of Europe. The very terms of the boundary description impress us with the vague idea they had of their possessions in America. After seven of the eight Proprietors who owned the American soil from the Virginia line to a point in Florida had relinquished to the crown their rights, Edward, Earl of Clarendon (Lord Granville), retained his portion. This territory of Lord Granville extended from the Virginia line to a point about seventy miles south, and according to the terms of the deed, from the Atlantic Ocean on the east to the Pacific Ocean on the west, or, as the Spangenberg papers describe it, "to the South sea." Thus, when the Moravian explorers began their journey, they had a strip of land seventy miles wide and three thousand miles long from which to select their tract.

A conference was held November 29, 1751, in Lindsay House, London, the seat of the government of the Moravian Church at that time, and it was decided to accept Lord Granville's offer. So much depended upon the choice of the proper location that the very best men were sent to North Carolina to survey the one hundred thousand acres of land. Among them was Bishop Spangenberg, a learned

Augustus Gottlieb Spangenberg

SPANGENBERG'S EXPLORATION TOUR 5

man, and possessed of an unusual degree of practical knowledge. He, with his companions, made the journey, and he described it in what are commonly known as "The Spangenberg Papers." These are in the possession of the Wachovia Land Office, and have been in part translated from the German and published in the "Colonial Records of North Carolina," Vol. V, pp. 1 to 14. The first twelve papers describe the journey from place to place, and from camp to camp in western Carolina, till at last Wachovia itself is discovered and surveyed. Papers 13 to 23, inclusive, contained the maps, but these have unfortunately been lost. Possibly they were sent to Edenton, and not returned, or possibly they are in some archive house in some other portion of the Unity. Papers 24 to 35, inclusive, give information in regard to the people, the climate, the rivers, soil, and fruits. There is also a carefully written paper describing the political status, how taxes are collected, laws made, and officials elected. The Spangenberg papers are valuable documents. The journey from Edenton to the far western portion was difficult. It is not possible to definitely locate their various camps, but it is possible to follow them with sufficient certainty to make the general route clear.

Having left Edenton in the northeastern section of the colony, the surveying party made its way in a southwesterly direction to the Catawba River. The survey began in the general neighbourhood of Hickory or Morganton. Thence westward for some distance they journeyed. Next they proceeded northward and travelled over mountains and through untrodden wilderness. They then changed their course and with great difficulty made their way in a southeasterly direction till they came to Moravian Falls, near the present site of Wilkesboro.

Following the course of the river, they were later informed of a very desirable tract of land on Muddy Creek, several miles from the river, and this they visited, surveyed, and later purchased.

The journey was fraught with so much that was thrilling and hazardous that it would well form the basis of a story of adventure and travel.

On the 25th of August, 1752, a party of five men left Bethlehem, Pennsylvania, on their way to North Carolina. The following day one more joined them, and on August 29 they left Philadelphia. The names were Bishop Spangenberg, Timothy Horsefield, Joseph Miller, Herman Loesch, John Merk, and Henry Antes. The journey from Philadelphia to North Carolina occupied thirteen days and was made in part by land and in part by water. September 10 they arrived at Edenton, where they were hospitably entertained by the Hon. Francis Corbin, the agent of Lord Granville. They remained in Edenton a week or more, and better would it have been for them if they had made the time less. Their systems were filled with malarial poisons, which prostrated all but two of their party of six. Horsefield's condition caused Miller to insist on the necessity of his remaining at the home of one Captain Sennet, until he could regain sufficient strength to join the party. Spangenberg was so ill with continuous fever that he fainted while on his horse, and often on account of weakness had to be assisted to mount and dismount. When urged by his brethren to remain till he was really able to go forward, he replied, "The Lord will give me the necessary health and strength. I will have to pass through much weakness, you will have to exercise much patience, but the Lord will help me through." With this spirit Spangenberg, Antes, Loesch,

SPANGENBERG'S EXPLORATION TOUR

and Merk continued their westward journey, while Horsefield and Miller remained. These two did not again join the others, but later returned to Pennsylvania. When the party arrived at the Catawba River it consisted of the four already named, together with Mr. Churton, the surveyer, and two men who were acquainted with life in the forest, and who could act in the double capacity of carrying the surveyor's chain and supplying the party with game. As we have already stated, they began surveying in the general neighbourhood of Hickory and Morganton. The first tract consisted of one thousand acres, to which it was proposed to give the name "Gruenau," (green meadow) because of the fine pasture land. The second tract, two miles distant, was two hundred acres in extent, and was called " Merkfield," in honour of one of the party. Later one thousand acres were selected. This valley on the Catawba was called " Schoenthal " (beautiful valley). Fifty miles from their first camp six thousand acres were surveyed, and because of the beautiful mountains this land was given the name " Reichmont " (rich in mountains). Thus in succession they surveyed and named "Loesch Creek," " Montfort," "Oli" (the kettle, because of its shape), "Freydeck" (secluded corner), "Forkland," "New Hope," and last of all "Wachau" or "Wachovia."

They passed over the first seventy miles of the wilderness with no great inconvenience, though obliged to make their way over Indian trails and along paths made by buffalo to and from the streams. At times they were followed by the Indians and watched with suspicious eye. When they came to the most western point of their journey, their real sorrows began. They were in a wilderness unfrequented by even a wandering hunter or Indian. The mountain peaks spread out on all sides like the waves of the ocean. It was the beginning of December. A hunter who was acting as their guide missed his way, and they were lost in the wilds of western Carolina. They found it necessary to scale a steep mountain, with precipices all about them. The baggage was removed from the horses to prevent them from being hurled backward. The poor beasts trembled with fear. At last, having braved a multitude of difficulties and dangers, the top was gained. Here the party rested and partook of a morsel from their scant stock of provisions. Their faithful horses had nothing except the dry leaves. The descent was not quite so precipitous, but night came on and there was neither water nor pasture land, and the condition of man and beast was pitiful. At night they were not able to erect a tent because of a wind storm.

The second day they found pasturage for their horses, and killed two stags, so that all were somewhat refreshed; but as they were in the midst of the beaver dams they had to cut their way through the obstructions, and the exertions greatly weakened them.

Continuing their wanderings, they came on the third day to a rocky stream, which they could not cross. On both sides precipices arose, impossible to scale. Food for the horses could not be found. One of the hunters was sent forward to examine the character of the land. He returned and stated that from the top of the ravine he could see a large valley with pasturage for the horses, and a camping ground for the party. With renewed hope they pressed forward, cutting away the undergrowth as they advanced. At last the mountain was crossed and the valley reached, but their troubles were not yet at an end. Before the tents could be erected a terrible

SPANGENBERG'S EXPLORATION TOUR

blizzard swept down and then it was that hope forsook them. A hundred miles from civilization, lost in the mountains, no food for the horses, and little for the human beings, the weather at zero, and the ground covered with a deep snow, — we do not wonder that they exclaimed in despair, "What shall we do? Our horses will perish and we with them!"

The night passed, and Bishop Spangenberg writes that he could not remember ever to have felt so cold a wind as that in the December blizzard in the mountains of North Carolina. A bright sunshine greeted them the next day, and though the nights were terribly cold all were mercifully spared.

Later they travelled by the aid of the compass directly to the southeast, climbed boldly over all obstacles, and at last reached the Yadkin Valley, after having been lost in the mountains nearly two weeks, and during which time they had suffered great hardships and dangers. Antes was enduring intense pain from an accident, when they providentially came to the home of Mr. Owens, where he received tender care.

December 27 they reached the site of Wachovia, on Muddy Creek. Fourteen sections were surveyed, a total of seventy-three thousand acres, ten miles wide and eleven miles long. More land was later added, increasing the amount to nearly one hundred thousand acres. The record describes it as being one-half good, one-fourth medium, and one-fourth bad. Well watered, springs perennial, good timber, and good fishing and hunting.

Bishop Spangenberg examined the fine meadows, which called to mind the home of the Zinzendorfs in Austria. He remembered the rich and well-watered ancestral estates had been given the name "Wachau," from "wach," a stream, and "aue," a meadow. Hence, he said, let us give a fitting name to our new possessions and renew the old title; and on January 25, 1753, Spangenberg named the tract which has through a century and a half retained the title

"WACHOVIA"

In addition to the information which served as a basis for the foregoing account of the search for and the discovery of Wachovia, Spangenberg comments on the condition of affairs in North Carolina one hundred and fifty years ago. He speaks of politics, describing the troubles which arose between the old and the new counties in the way of legislative representation. He draws a comparison between the government of North Carolina and that of South Carolina and Pennsylvania, and suggests possible remedies for existing evils. What he says of the inhabitants throws light on the persecutions which Wachovia endured twenty years later. His thirty-third paper says: "Some of the people are native, and these are lazy. They cannot be compared with those who live in sections farther north. Others are from foreign parts, too poor to buy land in New York and Pennsylvania, hence they have come here, where land is cheap. These are harmless people. There are men here who have run away on account of debt, or have deserted their families and are fleeing from justice. Whole bands of horse thieves are exercising their art. For these reasons North Carolina has received a bad name. On the other hand, many fine families are coming from the northern colonies to western Carolina, and they will raise the standard." The three nations most largely represented in western North Carolina at that time were the English, German, and Irish.

The Spangenberg papers tell us of the condition of the

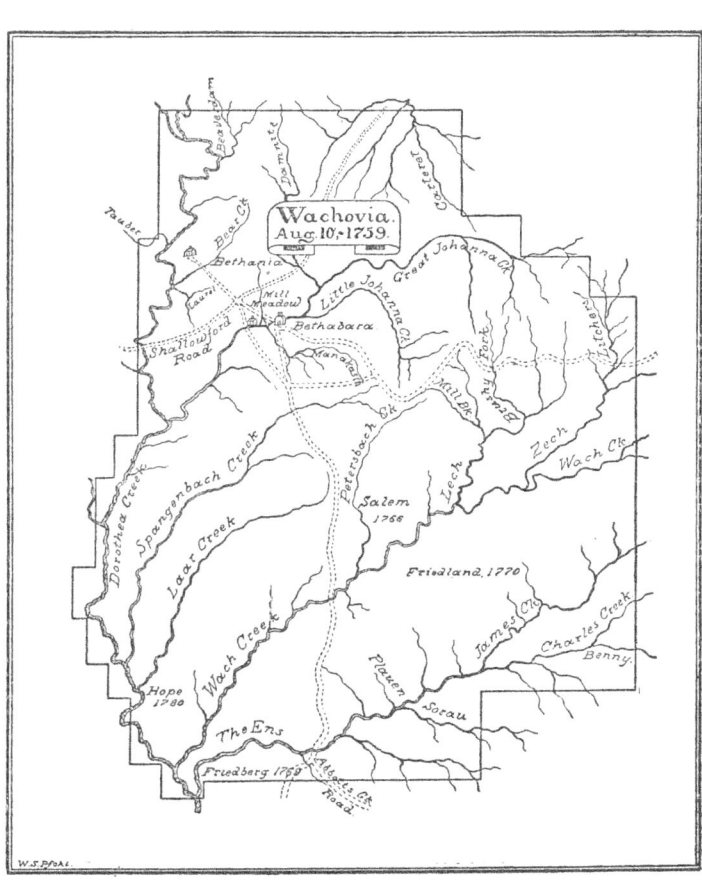

Indians, also of the negroes. They give a list of the counties, and they tell of the taxes, and tax gathering, and suggest that "it is well to keep tax receipts."

In concluding this chapter we add the following facts: —

August 17 of the same year, 1753, the survey was approved by Lord Granville and nineteen deeds were made to James Hutton, of London, the agent of the Moravian Church. The first payment was £500 ($2500). The exact amount of land was 98,985 acres. In addition to this first payment a yearly rental of three shillings (seventy-five cents) formed a ground rent. This ground rent amounted to nearly $750.

We have already called attention to the stringency of money matters in the Moravian Church at large. Hence to secure funds for the purchase of the land, payment of the rent, transportation of colonists, and their support during the first five years, a land company was formed, in which friends in Holland were particularly interested. December 18, 1753, Bishop Spangenberg and Cornelius Van Laer were appointed directors of this company. They experienced some difficulty in securing all the money that was required, but in the end their efforts were crowned with success.

CHAPTER III

JOURNEY OF THE FIRST INHABITANTS OF WACHOVIA FROM PENNSYLVANIA TO NORTH CAROLINA

IN the archives of the Bethlehem congregation is a paper written in quaint English, containing an account of the journey of the little colony which left that town early in the autumn of 1753 to begin the settlement of Wachovia, North Carolina. The original document is in German, and it was for many years lost, but is now in the archives of the Salem congregation. The paper shows how difficult was travel in those early days; it gives information in regard to Virginia, through which they passed; it makes clear the perfect consecration of the men who began the settlement of Wachovia. As the reader follows the party over the six weeks of their trip of five hundred miles, and then recalls how comfortable and pleasant is this same journey in our day, the contrast is indeed striking.

All the negotiations between Lord Granville and the church authorities had been completed. Wachovia had been purchased and plans made in 1753 to begin the settlement. The further details were carefully arranged, and it was decided in the beginning to send a small colony of carefully chosen single men. The new settlement was to have a minister to care for the spiritual needs, a physician for their bodily health, a business man of ability to guard the temporal affairs, and to these were added men who represented several trades, and two farmers. They were to live as one household, and thus would be so situated as best to endure hardships, brave dangers, and overcome difficulties.

The following is the list of those who located in Wachovia, and founded the village of Bethabara: —

1. Rev. Bernhard Adam Grube, a German by birth, age 37 years, the first minister.
2. Jacob Loesch (Lash), born in New York, age 31 years, the warden.
3. Dr. Hans Martin Kalberlahn, born in Norway, age 31 years, the physician.
4. Hans Peterson, born in Danish Holstein, age 28 years, a tailor.
5. Christopher Merkly, born in Germany, age 39 years, a baker.
6. Herman Loesch (Lash), born in Pennsylvania, age 27 years, a farmer.
7. Erich Ingebretsen, born in Norway, age 31 years, a carpenter.
8. Henrich Feldhausen, born in Holstein, age 38 years, a carpenter.
9. Johannes Lisher, a farmer.
10. Jacob Lung, born in Germany, age 40 years, a gardener.
11. Friedrich Jacob Pfeil, born in Germany, age 42 years, a shoemaker and tanner.
12. Jacob Beroth, born in Germany, age 28 years, a farmer.

With these twelve came the brethren, Gottlob Koenigsderfer, Nathaniel Seidel, and Joseph Haberland. After a brief visit these three returned to Bethlehem.

The little colony left Bethlehem, October 8th, 1753, with their goods stored in a large wagon. The route was

JOURNEY TO NORTH CAROLINA

almost in a direct line to Wachovia. The night before arriving at the Susquehanna they sojourned at the house of Mr. Loesch, the father of Jacob and Herman. Here they were hospitably entertained, the mother filling their boxes with provisions, and the father placing a part of the load in his own wagon till the river had been forded. The width of the Susquehanna was a surprise to them. Continuing southward, they crossed the border line between Pennsylvania and Maryland, and arrived at Frederick October 18th. Frederick was then a village of sixty houses. Entering the famous Shenandoah Valley, they continued southward by the present town of Staunton, then called Augusta Court-house. They crossed in succession the Potomac, the James, and the Roanoke rivers, and probably passed near the present site of the cities of Lexington and Roanoke. In due time the Pilot Mountain, so well known to all the inhabitants of northwestern North Carolina, came in sight. The Mayo River was reached and followed till they arrived at the junction of the Mayo and Dan rivers, where are situated the present Mayodan village and mills. A short journey and they reached the general section of the present town of Walnut Cove, and soon thereafter they crossed the borders of Wachovia.

Great difficulties confronted them at every stage of their journey. Their heavily loaded wagon was too much for the poorly built bridges, and in one instance the bridge gave way just as the horses and the fore part of the wagon were safely over. With a great effort they climbed the steep hills, at times being compelled to carry the load to the top, as the empty wagon was all the three pair of horses could draw. Nor were their troubles ended when the top was reached, for the steep descent was very dangerous. Having cut down a tree and fastened it to the rear of the wagon, and having locked the wheels, it was even then with difficulty that the descent was made. During the early part of the journey the heat was at times quite oppressive, and before North Carolina was reached the snow lay upon the ground. Heavy rains caused high waters which detained them days, and even when this trouble did not exist, the steep banks had often to be dug down before they could enter and leave the stream, while it was not uncommon to be obliged to clear a road of trees and undergrowth before they could proceed. The search for food was no small item, and the accidents to the wagon, as well as the sickness of the horses, often caused the deepest anxiety. We will devote space to but two incidents, to convey the impression of what was almost a daily occurrence.

The party arrived in the neighbourhood of the Roanoke River about the end of October. It was cold, wet, and had been snowing. Hill after hill had been climbed, and the night was coming on apace. Before them was a long and very steep ascent up the mountain side. A man approached and was asked whether it was possible to cross the hill before night. He answered in the affirmative. He added that at the top of the hill was a house at which they could spend the night. As the hill was too steep to allow the horses to draw the wagon and the load, the horses were taken from the wagon and the goods placed upon their backs. Then a part of the company journeyed on and a part remained with the wagon. Before the ascent was half made they were surrounded by storm and darkness, and when the top was reached they found that they had been deceived by the traveller. No house was on the top of the hill nor on the other side of the mountain, and as they pressed forward in the rain and darkness, they at

JOURNEY TO NORTH CAROLINA

last discovered that the distance between them and their companions was too great for them to rejoin those who had remained with the wagon. It was a dismal experience, and with great thankfulness they met again on the morrow by the aid of daylight and sunshine.

The second instance took place two weeks later. They had crossed the border line between Virginia and North Carolina. They determined if possible to reach the Dan River that day. The journey was begun at three o'clock in the morning, but storms and bad weather detained them. They missed the right road, and by nightfall found that they were still about seven miles from their destination. They were obliged to stop till the storm abated. At midnight the rain ceased, the horses were attached to the wagon, and with lighted torches to guide the driver, the journey was continued to Dan River. What a picture is presented by these sturdy Christian men as in the midnight hour, with flaring torches, they made their way through the mountain wilds, happy and cheerful, reminding themselves that the day was November 13, a great festival day of the church. As the traveller now passes over this same ground he can easily imagine this midnight scene as he looks upon the rugged hillsides, in the neighbourhood of Mayodan and Avalon, two places where Moravian churches have recently been erected.

The paper to which reference was made earlier in the chapter speaks of the inhabitants of Virginia, in the section through which they passed. They met travellers, they conversed with farmers and merchants, they came in contact with many nationalities, they saw some who were worthless and "lived like beasts," but others showed deep piety in their words and actions.

Whatever else the paper sets forth, the one picture which

stands in the clearest light is the great piety of this company, and their perfect devotion to Jesus Christ and his service. Night and morning they rejoiced in the spiritual food afforded by the songs, the prayers, the Scripture, and the words of admonition spoken by the ministers who accompanied them. Wherever they tarried, day or night, all men recognized that they were a company of Christians. Believers confided to them their faith in Jesus Christ, invited them to preach, and wished them Godspeed when they departed. Not only did their zeal and piety cause these devoted men to seek the souls of those who came in contact with them, but this spirit of devotion knit them together in the bonds of love and affection. Neither hardships nor perils, toils nor sufferings, could separate them. In this little company travelling from Pennsylvania to North Carolina we have a picture of the power of Christian fellowship which is delightful to contemplate.

After a delay of several days at the Dan River because of the high water, the crossing was finally made, and the last section of the journey was begun. Several members of the party had gone over in a canoe and had made a tour of inspection. Returning, they met the party with the wagon. The previous night had been very cold. A dull, leaden, November sky threatened snow. The progress was slow. They paused for a noonday lunch, after which, continuing their journey, the travel-worn company crossed the border line of Wachovia a little after noon, November 17, 1753.

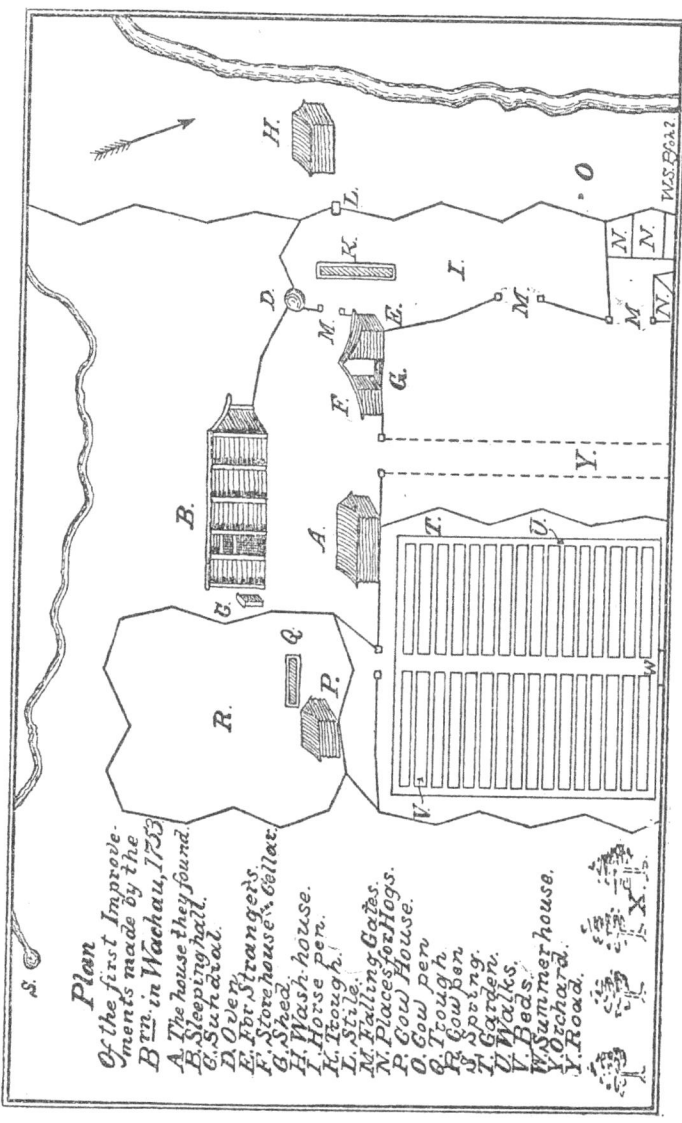

CHAPTER IV

THE FIRST YEAR IN WACHOVIA

WHEN the little company of fifteen persons crossed the borders of Wachovia at noon, November 17, 1753, they were still six miles from the cabin which was to shelter them. Half this distance they had to cut a new road, but willing hands and happy hearts made the labour light, and ere long they reached the deserted hut. It was an humble abode, without floor, and with a roof that did not protect them from the weather. Yet it offered comforts and pleasures compared with the experiences of the preceding weeks. Their joy knew no bounds, and so happy were they that they were more like little children in the exuberance of their spirits, than like the travel-worn pioneers on their earnest errand. Turning to the text for November 17, they found that it was indeed suited to their case, "I know where thou dwellest." (Rev. 2:13.)

As the early Christians were accustomed to celebrate all special occasions with "agapæ" or "love-feasts," in like manner these weary travellers made their first meal a love-feast, thus consecrating it to their Lord and Master, and making it an emblem of the strong bond of brotherly love which held them together. This happy duty performed, they felt that they had arrived at a place which they could call home, and how blessed was the beginning of this new home with Jesus speaking to them in the text of the day, "I know where thou dwellest," and they responding by making their first meal a solemn but happy love-

THE FIRST YEAR IN WACHOVIA

1. Herba Mentha. Curly Mint.
2. Herba Mentha. Curly Mint.
3. Semen Anisi. Anise Seed.
4. Nasturtium.
5. Semen Fœniculi. Fennel Seed.
6. Nasturtium.
7. Semen Carui. Caraway Seed.
8. Semen Carui. Caraway Seed.
9 a. Artemisia. Mugwort.
9 b. Violex. Knot Grass.
9 c. Semen Carvi.
10. Flores Lavenduli. Lavender.
11. Semen Anethi. Dill.
12. Centaurea Minor. Centaury.
13. Salvia. Sage.
14. Salvia. Sage.
15. Artemisia. Mugwort.
16. Artemisia. Mugwort.
17. Rumex Acet. Sorrel.
18. Rumex Acet. Sorrel.
19. Rumex Acet. Sorrel.
20. Millifolium. Yarrow.
21. (Empty.)
22. " Mundrosen."
23. Petroselinum. Parsley.
24. Calcatrippa. Larkspur.
25. (Empty.)
26. Abrotan. A Small Cypress.
27. Abrotan. A Small Cypress.
28. Abrotan. A Small Cypress.
29. Basilicon. Sweet Basil. Marjorana. Sweet Marjoram.
30. Basilicon. Sweet Basil. Marjorana. Sweet Marjoram.
31. Abrotan. Small Cypress.
32. Abrotan. Small Cypress.
33. Abrotan. Small Cypress.
34. (Empty.)
35. Calcatrippa. Larkspur.
36. (Empty.)
37. Flor. Papaver Alb. White Poppy.
38. (Empty.)
39. (Empty.)
40. Aquilegia. Columbine. Papaver Rubra. Red Poppy.
41. Semen Papaver Rubra. Seed Red Poppy.
42. Semen Papaver Rubra. Seed Red Poppy.
43. Angelica Hortensis. Angelica.
44. Millefolium. Yarrow.
45. Safflore. Wild Saffron.
46 a. Carduus Mariæ. Mary Thistle.
46 b. Fumaria. Fumitory.
47. Levisticum. Lovage.
48. Levisticum. Lovage.
49. Angelica Hortensis. Angelica.
50. Rumex Acetosa. Sorrel.
51. Fumaria. Fumitory.
52. Chamomilla Rub. Red Chamomile. Lilium Album. White Lily.
53. Lilium Album. White Lily.
54. Rosa Rub. et Alb. Red and White Rose.
55 a. Semen Citri. Seed of Citron.
55 b. Vicus Hispanio.
56. Rosa Rubra. Red Rose.
57. Lilium Album. White Lily.
58. Chamomilla. Chamomile. Semen Coriander. Coriander Seed.
59. Plantago Minor. Small Plantain. Marrubium. Hoarhound.
60. Santonicum.
61. Lavendula. Lavender. Hormium Clary.
62. Nigellum. Fennel.
63. Scurvy Grass and Lavender.
64. White Poppy.
65. Hyssop.
66. Larkspur.
67. Flor. Belidor Min.
68. Chamomile and Hyssop.
69. Sage.
70. Fennel.
71. Cardui Benedict.
72. Scurvy Grass.
73. Salsify.
74. Balm.
75. Herb. Absynth. Wormwood.
76. Herb. Ruth. Garden Rue.
77. Parthenium.
78. Wandering Poppy.
79. Chamomile.
80. Scabiosa.
81. Sage.
82. Sage.
83. Chamomile.
84. Chamomile.
85. Althea. Marsh Mallow.
86. Althea. Marsh Mallow.
87. Althea. Marsh Mallow.
88. Comfrey.
89. Marsh Mallow.
90. Sweet Clover.
91. Black Comfrey. (Black Bryony.)
92. Poppy.
93. Columbine.
94. Melons.
95. Cucumeris.
96. Comfrey.

THE FIRST YEAR IN WACHOVIA 23

feast. What mattered it that the space on the ground was cramped and small! What mattered it that the cold found its way through roof and wall! What mattered it that the howling of the wolves and the cry of the panthers greeted them as they entered their new abode! Religion came with them, love came with them, and on these two foundation stones they began a work on that dark and cheerless November day, which was destined to outlive many generations, a work which is still felt after the lapse of a century and a half.

The next day was Sunday. It was a real day of rest. They took great interest in examining their surroundings. Looking northward, they saw a forest-covered lowland, which in imagination, they could picture cleared and cultivated, or covered with luxuriant grass. Through this flowed a clear, strong stream which was destined to turn the wheel of the busy mill. This lowland was bordered by low hills, while in the distance could be seen the mountains, robed in their mantle of blue. Turning to the east and south, they saw a rolling country, suited for farm land. West of their cabin home, and overshadowing it, was a great bluff or hill, at the base of which flowed a rivulet of the clearest water. Could the newcomers have lifted the veil of the future, they would have beheld, on this same hillside, the most luxuriant ferns and rare wild flowers in profuse abundance. And on the top of this beautiful hill, with its covering of giant pines, chestnuts, and oaks, they would have beheld the graveyard, or, as they termed it, "God's Acre," in which one and another would find a peaceful home when life's duties were done. These were the surroundings which appeared to the twelve settlers as they arose and greeted the first Sabbath day in their new home in North Carolina.

A somewhat detailed account of the life of this little colony during the first year in Wachovia will serve as a description of the life in Wachovia for a generation and more, and will also bring before the mind of the reader the experiences in the several congregations which were founded after Bethabara. It is true that never were the struggles so difficult as during this first year, at the same time they were so brave and hopeful, that the picture is really a pleasant one to study.

Refreshed by the day of rest, the brethren arose Monday morning, ready for the task of making a home in the wilderness. We are impressed with the businesslike manner in which they began the work. With the implements brought with them, they commenced clearing a tract of land to sow with winter wheat, and within three weeks from the date of their arrival, six acres had been cleared and planted. During the first year not less than fifty acres of land had been prepared for farming purposes. They recognized that, in this sparsely settled section, it would be difficult to secure provisions, hence at the very outset they began to raise cattle and to plant a variety of grain for their future use and comfort. In the first summer, they gathered wheat, corn, flax, millet, barley, oats, buckwheat, turnips, cotton, and tobacco, in addition to the garden vegetables. Fruit trees were planted, and various kinds of medicinal herbs. A most interesting map of a "medical garden" (see page 22) is in the Wachovia Land Office. This map shows the garden divided into squares and sections, and each square named. It is of great interest to the medical profession as indicating what medicines were produced in western Carolina, a hundred and fifty years ago.

Diversity of industries is said to be the real test of the

THE FIRST YEAR IN WACHOVIA 25

prosperity of a place. In 1754, with the great strain of clearing land and building houses, we find the record of trade commenced with their neighbours, and the notes indicate that they had in operation the following:—

Carpenter shop.   Shoe shop.
Tailor establishment.   Tannery.
Pottery.   Cooper shop.
Blacksmith shop.

Under the head of prices, we note the value of a pair of shoes. A stranger passing through Wachovia desired to purchase a pair of shoes. He evidently had no money. To overcome this difficulty and secure them, he was willing to cut down and trim one hundred forest trees as a compensation.

The company of twelve men were very busy during the first year. They had roads to cut, journeys to make, farming work to attend to, and houses to erect. But their greatest undertaking was the building of the mill, though this was not entirely finished in 1754. The magnitude of the undertaking will be understood, when we recall the fact that all the needed articles had to be made by the members of the little company. The site for the mill was selected a mile or more down the stream. The dam was built, and the race constructed. The foundation stones were large, as is indicated by the one used as a step before the door; this is now in the possession of the Wachovia Historical Society. Timber they had in abundance, but old persons who remember the mill express surprise at the great size of the beams and timbers used in its construction. Then the wheel had to be built; forging metal bearings for the wheel was no small task; suitable millstones had to be found, quarried, shaped, and dressed. They were discovered on Muddy Creek, in the general neighbourhood of Friedberg. Before the second year of their stay in Wachovia had passed, the mill was completed and was busily grinding. It was a great blessing to this entire section, and the maps of those days show roads leading from the mill to all points, north, south, east, and west, and the records indicate that not only from a commercial standpoint was the mill important, but in the Indian War, and in the days of the American Revolution citizens and refugees were fed, and the soldiers of both armies made demands upon it from time to time. Hence, at this early day, the mill was of importance to the entire western section of the colony.

The live-stock industry shows sixty-nine head of cattle and pigs.

It was apparent to the company the first night of their arrival that larger accommodations would have to be provided. The Hans Wagner hut, which they found upon their arrival, a picture of which is given in this volume, was not large enough to allow sleeping room, and a second story was improvised by stretching hammocks from wall to wall. Strangers often came, and it was not an uncommon thing to give the law of hospitality the precedence, and this sent a number of the company to sleep beneath the stars, a thing which was not pleasant in January in North Carolina.

As soon as it became known that there was an able physician and a skilled surgeon in Wachovia, many persons came for medical treatment. As the original cabin was too small for their own comfort, they resolved to build a "stranger's house," that is, a modest hotel, the first one in Wachovia. It was indeed an humble strangers' house, not much larger

THE FIRST YEAR IN WACHOVIA

than the first hut. February 9 this second building was finished, and four days later a man arrived from his home fifty miles away, with his invalid wife. These were the first to use the new house.

As soon as the little house for strangers was completed, work on the dormitory was begun, and though crudely constructed, it afforded sufficient room, being thirteen feet wide and fifty feet long. With the addition of some small shelters for the grain, etc., the above-mentioned buildings were all that were completed within twelve months after their arrival, though the work on the mill was being actively pushed, and the foundations for a large dwelling house had been laid.

The many duties left little time for social enjoyments, yet the narrative pictures a carefully arranged plan by means of which they did enjoy the home life. The table fare was simple but varied, and when the work was unusually hard the kind and supply of the food was adapted to the needs of the body. Not only when the days were marked by inclement weather do we find them in the house, but on other occasions they gathered together to plan the work, to read letters or hear church news from other parts of the world, and to hold sessions of what they called their "society."

They were not fond of hunting. They did not like it as a sport, and they concluded that it was not profitable as a business pursuit. When it was necessary to kill a bear or scatter a pack of wolves or hunt down a panther in order to protect their own animals, they entered energetically into the duty and did their work well.

The life of the first settlers in Wachovia was by no means a quiet and retired one. The Moravian brethren were busy travellers. Their first journeys were to inspect their possessions. They journeyed to the Black Walnut Bottom, where later Bethania was located. They went down to Muddy Creek, where lived Adam Spach, later the well-known member of the Friedberg congregation. They made so many trips to the well-watered and productive Yadkin River Valley that a road was cut through to the river. The diary gives a condensed list of the visits of Lash, the business manager, and Kalberlahn, the physician. The former went hither and thither to buy and to sell. The latter was called to go twenty, fifty, even one hundred miles through the forests to minister to the sick and those who were suffering from accidents. Several trips were made to Fayetteville and Wilmington to consider the arrangements for their later commercial interests, and to interview the authorities on legal points. Then, too, we find accounts of the arrivals from and the departures to Bethlehem. It is a tender and beautiful picture to see how with tears and prayers they bade farewell to the brethren, Koenigsderfer, Seidel, and Haberland, as they began the return journey to Pennsylvania. This is in strong contrast to the note of joy with which they welcomed the brethren, Fries and Lisher, on the 15th of April. The former arrived as minister, and it is to his interesting and clearly written record that we are indebted for the facts which have come down to us in connection with 1754 and 1755. In September the famous Peter Boehler visited them. In a love-feast held soon after his arrival, the bishop announced that the name which Spangenberg had selected last year had been indorsed by the authorities, and our land would in future be officially known as "Wachovia."

In addition to the visitors from Bethlehem and the visits made by the brethren themselves, many strangers came on matters of business or for professional advice. In 1754,

THE FIRST YEAR IN WACHOVIA

within three months they had 103 guests, and in 1755 not less than 426 persons visited Bethabara. All this shows that while the Moravians carried out their idea of retaining Wachovia for themselves, they also came into close contact with the outside world.

Their relations to others were pleasant and satisfactory. They paid their taxes promptly and without protest. They refused to take an oath, and declined to perform military duty, but socially they were on the best terms with all their neighbours near and far. The many presents sent to them showed the kindly feelings which existed.

The first year in Wachovia was not entirely free from sufferings. It is true that there was no death and no alarming illness, but two accidents threatened serious results. On New Year's Day the roof of their little home, their only shelter at this time, was discovered to be in flames. In the struggle to save the building from destruction, Kalberlahn was severely burned. While he was suffering from his wound, some members of the company were cutting timber. As one giant of the forest came crashing to the ground, Peterson was struck by a limb, and when his companions rushed to his aid, it appeared to them that he was fatally hurt. With heavy hearts they bore him home. An examination was not possible that day, but the following day, Dr. Kalberlahn discovered that the skull had not been broken; and though the wound was both serious and painful, he recovered, as did also the victim of the fire on New Year's Day.

To the student of the weather bureau, it is interesting to note that the same general conditions prevailed then as now. It is sometimes claimed that climatic conditions have changed in a century and a half. Such is not the case, as the sketch of each month's weather given in the diary will show.

The love for music appeared at the very outset. Singing formed a large part of their worship, and liturgical services with hymns specially composed for the occasion were not infrequent. The first mention of instrumental music is found under date of February 23, 1754, when it is said that the evening singing was accompanied by the playing of a trumpet, which would compare favourably with the excellent instruments used in the Bethlehem congregation. A year later the music is mentioned as having been very good. On this occasion the singing was accompanied with flutes and trumpets.

We close this account of the first year by referring to their religious life. We have already spoken of their deep piety and perfect consecration. Their worship formed a regular part of the programme of each day. They frequently had the meal in common, as a religious observance. With joy they mentioned the fact that in late summer a love-feast was provided with buns from the flour made of the first fruits of their wheat fields. Saturday afternoon was observed as a preparation time for the approaching Sunday. Only on a few occasions, when special conditions made it necessary, did they labour on Saturday afternoon. Sunday was observed in about the same manner as we observe it at the present day, though modified to suit their circumstances. At Easter they celebrated all the occasions of that festival, greeting each other on the resurrection morning with the happy "Ave!"

A touching and beautiful sketch might be written of the first Christmas, when they related the ever sweet and tender story of the Christ Child, as they gathered in the

Christmas vigils. These are the words of the journal, "We had a little love-feast; then near the Christ Child we had our first Christmas Eve in North Carolina, and rested in peace in this hope and faith;" and a later writer says, "All this while the wolves and panthers howled and screamed in the forests near by."

CHAPTER V

INDIAN TROUBLES THREATEN WACHOVIA, AND THE BETHABARA FORT ERECTED

THE war between France and England, including the period of which we are now writing, dates its origin to the time of Washington's campaign in 1754. The time of the treaty between England and France in 1763 is considered the conclusion of the war. The progress of hostilities was not as rapid as in our day of steam, telegraph, and telephone, hence not till the summer of 1755 did disquieting influences reach the Indians of North Carolina. Alarming rumours then began to fill the air, and during the following four years the situation became increasingly worse, though actual war did not break out till 1759. The delay of open hostilities was due to the fact that the centre was far north of the Carolinas, in the neighbourhood of the Great Lakes, in New York, and in Pennsylvania. The Moravians in Pennsylvania experienced the horrors of the struggle several years before bloodshed began in North Carolina. Another reason for the delay was that the Cherokees, Creeks, and Catawbas were friendly to the whites. In time they were won over by their red brethren. First secretly and then openly, they espoused the cause of the hostile Indians against the white men, and from 1759 we may consider Wachovia as in the midst of a bloody Indian war. Toward the end of 1761 the troops conducted a campaign of destruction against the Indians of western Carolina, and at the same time a similar cam-

INDIAN TROUBLES; FORT ERECTED 33

paign was carried on in the western portion of Virginia. This really brought the war to a close in these sections, though it was two years later before the peace negotiations were concluded between England and France. The present chapter will deal with the period of four years of unrest which gradually led up to open warfare.

As a sudden storm will rise without previous warning and in an hour cover everything with dark and threatening clouds, so, in 1755, the prosperous and thrifty little settlement in Wachovia within a day found its peace had departed. On July 22, a Dunkard with his family arrived from New River. He had travelled seventy miles in a circuitous route, and reported the beginning of Indian outrages in his section, relating many instances of cruelty and bloodshed. One of his more distant friends had been attacked, his family murdered, and he himself carried to the torture. The night before the Dunkard fled, his nearest neighbour's family had been slain. Twenty-eight persons were known to have been captured or killed.

A little later in the evening a man came to Bethabara to seek for his strayed horses. The man's name was Benner. After a time he departed. About four o'clock in the morning they were awakened by cries of distress. Upon investigation they found that it was the same man Benner who had been searching for his horses the evening before. He told them that he had returned to his home only to find it robbed and his family gone. They could do nothing to comfort him in his great distress. A little later the brethren engaged in their morning devotions, using the trumpet with the singing. This was not usually done, but it was thought the trumpet might attract the attention of any friend who happened to be in the forest, or to warn the foe that the inmates of the house were not sleeping. When they had concluded their devotional exercises, one of the party went into the yard and fired a gun to warn enemies or attract friends. Blowing the trumpet and firing the gun was continued, and after a time they heard a call. Hastening to the spot, they found the wife of the distressed man with her four children. The smallest child was a babe in the arms of the mother. The joy at this unexpected meeting was touching and pathetic. After the needs of the woman had been attended to and she had somewhat recovered, she related her experiences. Night had come on, and she was awaiting her husband's return. Suddenly the dogs rushed barking into the woods, but returned howling with fear. As she went to the door several stones whizzed by her head. She closed the door and fled from the house, her children with her. As she entered the shelter of the forest, she turned once more toward the house, and by the light within the room saw three men spring in. Continuing her flight, she wandered all night hither and thither, and was providentially guided to Bethabara, where the blowing of the trumpet and the reports of the gun reassured her, and she called for help which was right willingly given.

This incident illustrates the condition of things in the entire section. The most alarming intelligence continued to reach them. Haltem and Owens came from the section north of Wachovia, and said that all the families in that neighbourhood were leaving their homes. A man arrived from the Yadkin Valley, and reported that the neighbours up and down the river were gathering together for mutual protection against either wandering bands of savages, or an organized attack. Even from Haw River came an appeal for help.

With the same thoroughness that characterized all their

INDIAN TROUBLES; FORT ERECTED

actions, the men of Wachovia made their plans. They reasoned among themselves as follows: If the Indians who are causing all the trouble are only in scattered bands, watchfulness and ready rifles will be sufficient. Therefore a watch was established, and their work was so arranged that they remained close to each other. If an alarm had to be given, they could readily assemble. They were not panic-stricken, but continued to run the mill and pushed forward the work on the large building which they were erecting. They further argued that if a large body of Indians was moving against the western part of North Carolina, the only hope would be instant flight. But they determined in the conference which was held that all things should be done wisely. Accordingly the following plan in regard to their property was approved by all. This plan was to be carried out in the event of the approach of a large body of Indians.

1. All the iron was to be hid in the creek, as iron was a precious metal in those days.
2. All the wooden materials were to be buried in the ground.
3. The house was to be fortified so that resistance could be made in case of a sudden attack by a large company of savages.
4. A stock of provisions was stored in the house, especially flour. The miller could not remain at the mill, still the mill was left open for the use of customers who might wish to grind their grain.

These plans and precautions having all been made, they continued with their usual work, and during the following weeks the excitement subsided and many of the refugees left Bethabara to return to their own homes. Some moved away from the section altogether, and the Bethabara warden purchased their cattle and grain from time to time, as it was his policy to provide for the future as well as the present. This policy of providing for the future was a great blessing to many in the later experiences of the war.

Six months passed. In January, 1756, rumours again began to fill them with alarm. This time the reports related to the Moravian congregations in Pennsylvania. Again and again the stories were told, sometimes in one form and sometimes in another, but always the one fact of a massacre was incorporated. Finally they heard the true statement, and though the calamity was not as widespread as they had at first been led to fear, still it was terrible, and might well fill them with forebodings as to their possible fate. Hamilton in his history of the Moravian Church describes the massacre in the colony of Pennsylvania to which the rumours and later reports referred. He says:—

"On November 24 the worst fears were realized at the Gnadenhuetten station on the Mahoni. As the evening shadows lengthened, and the occupants of the Mission House were gathered for their evening meal, the dreaded war-whoops suddenly rang out, and the reports of firearms reëchoed among the hills. When the startled men and women darted from the lower story to the room above, and barricaded the entrance, fire was applied to the house. Those who fled from the flames by leaping from the windows were pierced by bullets or slashed by tomahawks. Out of fifteen only four persons escaped to tell the manner of their companions' martyrdom. The raiders soon left only ashes and charred fragments to tell where once church and school and dwellings had stood."

The inhabitants of Bethlehem and other Moravian towns

INDIAN TROUBLES; FORT ERECTED

escaped, though all these places were threatened at the time of which we write, and Bethlehem had been surrounded by a stockade fort, and two swivel guns had been mounted.

Reference is several times made to a certain body of men whom the diary calls "outlaws." This company had organized and erected a fortification. The colonial authorities sent troops who attacked their stronghold. The men fled, leaving the women and children. One of the outlaws requested the Moravians to adopt his two boys. Just what influence brought these people together is not made clear by the Bethabara journal, nor can we assume with certainty that they were desperadoes. Owens was one of them, and in earlier days he frequently visited Bethabara, and nothing is said against him in the diary. In those days even good men were often styled outlaws by the colonial authorities if perchance they did not belong to the king's party.

The spring of 1756 approached, and the rumours of Indian atrocities continued to reach them. Fearing that because of some neglect disaster might overwhelm the little colony, it was decided to appoint additional watchmen as a precaution against a possible surprise.

In May there were several experiences which indicated the increasing tension between the Indians and white people. Lash was making a trip to some point in the neighbourhood for the purpose of buying oil. He had with him a small keg in which to carry it. Suddenly he was confronted by eleven Indians accompanied by a white woman. The Indians began to revile and abuse him, and ordered him to dismount. Lash refused, knowing that to do so was to surrender to them his horse. Then they pointed to the keg and demanded "fire-water." He told them that he had none, and tapped the head of the little keg to show them that it was empty. Then they became still more excited, and feeling that at any moment they might resort to personal violence, and recalling the many murders in more distant sections, he made an attempt to divert their minds. He told them that he lived twelve miles away, and that he had a good meal awaiting them if they would visit him. This pleased the savages; but the white woman turned in surprise to Lash, told him that he was a fool, and assured him that this band would visit him and steal all that he owned. The savages agreed to come, and the record says that Lash rode away with "great speed."

As soon as Lash arrived at Bethabara, a conference was held and a messenger was sent to the house of Hughes and Banner. The latter gathered men quickly, and when the Indians arrived they found that the number of the white men exceeded their own numbers, and therefore they behaved well. Some distance farther on they continued their depredations, were captured, and taken to Salisbury.

Two weeks later Indians suddenly appeared at Bethabara. No special notice was taken of them. The people acted as though they took it as a matter of course that they should come. The diary says that they pursued their usual duties, but that they were careful to so dispose themselves that the Indians could recognize their strength. Lash went to them, showed them the mill, furnished them with a good meal, and presented them with pipes and tobacco. This greatly pleased them. While eating the meal they talked with each other in signs, and in this way informed Lash that eight more Indians were on their way to Bethabara. That night they slept in the woods. The next morning they returned, were given a good breakfast, and then proceeded on their journey.

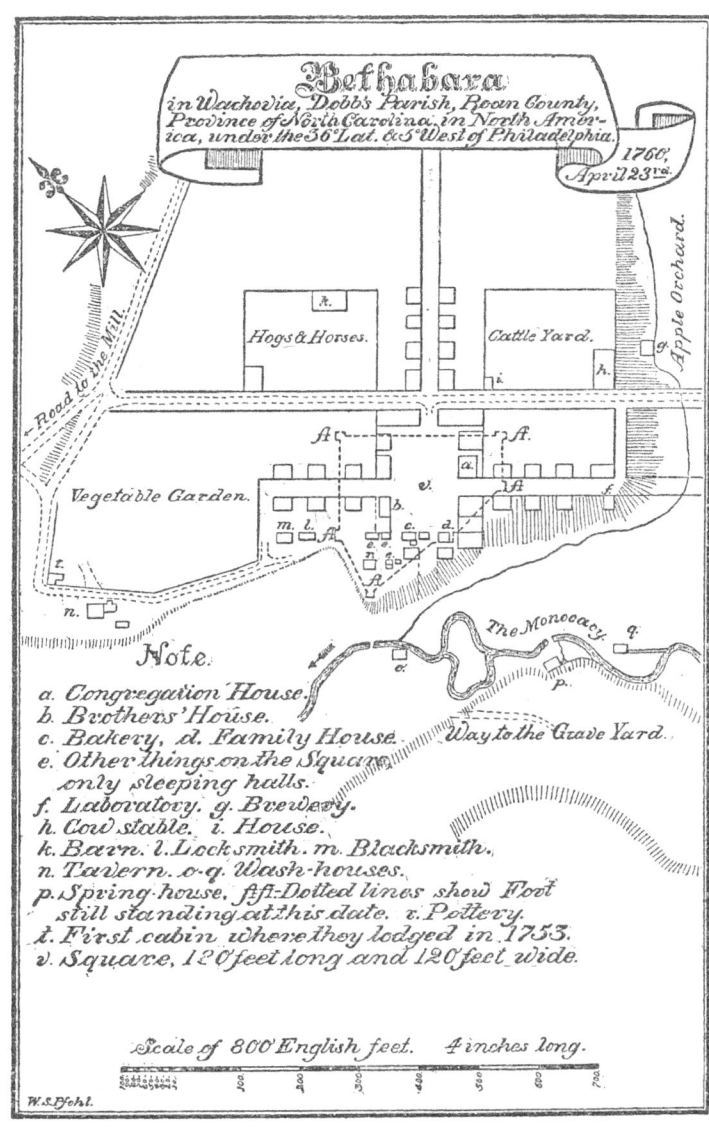

The repeated visits of these increasingly hostile bands of Cherokees made them feel that more decided measures should be taken to protect the colony, especially the women and children, for Wachovia now had a number of families in the village.

One year from the time that the first alarm reached them, that is in July, 1756, an important conference was held. Rauch, the pastor, explained to them that now he had certain knowledge of the hostility of the Cherokees, as they had secretly espoused the cause of the French. He furthermore called attention to the fact that Wachovia was on the frontier, and Bethabara would be one of the first points attacked by the cruel redmen. Two letters were read describing what Bethlehem had done in the midst of troubles similar to their own. These letters told how the town had been surrounded by a stockade, this converting it into a fort, affording protection to life and property. Rauch continued his earnest address, and opened his heart to his congregation. He said that for himself he had no fear; he felt that his life was in the hands of his Saviour; at the same time precaution was wisdom worthy of the people of God, and any neglect which endangered the lives of the helpless ones committed to their care would be a great wrong. The decision was deferred to the next afternoon.

A parenthetical clause in the diary says that although the question of the fortification was deferred till the next afternoon, early in the morning Peterson was sent for more powder and lead.

The afternoon of the following day a second conference was called, and at this meeting it was decided to erect the stockade fortification which became the well-known "Fort," and played a prominent part in the Indian War, being a

INDIAN TROUBLES; FORT ERECTED 41

place of refuge for many unfortunate people, and affording protection for themselves and their families.

All other work was temporarily suspended. One detachment of men went to the forest to cut down and prepare timber; another party transported it to the village; while still another company dug the trenches and placed the timbers in an upright position. Gates were arranged, and when these were secured the inmates were reasonably safe. A good map exists, giving the plan of the fort drawn to scale. Fortunately we are able to locate the foundation of one house which formed a part of the line of the stockade, and with this as a starting-point we can easily trace the outlines. (See d on map, p. 39.)

If the visitor of to-day will enter the grounds just above the "garden," that is about one hundred feet north of the Bethabara church building, and will walk westward toward the graveyard a hundred and fifty feet, where the ground descends to the level of the meadow, he will find himself at the location of the house that formed a part of the stockade line. From this point the line of the fort ran southeast to the site of the present church. Thence north to the brick residence of Mr. Calvin Hauser, about three hundred feet. Thence toward the graveyard hill, to a point near the little bridge. The stockade enclosed all the space from the little bridge southeast to the church, and northeast to Mr. Hauser's house, the eastern boundary extending along the main road. The shape of the fort was triangular, each of the sides being three hundred feet or more. Within the enclosure were the main buildings, that is, the home of the single men, the large congregation house in which the married people lived, as well as a number of other buildings, including the various workshops. The first cabin was not within the stockade.

The further history of the fort will appear as the events of the war develop, but we will add that a spot so rich in historical associations ought to be carefully measured, by means of the map, and the location made plain to all visitors by stone pillars.

The actual work was begun on the 13th of July, 1756, and within ten days the enclosure was finished, except the gates, these having been added a few days later. The news that there was a place of refuge in Wachovia spread rapidly, and from that time forth so great was the company of refugees that special provisions had to be made for them. A village grew up at the mill, which was also surrounded by a stockade. When the record mentions "the people at the mill," reference is made to this second portion of the village of Bethabara.

The following two years brought with them a continuation of the experiences we have just described. The Indians were nominally friendly, but were becoming more and more restless. Bands passed and repassed. Sometimes as many as a hundred warriors would make their appearance at one time, and the number of Indians who visited Bethabara in 1757–1758 was very large. The company of fugitives became larger and larger. The committee endeavoured to dissuade people from moving to Bethabara, unless in case of dire distress, but even this did not prevent them from coming. Every house and every place of temporary abode was filled with the terrified refugees. The behaviour of the Indians was one thing at a strongly guarded fort, but it was quite another thing at a lonely farmhouse in the wilderness.

A petition asking the governor to provide a company of troops to guard this section was one day presented with a request that they sign it. They declined to do so. They

INDIAN TROUBLES; FORT ERECTED   43

argued that if they were not willing to take part in military affairs, they could not logically ask for military aid. They were willing to be assessed to pay money for the support of the soldiers, but the question of sending troops must rest with the governor.

The preparation for the impending struggle was pushed forward from week to week, and every precaution taken. By this time every one felt convinced that the struggle must come. Well it was that they had this time of preparation, and well it was that they used it to complete their defences. Otherwise it might readily have been with them as it was with the martyrs in Pennsylvania and Ohio, and with scores of families in North Carolina, a quick death in the light of their burning houses, or the slower and more terrible death by torture. As it was, by the blessing of the Lord upon their precautionary measures and upon their watchfulness and bravery, all escaped, though murder and bloodshed were all about them during the years that followed.

CHAPTER VI

WACHOVIA DURING THE FRENCH AND INDIAN WAR

NOWHERE does the wisdom of our forefathers call for our admiration more than during the years from 1755 to 1763. So long as it was possible to maintain peaceful relations with the Indians, this was done. When this was no longer possible they made a sudden change of base, and presented a front to the enemy which completely outwitted the utmost cunning of the wily savage. The first statement is proved by the fact that when men and women were being driven in terror from their homes in the neighbourhood of Wachovia, the Indians who caused the trouble came peacefully to Bethabara, enjoyed the fine meals which were prepared for them, rejoiced in the gifts of pipes and tobacco, and far and wide among the redmen spread the fame of Bethabara, a place "where there are good people and much bread." This policy was supplemented by every precaution and every provision for defence. Then there came a sudden turn in affairs, when peace was no longer possible; in a day "the good people and much bread" principle had disappeared, and thenceforth no Indians were allowed to approach. We admire the sagacity which preserved peace as long as peace was possible, as well as the wisdom which carried the community safely through the treacherous and tortuous windings of a cruel war.

When we speak of the Indian War, we must recall the

DURING FRENCH AND INDIAN WAR 45

fact that the Indians always employed a method of warfare different from that of civilized nations. We must not think of planned battles nor of large bodies of moving soldiers. The picture shows us the stealthy warrior destroying the isolated home, or waylaying the unsuspecting traveller. At times they gathered in sufficient numbers to attack a wagon train or even resist a body of troops, but this was not the rule. It will not be our object to give a full list of the sickening atrocities which took place in and around Wachovia, but we will describe a sufficient number to impress the fact that Bethabara was really in the midst of the terrors of this war which swept over the American colonies.

Allusion has already been made to the fact that open hostilities in North Carolina began later than elsewhere, because the Indians in this colony were friendly toward the whites. This friendship became weaker and then disappeared. For a time the semblance of a neutral position was maintained. But the actions of the Indian bands proclaimed a spirit of growing hostility. Finally, when their true position could no longer be concealed by artifice, the Cherokees and Creeks declared war, and the news was announced to the Bethabara settlement in October, 1759. From that time on there was no further attempt on either side to maintain even the semblance of friendship. It is true that we find, recorded in the diary, the statement that they did not seek the destruction of their enemies as in the Old Testament days, but at the same time we see no further personal contact with the redmen. The "good people with plenty of bread" entertained no more bands of Indians, nor was the pipe of peace, nor any other pipe, presented to the passing savages. When the tribes declared war, the Bethabara settlers accepted the situation, and thenceforward even the wary spies were detected and promptly fired upon.

After the news of the declaration of war reached them, they carefully cleared all the undergrowth from the forest around the towns (for Bethania had been begun three miles northwest of Bethabara), and made the road wider between these two places, to prevent ambuscade. The high hill west of Bethabara became a watch tower, and in time of special peril the watchman scanned the horizon for miles around to detect the first sign of the approach of the enemy. The visitor of to-day should always pause as he ascends the steep hill leading to the Bethabara graveyard, and admire the broad expanse of hill and valley spread out before him, and as he admires the beauties of nature, he should recall the perilous task of the solitary watchman of 1759.

The first duty was to rescue their good friend and neighbour, Justice Hughes. He sent a messenger to the village asking for assistance, as the Indians were surrounding him and would soon attack his home. Help was sent, and when they saw the relief approaching they fled.

From Salisbury came the most alarming reports. Men bore testimony to the dreadful atrocities which they themselves had witnessed. The authorities considered the question of drafting every third man for service, but this was not done, as there were enough volunteers. Fort Dobbs, about forty miles west of Wachovia, had within it a number of friendly Indians. Hostile redmen tried to entice them from the fort, but were unsuccessful. Fighting occurred at and around the fort. It was at this time that the authorities began to press the campaign against the Indians. Some of the Cherokees still maintained the

DURING FRENCH AND INDIAN WAR 47

semblance of friendship, and they gave a score or more hostages for the murders which had occurred.

Bethabara now made its final plan in case of an attack, as everything indicated that the savages were all about them and drawing nearer and nearer. They received one hundred pounds of powder from the fort as an additional supply. Spies approached, and they were promptly driven away from the mill, from the fort, and from Bethania. At the latter place they were fired upon by the guards and quickly disappeared in the forest. The volley from the guns of the sentinels was replied to by the war-whoop of the Indians concealed in the woods, and the diary says it sounded like the "howling of a hundred wolves." The scouts sent out from the settlement discovered tracks of Indians in all this section, a large company having encamped for six weeks a short distance from Bethabara.

Much has been written of the New England Pilgrim attending to his religious duty with his gun on his shoulder as he trudged along over the snow. Should the artist of the future depict these godly men in the forests of North Carolina, he will show how, with equal piety, they did not neglect their religious duty. With his Bible in his hand, and with his trusty rifle on his shoulder, with the most pressing dangers about him, the inhabitant of Wachovia went to his usual place of worship. Or again, the picture may be drawn, showing the congregation devoutly singing and praying in the church, while in front are stacked the guns, the sentinel pacing up and down to guard against sudden attacks.

The month of March was a month of terror. On the 9th of the month a man arrived at Bethabara, who had fallen into the hands of the murderous bands. He had escaped and fled to Bethabara. There were among the refugees at the latter place a Mr. Fish and his son, who had been driven from home on the Yadkin River. The father and son asked this man to whom we have referred to accompany them, to see whether their house had escaped the torch of the redman. Before they reached the Fish homestead they entered an ambush from which the arrows flew thick and fast. Father and son fell dead. The stranger was wounded in two places, one arrow passing through his body and protruding from his back. He fled from his enemies and escaped by fording the Yadkin River. He did not draw out the arrows, knowing that without medical aid he would bleed to death. In fact, he felt that he could not survive the effects of his wounds, and he wished to receive spiritual advice before he died. Accordingly he turned toward Bethabara. In his wounded and suffering condition he suddenly saw a company of savages approaching. Plunging into the river, he again crossed and eluded the Indians. By this time night was approaching and it began to rain. How pitiful the condition of this wounded man, as all night long, in the rain and darkness, he wandered in pain and dread of meeting another company of murderers! At the end of twenty-four hours he arrived at Bethabara, and the arrows were extracted by a skilful physician, Dr. Bonn.

A detachment of soldiers were near, and with Lash and others as guides they determined to march to the scene of the murder and give the bodies Christian burial. Before reaching their destination a new trouble met them. A farmer had been besieged in his home, and with his trusty rifle was defending himself and his family. The savages had succeeded in setting fire to the house, and the experience on the Mahoni was about to be

DURING FRENCH AND INDIAN WAR 49

repeated. The flames were taking hold of the building, and in a few moments more the atrocious work of the pitiless band would be completed. Suddenly the sharp report of the guns of the soldiers were heard, one savage fell dead, and the remainder saved themselves by flight. The soldiers did not feel that they dared pursue the Indians, nor did they continue their march to the scene of the Fish murder, as they discovered how large was the number of the enemy. They were satisfied to have rescued the farmer and his family, all of whom they took to Bethabara for protection. This occurred March 11.

The next day an appeal for help came from the neighbourhood of what is now Walnut Cove, the inhabitants stating that they were surrounded by the enemy. A company made up of soldiers and others hurried to the relief of the besieged. They returned and brought with them those who still survived, but help came too late for two families, Robinson and Leslie. One case is particularly pitiful. This man had surrounded his humble home with an outer defence, a small palisade. When the enemy approached, he took shelter behind his improvised fortification. He was driven from his yard into his log house. But still he resisted. Only when his last load of powder had been used did his enemies overcome him; he and his family fell victims to the tomahawk, and in a brief space only a few ashes remained where was before a happy home — truly an experience as thrilling as any related in the Leather Stocking Tales.

One week after the rescue of the people of Town Fork neighbourhood, three ministers were journeying south to where Salem was later founded. One was a Baptist minister by name Thomas. They were attacked by the Indians, Thomas was slain, and later his body was found.

The second minister escaped, but of the third nothing was ever heard. He was doubtless captured and reserved for the torture.

Does the reader ask how fared Bethabara itself? Indians were all about them. Two refugees residing at the mill, by name Makefy and Woodman, went into the forest. Having ventured too far from the protection of the company residing there, Makefy was shot and left by the Indians, who thought him dead. A passing stranger brought him to us. Woodman was captured by the enemy, and of him nothing more was heard.

Even those within the fort were not secure. Two women were milking the cows near the stockade, quite unconscious of impending danger. Looking up, they saw two Indians peering over the fortifications, with their faces disfigured with war-paint. A scream of terror sounded through the enclosure. The Indians fled, but this incident, coupled with the murder at the mill, illustrates their danger.

Not until some time later did the Bethabara people know their peril at this time. A large body of Cherokees, having lost a distinguished chief, determined to take revenge. This was doubtless the party who committed the murders we have described. They had planned on a number of occasions to attack and destroy the village. When approaching the fortifications, they heard the ringing of the bell, and by this they understood that they had been discovered. They then withdrew. The bell was only intended to call the congregation to their evening service. Again the redmen planned an attack, and when stealthily surrounding the fort they heard a trumpet sound out in the stillness of the night, and thinking that their plan had been discovered, they hastily retreated. The trumpet

DURING FRENCH AND INDIAN WAR 51

was really that of the night watchman, who was only announcing that another hour had passed. Little he knew that he was wielding a protection which was as potent as would have been the rifles of the soldiers. Thus a number of weeks passed, and a kind Providence held his protecting hand over his people till the hostile Cherokees moved to another section.

The information in regard to the action of the band of Cherokees around Bethabara, and who were repeatedly prevented from attacking the fort, was received from two interpreters, by name William Priest and Aaron Rice, and they received the information from the well-known chief, "Little Carpenter."

It became evident that this state of affairs would have to be brought to an end, and toward the close of 1760, and especially in 1761, larger bodies of troops began to move here and there, with the determination to check the heartless murders of harmless settlers and helpless women and children. In place of the continued tales of woe and suffering which had reached Bethabara the past two years, came the news of the successes of the militia. One of the murdering bands had been discovered on the Catawba, and before they could escape twenty of their number had been killed. The Indians did not always submit to the soldiers, but in some cases were very bold. A wagon train, with an escort of five hundred soldiers, was attacked near the South Carolina line, and a desperate battle followed. There were one thousand Indians in the attacking party.

This new phase of the war changed the situation of things, and brought about its peculiar experiences. Farming had been greatly neglected in many sections during this time, and yet the soldiers had to be fed. The demands upon Wachovia were great, and well it was that they sowed and reaped and bought grain. They complied with all the demands of the increasing number of soldiers. Even with the arrival of the troops their experiences were not always pleasant. As a Virginia regiment passed through Bethabara, discontent was abroad among the soldiers. When they neared Bethania it culminated in a mutiny. Lash recognized the situation, and persuaded them to camp on the creek, away from the village. That night a court martial was held, and the record says "a dreadful execution took place."

The last important event in the war occurred in June, 1761. Colonel Bird sent a messenger to Wachovia, informing them that an invasion had been made into the middle section of the Cherokees. The most severe measures were necessary. Accordingly the soldiers burned fifteen villages, in which there were eight hundred houses, and they also destroyed eighteen hundred acres of corn. A similar campaign was entered upon in Virginia, and these two efforts broke the power of the Indians.

It was some time before the usual quiet was restored. Many desperate characters were passing hither and thither. Murders still occurred in various sections. The people at the mill were not always upright, still, in a time of danger they could not be ordered off. Famine, too, was abroad in the land, but they rose to the needs of the times, and the writer of the Bethabara diary says, "This year we became a storehouse (bread room) for the entire western portion of North Carolina."

CHAPTER VII

THE FOUNDING OF BETHANIA AND A TIME OF SORROW

BEFORE leaving the period of the Indian War, we will study the internal history of Wachovia. It might well be supposed that with all the difficulties there could be little progress, yet the contrary is true. All their trades and industries increased because of the needs of the times. Their farming operations were on a larger scale than usual. Their wagons were going hither and thither, and their store and mill were centres of activity.

After the arrival of the first twelve settlers, others journeyed from Pennsylvania from time to time. Some of these came to direct and plan, and to establish the proper relationship between Wachovia and the central church government in Germany. Among these were Spangenberg, Nitschman, Boehler, Zeisberger, Hehl, and others. Some came as leaders and directors of the communities, and remained several years. Still others came to make North Carolina their permanent home. Single men arrived in larger or smaller companies. A band of boys walked the entire distance from Bethlehem, and entered the various trades to " grow up with the country."

The advent of the first married couples was a marked event. Two years had passed since the first twelve men had entered the little hut built by Hans Wagner. These years had been busy years, but no doubt there was often the desire for the pleasures of home life. These unmarried men had erected a large house which they now occupied, and when they heard that the first married couples were on their way to Wachovia, they began to prepare with great zeal for the erection of what was termed a "Congregation House." In this building the married people would reside, and in the same house would be located the new meeting hall or chapel. As the days and weeks went by, the interest in the approaching company increased, and when it was finally announced that on the morrow they would reach Bethabara, we can well imagine the hurry and bustle which attended the final preparation. Toward evening, November 4, 1755, the long-expected company arrived. A formal reception was tendered them that evening. There were twenty-nine in the party, fourteen of whom were married people. Including all who came since the beginning, we find that there were sixty members in the congregation at the end of the second year.

On the evening of November 9, Fries writes: "This closes the diary of the single brethren. What shall I say who have served a year and a half in this field? Praise the Lord for all his blessings!"

Heretofore they lived in one house, sat down to one table, and conferred as "a committee of the whole," on all subjects relating to the work of the community, and the record says "nothing was decided without the advice of all having been given." It was a happy collegiate life in which they were joined very closely together. It was said that Fries, who was their devoted spiritual adviser during this time, and who later served the church faithfully elsewhere, always spoke in the warmest terms of the happiness of those days, when they made the beginning of the new work in North Carolina.

At this time we find a note in regard to what is termed

BETHANIA AND A TIME OF SORROW   55

the smaller conference, "Enge Conferenz." As their number had now increased so as to make it impossible to gather together the entire community for the consideration of each and every question, and as the company was now made up of men, women, and children, the smaller conference was begun, and was no doubt composed of the ministers and the heads of the several divisions of the congregation. It was the beginning of the government by elected or *ex-officio* boards.

More space might be given to the visitors of note, either Moravians or others. We might speak of Bishop Spangenberg, who is so well known because of his writings, and is beloved because of his godly life and his genial disposition, as well as his scholarly attainments. We could expand on the visit of Bishop Boehler, so well known to all Methodists, the friend and spiritual adviser of John Wesley when he was being prepared for his great work by the spirit of God. We might mention more at length the great Indian missionary, David Zeisberger, who spent sixty years in missionary labours, and whose body is buried on the banks of the beautiful Tuscarawas River, in Ohio. To these could be added the names of Hehl and Nitschman, and others, who, by their successful labours and devoted lives, have come down in history as great men in the cause of Jesus Christ.

In like manner we could relate how the village was visited by the chief justice on more than one occasion, how they welcomed Colonel Bird and Colonel Frohok, and other well-known military men of their day, nor would it be right to forget the Philadelphia botanist who spent some time in Wachovia, and declared that the hillside west of Bethabara was a "treasure-house for the botanist." We might tell of the cultured and refined Swiss

56 HISTORY OF WACHOVIA

lady who came many miles to make purchases of goods, and who left greatly pleased by the visit, but who met with an untimely end on her return journey, probably drowned while crossing one of the streams. The entire subject of the arrivals and the departures we will include in the following list of all who came and went from 1753 to 1762. In the later years the numbers were so great that this list will be the only one which can include the entire membership.

Grube, Rev. Bernhard Adam.
Lash, Jacob.
Kalberlahn, Dr. Hans Martin.
Peterson, Hans.
Merkly, Christoph.
Lash, Herman.
Ingebretsen, Erich.
Feldhausen, Henrich.
Lischer, John.
Lung, Jacob.
Pfeil, Friedrich Jacob.
Beroth, Jacob.
Koenigsderfer, Rev. Gottlob.
Seidel, Rev. Nathaniel.
Haberland, Rev. Joseph.
April 15, 1754.
Fries, Rev. Jacob.
Sept. 10, 1754.
Boehler, Bishop Peter.
Hoeger, Andrew (Surveyor).
Oct. 26, 1754.
Christensen, Hans Christoph.
(For the mill).
von der Merk, Jacob.
Schmidt, George.
Kapp, Jacob.
Bez, Andrew.
Holder, George.

Rancke, John.
Nagel, John.
April 28, 1755.
Nitschman, Bishop David.
Benzien, Rev. Christian Thomas.
Stauber, ———.
June 13, 1755.
Rancke, Michael.
Steiner, Jacob.
Baumgarten, John George.
Aug. 1, 1755.
Sauter, John Michael.
Kreiter, ———.
Mueller, Joseph.
Sept. 15, 1755.
Wutke, Samuel.
Goss, Andrew.
Richter, John.
Goepfert, George.
Oct. 11, 1755.
Friebel, Christian.
Kuerschner, Christoph.
Angel, William (England).
Pfeiffer, Christian.
Nov. 4, 1755.
Hoffman, Rev. Gottlob.
Bachhoff, Rev. Ludwig.
Fogle (Fockel), Gottlieb.

Kremer (Cramer), Adam.
Aust, Gottfried.
Myers, Stephen.
Rasp, Melchior.
Renner, John George.
Muenster, Melchior.
Rauch, Rev. and Mrs. Christian.
Kuehnast, Mr. and Mrs. Christoph.
Opiz, Mr. and Mrs. Charles.
Krause, Mr. and Mrs. Matthew.
Bieffel, Mr. and Mrs. Henry.
Schmidt, Mr. and Mrs. Christoph.
Schaub, Mr. and Mrs. John Frederich.
May 28, 1756.
Zeisberger, Rev. David.
Aug. 22, 1756.
Hehl, Bishop Matthew.
Seidel, Rev. Christian.
Sept. 12, 1756.
Bischoff, Rev. and Mrs. David.
Oct. 29, 1756.
Grabs, Mr. and Mrs. Gottfried.
Grabs, William (nine months old).
Straus, Abraham.
Schaaf, Jeremiah.
Heckedorn, Erhard.
Hoffman, Thomas.
Anspach, Nicholas.
Dec. 31, 1756.
Mack, Martin.
Garrison, Nicholas.
June 28, 1757.
Pizman, ——.
Nov. 17, 1757.
Lawatsch, Mr. and Mrs. Anton.
Lueck, Mr. and Mrs. Martin.
Lueck, Magdalin.
Hege, Mr. and Mrs. Balthasar.

Lash, Mrs. Anna.
July 22, 1758.
Ettwein, Rev. John.
Rogers, Rev. and Mrs. Jacob.
Nilson, Mr. and Mrs. Jonas.
Reuter, Gottlieb (surveyor).
Lenzner, Henry.
Wuertele, John.
Blum, Jacob.
Lash, George.
Nov. 11, 1758.
Bonn, Dr. Jacob.
May 30, 1759.
Seidel, Catharina.
Kalberlahn, Catharina.
Lash, Barbara.
Ranke, Elizabeth.
Beroth, Maria Elizabeth.
Kremer, Barbara.
Ettwein, Johanna Maria.
June 5, 1759.
Spangenberg, Bishop and Mrs.
Buerstler, John.
June 25, 1759.
Schaus, Andrew.
Dec. 31, 1759.
Odenwald, Michael.
July 23, 1760.
Dickson, Mr. and Mrs. Christian.
von der Merk, Christina.
Schubert, Dr. John A.
Edwards, William.
Feb. 15, 1761.
Post, John Frederick.
Bonn, John.
June 8, 1762.
Graff, Rev. and Mrs. John Michael.
von Gammon, Mr. and Mrs. Abraham.

Transsou, Mr. and Mrs. Philip.
Transou, Abraham.
Transou, Philip.
Transou, Maria.
Herbst, John Henry.
Witke, Elizabeth.
Leibert, Maria.
Grosh, Felicitas.
Holder, Elizabeth.
Palmer, Elizabeth.
                Nov. 14, 1762.
Koffler, Adam.
Stoz, Peter.

Although we have devoted some space to the industrial features of the first year, it is necessary to allude to these matters in the period now under consideration.

In the year 1755 six houses were finished, or nearly finished, in addition to the smaller ones described earlier in the history.

Mill.
Congregation house.
Single brethren's house.
Kitchen.
Smith shop.
Home for the miller.

The erection of all these was accomplished without serious accident, though one of the workmen had his arm broken, and on New Year's Day, 1756, the large framework in one of the buildings fell, but providentially all the workmen were away at the time. The mill gave them some trouble before all was in order. The iron bearings of the large wheel were defective, hence they had to be taken out and repaired. The first millstones were found to be too soft, therefore another set had to be quarried and dressed. Gradually all things were arranged. The married people moved into their house March 5, 1756, and the single men were again given possession of their home. A bell was placed in position, the same that alarmed the Indians when they had gathered for the attack. This bell was blown down from its frame about the close of the Indian War, and was broken. An organ was brought to Bethabara in 1762.

BETHANIA AND A TIME OF SORROW 59

The farming was successful during these years. They understood how to get the best results. One year during the war they planted an additional sixty acres in wheat, because they thought the demands would be greater than usual.

In 1759 they harvested 1400 bushels of grain.

In 1761 the harvest is described as follows: —

1984 shocks of wheat.   7 wagon loads of barley.
304 shocks of rye.

The harvest of 1762 was as follows: —

1009 bushels of wheat.   40 bushels of buckwheat.
163 bushels of rye.   73 bushels of flaxseed.
328 bushels of barley.   114 bushels of corn.
300 bushels of oats.
                         ———
                         2027 total.

This was several hundred bushels more than the year before.

The commercial interests were not as great prior to 1763 as after that date. At the same time, some of the industries had assumed creditable proportions, among them the pottery trade. When it was known that a kiln would be burned, large crowds gathered, and the ware was sold as soon as taken out. People came fifty miles and more to the mill for flour and meal.

We notice a number of entries in the diary which cannot be classified, but must be given as independent items. As early as this we note the request of parents to have their children cared for by the Moravians, as if the love of the church for children had been recognized before the day of schools.

There is a record of the appointment of fire inspectors, that is, men whose duty it was to inspect the condition of each house, to be sure that there was no risk of fire from neglect or defect.

A request came to them from South Carolina to establish a colony, a grant of land having been offered them. Request also came from Fayetteville to establish a warehouse, in order that their commercial interests might be furthered.

We read that on a certain day all engaged in opening a new road which they termed "The king's highway."

The government paid the usual bounty for all the wolf scalps which were presented to the proper authorities.

Wild pigeons passed in great flocks; so numerous were they that the air was darkened by their numbers, and when they settled for the night great limbs of trees were broken by the weight of their numbers.

The poll tax was a little more than $2.

The professional work done by Kalberlahn and Bonn is worthy of our admiration. Not only were they called upon to attend to the ordinary forms of illness, but especially difficult cases arose. Wounded men were brought to Bethabara, and received the best care and interest. We are told of one man who had his skull fractured. A part of the skull pressed upon the brain, and his mind was affected. By a skilful operation the splinter of bone was removed and the man's reason was restored. It is of interest to note the visit of the Bethabara physician to Hans Wagner, the same farmer whose hut had sheltered the first settlers when they arrived in 1753. In the records we find the note that on a certain occasion "all the people in Bethania were bled by the direction of the physician." A list of the medical herbs gathered is recorded and a laboratory and a drug store established. During this period the good and famous physician Kalberlahn died, and Bonn arrived. The latter won great honour in the War of the American Revolution, as a physician and surgeon.

BETHANIA AND A TIME OF SORROW 61

In the domestic life we find among the arrivals, which were now increasingly frequent, the names of a number of single women who came in 1762. It is but logical to find, later in the year, the record of the first marriages in Wachovia.

The first death occurred December 26th, 1757, — a little child, the infant daughter of Mr. and Mrs. Opiz, by name,

ANNA MARIA.

In speaking of this death the diary says, "She was gathered in as the first flowret in Wachovia by our Heavenly Gardener, and her little tenement was sown as the first grain of wheat in this God's acre, which upon this occasion was consecrated."

The first child born in Bethabara was a little girl, the daughter of Mr. and Mrs. Krause, the date being May 11, 1756. The name was

ANNA JOHANNA.

The political history of Wachovia during this period is both interesting and important, and parts are given in detail in the record. In 1755 the legislature was petitioned to constitute Wachovia a separate parish. This petition was granted. Benzien and Stauber were the representatives from Wachovia to present the petition. Jacob and Herman Lash waited on the governor in Newberne, in December, and received official notice that the bill was a law. The representatives of the Bethabara congregation were graciously received by Governor Dobbs.

In April, 1756, the Act of the Assembly was communicated to the congregation by Rauch and Angel. By this act twenty men were created freeholders, and each man received fifty acres of land. In May these twenty men were summoned to Salisbury to be invested with their new powers. The journey was somewhat difficult for so large a company, but at nine o'clock, June 1, all arrived in Salisbury. The record gives a detailed account of the visit, and we copy the extract, which throws light upon the experiences at court one hundred and fifty years ago: —

"In Salisbury some lodged at Mr. Burry's in a little room. Hughes and the Sheriff welcomed them. Weidell, a captain of the fort, of nice appearance, paid his respects. He had met Benzien at Newbern. In his reception he was very kind. They had a short discussion and all went to the court house to elect vestrymen. A herald took their names, and then made known to them their duties. The vote of the Freeholders was taken, and the names of the vestrymen made known to the public. When this was done the Chief Justice announced to the vestrymen that they would have to appear at court and select two wardens. The Sheriff said that as it would be a task for so many to travel to Salisbury he would himself come to Bethabara to qualify them. They gladly accepted his offer. Twelve vestrymen were chosen. Thus the affair happily ended.

"Chief Justice Handely and other gentlemen were invited to dine with us, but the Chief Justice had to continue the sitting of the court. The Sheriff with Hughes and Carter came and sat down with us. We had an enjoyable time in our social intercourse. After the meal we bade them farewell. The Sheriff took Lash and Rauch to pay their respects to the Chief Justice, who was profuse in his professions of friendship.

"After this we got ready for our journey, which began at three o'clock. We went eighteen miles and camped where we had been the day before for dinner. Haltem and two others were with us. Haltem had recovered his stolen horse. He went on to Wachovia, as his family was at Bethabara. A thunderstorm drenched the party, as it poured rain for two hours. We arrived well and happy. In the evening meeting Rauch gave an account of the visit to Salisbury."

June 21, Justice Hughes visited Wachovia to complete the organization of Dobbs Parish. The record says:—

"The Vestrymen gathered in Lash's room before breakfast. There the oath was taken. We answered "yes." Thus we were qualified to legally act. Our first step was to select two wardens. We elected Lash and Wutke. The organization was now complete according to the wish of our hearts. We thanked the Lord that it is so. A breakfast was served, and remuneration given to the officials."

The vestry meeting was held the first month of each year, and the proper officials elected.

Rogers, an English-speaking minister, came to Bethabara, this evidently being one of the requirements of the regulations of Dobbs Parish. In August formal notice was sent to the governor that the English pastor had arrived, and that he would later present himself in person. In January he visited both Newbern and Brunswick, and was formally presented to Governor Dobbs. Several visits to the governor were made by others. On one of these visits, Lash was made justice of the peace, and during the war he was appointed official commander of the men at Bethabara and Bethania, so that in case of emergency he could act with full military authority. This authority was called into use on more than one occasion when turbulent crowds threatened harm. The freeholders were authorized to vote for members of the legislature.

The festival services were held regularly, and special mention is made of Christmas and Easter. At the Christmas meetings there was great rejoicing, and we are told that the presentation of lighted wax candles to the children was begun thus early. On one Christmas eve the little children from the stranger families at the mill were invited to the church, and each child was presented with a little card, and was served with a love-feast bun and coffee. They were a ragged and neglected little company, "so poorly clad," says the diary, "that it seems the very stones would cry out in pity." In addition to the material pleasures, the minister gave good words of religious advice.

At the Easter services the company was increasingly large. These were soul-stirring occasions, and though many had strange and fantastic ideas in regard to what they expected to witness, all returned to their homes impressed with the deep religious spirit which actuated the congregation.

In 1763 they celebrated the tenth anniversary of the arrival of the first settlers in Wachovia, and by this time peace and prosperity were again abroad in the land.

Three miles north of Bethabara is located what was called the Black Walnut Bottom. Early in their history land was cleared, and in 1759 the question of providing for certain existing circumstances brought this section before them. A number of persons were drawn very close to them in sympathy and had expressed a desire to unite with the church. These outside friends could not readily be received into the congregation of Bethabara, since there was a certain community of material affairs which would have failed as soon as a strange or unsympathetic element was introduced. Hence these strangers had continued to live with or near the Moravians, but had not

BETHANIA AND A TIME OF SORROW 65

united with them. Furthermore, there were within the church a number of families who desired to have more individuality in their home interests. The condition of affairs in Wachovia made the community of interests very desirable at the beginning, but it was never the plan of the church to deprive the members of the right to own property. To meet the wants of these two classes it was decided to begin another village at the Black Walnut Bottom, in which the members could own their homes, conduct their own housekeeping independent of the general economy, and a part of the town was assigned to the strangers who had applied for membership and later became members. This village was to be only a village, as was also Bethabara. The larger central town was to be established at some point to be later selected. To this new settlement was given the name "Bethania."

Bishop Spangenberg came to Wachovia in 1759, six years after his first visit, when he and his party surveyed the land. June 12, Spangenberg, Seidel, and Jacob Lash decided the exact location of Bethania. It is on a gently sloping hillside, north of the Black Walnut Bottom. On the 30th of the same month the streets and lots were laid out. About thirty town lots were marked off, and two thousand acres set aside for the use of the Bethania congregation. This land was divided into smaller sections to be rented to the members. The records of the first days in the establishment of this new village of Bethania have a peculiar interest, because of the sad and even tragic circumstances connected with the writing. The diary was probably written by Christian Seidel. He was active in prosecuting the work at Bethania. At a certain point the handwriting in the original manuscript changes, and this is the exact time when Seidel was stricken with the fatal fever. Hence the extract which follows may be looked upon as one of the last acts of the good man who had followed the remains of his devoted wife to the grave, and who was himself carried thence so soon after. The journal says in regard to the founding of Bethania: —

"*July* 9, 1759. — In the morning we held a conference in regard to building Bethania. Reuter, the surveyor, was appointed to lay out the new road from the mill. *July* 10. — Seidel and Lash with eight men went early to make the road, and to cut down wood for the houses. Erected our tent in the midst of the forest in the centre of the location of the new town. *July* 11. — We had our morning devotions, in which Bishop Spangenberg gave his benediction to the whole company, but especially to the Bethania party who were beginning their work. The company began their labours by opening the road. They were served with breakfast, there being sixteen in the party. Noon arrived, and dinner was eaten in the tent in the Bethania square. After the meal we began transporting the timbers for the Grabs house. Reuter measured the square, and marked the location of the houses. In the latter part of the afternoon we had a religious service. *July* 12. — We were awakened by some of the brethren beginning to sing hymns, and when ready for the work of the day, we went to the place where the Grabs house is to be located. The morning prayers were conducted on this spot, and we prayed that those who would reside in the house, as well as all the future inhabitants of the town, might be blessed. The service drew us very near to each other in the bonds of brotherly love. Last evening we heard the Bethabara trumpet, three miles distant. Reuter and Peterson went back to Bethabara.

BETHANIA AND A TIME OF SORROW 67

Kapp became ill and had to remain in his tent. At ten o'clock the old man Hauser came to cut timber for his house. Jacob Steiner presented a pound of sugar to those who were sick. In the afternoon we had a heavy rain and thunder-storm. Spangenberg came soon after, and was pleased to see that the framework was up. We had a fine evening service. Spangenberg remained all night. *July* 13. — After the morning service we cut out the road to the stone quarry, and made a bridge over the creek. Later a number of men came from Bethabara. Holder and Spangenberg returned to Bethabara. The foundation stones of the Grabs house are in place, and the chimney commenced. Shingles placed on the roof. Sixteen at work. By sundown we had finished our work, and returned to Bethabara. *July* 15. — Conference about second house in Bethania. This house is to be thirty feet long and twenty feet wide, and is to serve as a model for the future dwelling-houses. At four o'clock Spangenberg notified us that on Wednesday, Brother Grabs would move to Bethania, and he designated other brethren who would live there. Brother Grabs has already been assigned to his house. The lots were divided as follows:—

No. 1. — Grabs.   No. 20. — Hege.
No. 2. — Beroth. No. 21. — Biefel.
No. 4. — Kremer. No. 22. — Opiz.
No. 5. — Ranke.   No. 23. — Schmidt.

July 16. — We went to Bethania and the wagons followed us. Lash came later. The day's work was to clear lot No. 6, for the meeting hall. This was to be the second building, and in addition to this we were to cut more logs. The chimney of the Grabs house finished. *July* 17. — Our morning prayers were held on the location of the second house. The text of the day was about the servants of the Lord, a fitting scripture for the day that we laid the foundation of the church. Grabs came from Bethabara, and Lash and Seidel returned. *July* 18. — Peterson went to Bethabara. Grabs, his wife, and his little son William moved into their new house; they are the first inhabitants of Bethania. Service conducted by Spangenberg on the site of the new church, his text being taken from the 23d Psalm. Shore received lot No. 10 and Strupe No. 17. [These two names are spelled in the old record Shoer and Strube.] *July* 19. — In the afternoon Lash returned. Seidel called home by the illness of his wife. Otherwise the work continued as usual. Reuter measured sixty acres of land to be cleared. He also laid out an orchard. A road was made from Dorothea Creek. Made shingles and nailed them on. One side of the meeting hall finished. Seidel sent word that Mrs. Rogers was dead. Most of the brethren went to the funeral. *July* 21. — Some of the members visited Bethania, among them Spangenberg. He conducted the meeting."

Here the diary suddenly stops. We know that on the next day Mrs. Seidel died, and a little later Seidel visited Bethania. While there he became ill and felt that his end was probably near. A few days later he entered into his rest.

This sad dispensation introduces us to the period which we have termed the time of sorrow. There is no chapter in the entire history of one hundred and fifty years so sad as that of the summer of 1759. The work of the Moravian colony had been blessed. Good and earnest men and women had come to North Carolina to make it their home. The village of Bethabara was growing. The new village of Bethania had been founded. Their har-

BETHANIA AND A TIME OF SORROW 69

vests were abundant, and their efforts in every direction were being crowned with success. Even the terrors of the Indian War did not ampen their ardour, yet at this time the saddest experience possible came upon them.

This terrible visitation was a deadly fever. We do not know what was the exact nature of the disease, but it was stated that it was contagious, that the blood of the patient became "boiling hot," that there was in some cases a white eruption, and that the sickness lasted only from two to four days. After considering all the symptoms described in the diary, medical men of our day give it as their opinion that it was probably typhus, or ship fever, no doubt brought to the settlement by one of the numerous strangers passing through from a seaport town. Whatever may have been the nature of the disease, the results were speedy and fatal. The first to succumb was Mrs. Rogers, the wife of the English pastor. She died at noon on the 19th of July, 1759. The next day her body was tenderly laid to rest in the graveyard on the hill, a large concourse of friends being present. Two days later Mrs. Seidel, the wife of the German pastor, died, and on July 23 she was buried in the same sacred spot, which they termed their "Hutberg." After three days the spirit of Seidel took its flight, and at that time Dr. Kalberlahn, the faithful and able physician, became ill. He heard of several cases of sickness in the town, and deplored the fact that he could not go to them, and relieve their suffering. Two days after the death of the minister the physician closed his eyes in the last long sleep, and on the 30th of the month, Ingebretzen, one of their business managers, died. He had a foreboding of his coming end. On the 27th of the month he closed his accounts, and going to his superior in office he stated that, though four days remained in the month, if his forebodings were fulfilled he could turn over all things in order. His premonitions were realized and the same day the fever took hold of him. Before the close of the month he had closed all his earthly accounts, and his body was laid to rest beneath the sighing pines.

To understand fully the dark cloud of sorrow which fell upon them, we must recall all the surrounding circumstances. Even though prosperity was smiling upon them, they were only a little band, a month's journey away from their nearest friends. A cruel and relentless war was in progress around them. How sad the company of mourners as they returned from the funeral of Mrs. Rogers, and how much heavier their hearts as the second consecrated woman was laid to rest beside her! Then the blow fell on their minister, and alarm began to mingle with heaviness of heart, only to be increased and intensified as their physician so soon followed. And when the warden and others were called home, no doubt the question uppermost in their minds was, "Where will this end?"

This time of sorrow needs no comment. It was so deep and terrible that even at this distant day our sympathy flows out to the stricken little colony. But their faith in an all-wise Providence was never shaken, and on the following Easter the congregation gathered on the hill at sunrise, in the midst of the green graves of their loved ones. The people from the mill joined the procession, and one hundred and fifty or more stood with bared heads, as good Bishop Spangenberg read aloud the confession of faith, and then solemnly repeated the words: —

"And keep us in everlasting fellowship with those of our brethren and sisters who since last Easter day have entered into the joy of their Lord."

BETHANIA AND A TIME OF SORROW

At this point in the prayers, he read in a clear and tender voice the names of the departed, —

Christian Seidel.	Samuel Wutke.
Hans Kalberlahn.	Samuel Shaub.
Henry Biefel.	Maria Rogers.
Eric Ingebretzen.	Catharine Seidel.
John Lentzner.	Anna Lash.
John Negel.	Anna Smith.

The sun rose and bathed the hills and meadows and the distant mountains with its glorious morning light. The well-armed guards gazed with unrelaxing vigilance into the gloomy shadows of the forest, lest the savages should choose this sunrise service as the time for a murderous assault. The procession was again formed at the conclusion of the prayers, and as it made its way down the hill the heavy tramp of soldiers was heard on the opposite side of the village. This Easter Day in 1760 should never be forgotten: the watchful sentinels, guarding the praying congregation; the silent graves, recalling the sorrows since last Easter; the clank of arms as the militia filed into the fortified village; the sunshine just as bright and gorgeous as if no sorrows threw their dark shadows athwart the months; and above all the triumphant faith of those true and brave men whose unwavering trust in God was never shaken, and was never more severely tried than in 1759 and 1760, and which never appeared in a brighter and grander light than on that glorious Easter morning one hundred and forty-two years ago.

CHAPTER VIII

BETWEEN THE INDIAN WAR AND THE AMERICAN REVOLUTION

1763-1773

THE thirty years from the founding of Bethabara, in 1753, to the celebration of the Peace Jubilee at the close of the Revolution are divided into three periods of ten years each. The first period includes the founding of Bethabara and Bethania; the second that of Salem; the third the formal organization of Friedberg, Friedland, and Hope.

The first of these ten-year periods brought the colony into touch with the natives, their cruelty and treachery, during the Indian War. The second introduced them to the royal governors, Dobbs, Martin, and Tryon. They were in the midst of the struggle which ended in the suppression of the Regulators, and for a time Tryon had his headquarters in Wachovia. During this decade they came into close contact with that type of men which passed away with the War of Independence. The last one introduced the new era, and includes the interesting experiences of the Revolution. There is a marked contrast between each one.

1753-1763, the redman: his friendship, his treachery, his cruel warfare.

1763-1773, the rough Regulators, and side by side with them the almost royal ceremonies of the ostentatious Tryon,

BETWEEN WAR AND REVOLUTION

and his struggle with and persecution of these misguided men.

1773-1783, the American patriot, driving before him the British army as the new era is ushered in.

These are the bold and striking characteristics. The Indian troubles have been studied. The period which includes the battle of Alamance is now before us.

We will first consider the affairs of the Province, then the founding of Salem; and finally the account of the two visits of Tryon will form a suitable introduction to the time of the Revolution.

1763-1773 were eventful years in the internal history of Wachovia, and witnessed many important constitutional changes. These will be considered in the next chapter. The present chapter will bring before the reader the affairs of the Province in general.

The Indian troubles were at an end. No doubt the redman suffered much at the hands of the whites, — a natural result of their own cruelties inflicted upon the rude settlers during the war. The diary says the inhabitants of Wachovia were uneasy regarding the rumours which came to them of the sufferings of converted Indians in Pennsylvania. In that state the frontiersmen were cruel and unjust in their broadcast attacks upon the redmen; they did not distinguish between the wild, marauding bands and the peaceful, civilized Christian Indians. The event to which these reports referred is thus described by Hamilton, " History of the Moravian Church," p. 240 : —

"Dreading a counterpart of the Conestoga massacre at their village, Governor Penn had, therefore, already ordered the Moravian Indians to remove to Philadelphia for safety, together with their missionaries, Zeisberger, Grube, Schmick, and Roth. Excitement ran high in the city. Members of the Society of Friends, setting aside their peace principles in the conflict of duties, took arms to defend their charges, against whom frontiersmen swore vengeance. For a time the lives of the missionaries and their converts seemed to be in serious danger. But actual strife was providentially averted, though the arrangements for their sustenance at Province Island, the summer quarantine of the port, were distressingly inadequate, and the evidences of insecurity and of possible inability to protect them led to an attempt to remove them to New York. Thither they proceeded under escort. But when Perth Amboy was reached, they were stopped by a peremptory inhibition of farther advance, and had to retrace their weary steps. Returned to Philadelphia, the barracks were assigned as their quarters. Now came a rumour that men from Lancaster and Reading were marching on the capital, bent on having the lives of the Moravian Indians. Philadelphia surged with excitement. A large part of the people sympathized with the Paxton party. Again blows were averted by the determined position of the governor and his associates, backed by the sober treaty-respecting majority. But terrible distress was experienced by the Indians and their teachers in their cramped quarters and from the unnatural life. Confinement enfeebled them. Dysentery and smallpox broke out. From January, 1764, to March, 1765, fifty-six victims of barrack life were laid in the potter's field."

No similar scenes were witnessed in North Carolina, for even when the military expeditions resorted to the severest measures, they merely destroyed the villages and farms, but spared their lives. "Little Carpenter" made overtures to Bethabara to establish friendly relations, but there is no notice of a response to his efforts at that time, though later the Moravians were very active in evangelistic efforts in his tribe. It was in these years that Governor Tryon made his expensive journey to the Indian reservation to locate their boundary line, and received the severe criticisms of his opponents for spending so much money to settle such a trivial matter; he greatly rejoiced the chief by presenting him with a suit of his own clothing, but the gift of the suit of clothing did not make the tribe accept his ruling in regard to the reservation lines. On this occasion the Indians gave the governor the sobriquet, "The Great Wolf of North Carolina," and the enemies of the governor continued to apply this title, though with a different meaning.

The religious work of the period was vigorously and successfully done. Within the church itself the services were carried on with great earnestness. A number of leading men came to Wachovia, either to assist in making the constitutional changes, or to permanently engage in the work of the province. We notice such names as De Watteville, Gregor, De Schweinitz, Marshall, Utley, Soelle, and others. A bishop for Wachovia was consecrated, and men were ordained to the ministry to serve as pastors or to superintend the various divisions of the congregations. Instruction was regularly given to the young people. They were active in the home mission work, and the foundation was laid for several new congregations. Had the church all through the succeeding years followed the example of men like Utley and Soelle, the Moravian Church in North Carolina would be a large and powerful organization. The fathers thought differently, and only under special circumstances did they allow an outside friend to join the church.

This decade witnessed the preliminary work of Friedberg, Friedland, and Hope. Friedberg is situated in a beautiful grove nine miles south of Salem, Friedland is five miles east, and Hope is west about eight miles. Reichel, in "Moravians in North Carolina," gives a carefully prepared account of the founding of these three congregations, pp. 69–79.

Friedberg

In August, 1754, not quite a year after the arrival of the first Moravians in Wachovia, Adam Spach settled about three miles from the southern line of the land of the brethren. In September he visited Bethabara for the first time, to become acquainted with his nearest German neighbours, and cut a road from his house to Bethabara. At a second visit, in December, he requested the brethren to send one of their number from time to time to hold meetings in his house; but, for various reasons, this request could not be complied with at that time. During the first alarms of the Indian War he and his wife were among those who took refuge in the fort.

At his oft-repeated and urgent solicitations, Bachhof visited Adam Spach on November 26, 1758, and preached in his house, eight German families having assembled there for the purpose. The commencement was thus made, and preaching at this place continued at intervals, the number of hearers gradually increasing, and at one time considerably augmented by the arrival of some families from Pennsylvania, previously in connection with the congregations at Heidelberg and York, who now settled in this neighbourhood.

A meeting-house would have been built by them at once if they could have received any promise or assurance of receiving a stationed minister. Thus matters remained

BETWEEN WAR AND REVOLUTION

till 1766, when, in answer to their petition, they received a promise that a minister would be stationed among them, which caused them to prepare immediately for the building of a meeting-house. During the preparations of the building, Peter Frey died, and was buried in the present Friedberg burying-ground.

The house being finished, Utley consecrated the same on March 11, 1769, and kept a love-feast for all those who desired to become members of the congregation. On the 12th he preached publicly, and baptized two children, viz. Joseph Frey and John Walk.

They now had stated services every four weeks, and very soon fourteen married couples pledged themselves to the support of a resident minister. Their names were:—

Valentine Frey.	Adam Hartman.	Christian Stauber.
Christian Frey.	John Mueller.	Martin Walk.
Peter Frey.	John N. Boeckel.	Peter Volts.
George Frey.	Frederick Boeckel.	Adam Spach.
George Hartman.	Jacob Graeter.	

On February 18, 1770, Bachhof was introduced as their minister by Graff and Utley.

In January, 1772, this society was formally consecrated a Moravian Brethren's Congregation, by the name of Friedberg (hill of peace), in which, besides the preaching of the gospel and other means of grace, the sacraments were henceforth regularly administered, the first communion being held January 17, 1772.

February 19, 1768, the corner-stone was laid for a larger church, and this building served till 1827, when the present church was finished and solemnly dedicated.

Friedland

In 1769, quite unexpectedly six German families arrived from Broad Bay in Maine. They originally belonged to a larger company of emigrants from Palatinate and Würtemberg, who, about the year 1738 or 1739 had landed near Broad Bay and the Muscongus River, in the province of Maine. There they had settled and founded the town of Waldoboro, so called in honour of the original proprietor of the soil, George Waldo. They were Protestants, either Lutherans or German Reformed, but for a long while destitute of the means of grace. Since 1762 George Soelle, who, before he entered the Church of the Brethren had been a Lutheran pastor in Denmark, visited them from time to time. Thus they became acquainted with the Brethren, and soon began to build a meeting-house with a view to retaining Soelle as their resident minister. But as there were legal difficulties concerning their title-deeds, and they could not enjoy full religious liberty, they resolved, according to Soelle's suggestion, to emigrate to North Carolina. Having been shipwrecked on the coast of North Carolina, they arrived by way of Wilmington, in November, 1769, on the Wachovia tract, poor, wayworn, and many of them in ill health.

As the brethren had not been apprised of their intentions, no preparations had been made for them. Some found a temporary home in Bethabara, others in Salem, where some new houses were yet unoccupied. In the following year they were joined by another company of eight families, with whom Soelle arrived. Not wishing to remain in Salem, they determined to commence a settlement of their own on the southeast corner of the Wachovia tract, where nine lots, of two hundred acres each, were sold to them, and thirty acres in the centre were reserved for a meeting-house, and for school purposes. In 1771 nine houses were finished and occupied, and the settlement received the name of Friedland (land of peace).

In February, 1772, the corner-stone was laid for the house destined for church and school purposes. This house was consecrated to the worship of the Lord on the 18th of February, 1775, and Tycho Nissen was introduced as minister. The names of the members of the society in connection with the Brethren's Church were: —

John Peter and Elizabeth Kroehn.	Melchior and Jacobina Schneider.
Michael and Catharine Rominger.	Frederick and Salome Kuenzel.
Christopher and Barbara Volger.	Michael and Elizabeth Seiz.
Jacob and Barbara Rominger.	John and Catharine Lanius.
Frederick and Anna Maria Miller.	Peter and Elizabeth Fiedler.
Jacob and Margaret Hein.	George Frederick and Gertrude
Peter and Elizabeth Schneider.	Hahn.

Jacob and Elizabeth Ried.

In September, 1780, this society had meanwhile increased to forty persons, and received a regular constitution as a congregation in full communion with the Brethren's Church.

Hope

As early as the year 1758 Rogers and Ettwein had kept meeting on the southwest borders of Wachovia, having been invited there by Christopher Elrod and John Douthit, who had enjoyed the protection and hospitality of the brethren, while fugitives to the fort, during the Indian War. They repeatedly expressed their desire of entering into a more close fellowship with the Moravian Church, and some attached themselves to the congregation at Friedberg.

But as this was an entirely German congregation, they desired to have an English minister residing in their midst. After some years their numbers increased by the arrival of several English families from Carrol's Manor, Maryland, where Joseph Powell had preached the gospel to them for some years. These were followed by others, a year or two later, all settling in the southwest corner of the Wachovia tract, near Muddy Creek. For the time they participated in the enjoyment of the means of grace in the neighbouring congregation of Friedberg, the Brethren Utley and Soelle attending to the English part of the congregation.

The church building for the Hope congregation was finished in 1780. On the 28th of March, of that year, the house was solemnly dedicated to the worship of God, and John Christian Fritz placed in charge of the little flock of Christ, which was, on the 28th of August following, fully constituted a congregation of the Brethren's Church. On this day, the 28th of August, two married couples, viz. John and Mary Padget, and Benjamin and Mary Chitty, were added to the congregation; and on the 24th of September the first children, William Pettycord and Elizabeth Elrod, were baptized. The holy communion was administered for the first time, on October 14, to eight communicants. The burial-ground of Hope was laid out during the same year.

The business interests of this period were large. The farming operations were carried on with success, the various trades flourished and increased, while the store drew customers from the entire region round about Wachovia. Certain articles were standard products of the country and were, no doubt, the same as currency or coin. One was deerskins. Notice is frequently given of wagons going

BETWEEN WAR AND REVOLUTION

to Charleston loaded with deerskins, and returning with goods for the store. While the diary does not give complete lists, the mention made from time to time shows that in seven shipments there was a total of thirty-five thousand pounds of deerskins. This being evidently only a small portion of the amount sent from the store, we can imagine how numerous were the deer in the forest at that time. On one occasion sixteen hundred pounds of butter were sent to Charleston, four hundred pounds of snakeroot, and a number of beaver skins. When the teams went to Newburn, shells were brought to burn for lime.

An interesting fact is stated in connection with orchard and garden. In 1768 apples were gathered which measured fourteen inches in circumference and weighed seventeen ounces. From the garden they gathered cabbages, specimen heads weighing eleven pounds, and these were raised from seed without transplanting.

No great dangers threatened the colony except in 1771, during the troubles with the Regulators, described in a later chapter. Still the country was a rough, wild section, filled with dangers for the individual. Many an hour could be occupied with fireside stories for young people, gleaned from the headings in the diary, "Preservations." The mention of a few will convey to the reader the picture of the surroundings. We find notices like these all through the period: To-day a very large bear was shot near the mill. A wolf attacked a sheep in the barnyard and wounded it so that it had to be killed. Snakes were numerous and deadly. They were found coiled around the vessels in the spring-house, lying on the ledges over the doors, or on the steps of the houses. Marshall was walking with a friend and had extended his hand to raise the latch of the gate. Some one spoke to him at that moment, and he turned to reply. As he did so a venomous serpent dropped from the latch which he had already extended his hand to raise, when interrupted by the voice of his friend. Graff was preserved from a great copperhead, and rattlesnakes of immense size were killed.

We note a few items which call for passing mention.

A meteor fell August 17, 1764. It was so large that the surroundings were brightly illuminated. It appeared to be very near. We know that large meteoric specimens have been found some miles south of Bethabara, possibly remains of the one which fell in 1764.

Mention is made in 1765 of a deadly disease in Wilmington, which, from the description given, is not unlike the fever in Bethabara in 1759.

Trombones were used for the first time at a funeral in 1768.

A Swiss miner visited Wachovia in 1767 in search of minerals. The people wished to find lime, so they joined him in his prospecting tours. It is claimed that two and a half miles west of Bethabara, on the Johanna Creek, lead was found, with a trace of silver. Copper ore was also found.

The original Hans Wagner hut was torn down November, 1768.

A number of new roads were opened to various sections.

The deed to Mulberry Fields was secured in 1769.

A number of boys arrived, and began to study the trades as apprentices. They were also taught the common school branches, and were well cared for. A few restless spirits made trouble, and several ran away, while others rebelled against authority. It was not an easy matter to adjust, but all save one returned to their duties.

An interesting episode was the unusual circumstances

BETWEEN WAR AND REVOLUTION 83

surrounding the offer of marriage to Mrs. Gammon a few years after the death of her husband. The offer was from an English nobleman, on a visit to Florida. He sent a prominent officer in his Majesty's service to formally represent him in this matter. The lady declined the offer, and later returned to her home in England.

During this decade there were a number of deaths in the colony, which were a heavy loss to the communities. Dixon, Schropp, Gammon, and Klein were among the number. Klein had come to fill an important office. He was drowned while trying to cross a stream swollen by recent rains. Gammon was the financial leader, a man of rare qualities both in his business and his social relations. When he was buried, a very large concourse of people gathered to pay their respect to his memory, and he was spoken of as being a "father to this section of the country." Lash was called to Pennsylvania in the period now before us. He was very prominent in the affairs of this section, having laboured with great faithfulness and ability during a residence of sixteen years in Wachovia.

The social relations of the people of Wachovia with others were pleasant. They were envied by some, and misunderstood by others; still all good people were their friends. Lash, Bonn, Holder, and others were appointed to civil offices. At times fears filled the hearts of the people, and we find the note is made that "many colonies have been blotted out in these unsettled times, but ours has been spared." They were visited by civil and military officials, with whom they discussed the odious "stamp act," the "threatened negro rebellion," which had been put down "by the aid of the Indians," and from the visitors they heard of the death of their friend, the aged Governor Dobbs, which occurred March 29, 1765.

CHAPTER IX

SALEM FOUNDED

1763-1773

THE founding of Salem was an important epoch in the history of Wachovia. The town, begun in 1766, has increased till, with Winston, it is now the home of fifteen thousand people or more. The towns Salem and Winston are divided by only the width of a street, and hence geographically are one town. The history of this twin city is interesting and important. The business enterprises, begun in a modest manner one hundred and thirty-six years ago, have continued to grow and increase, and we now have a progressive manufacturing town. The professional men of that day were well and favourably known, and if the history of these men and their successors were written, we would have an interesting volume. The management of the finances was difficult, but successful, and we find all through the generations that follow, men who, in a conservative and faithful manner, administer important interests. The care of the young people was a prime consideration from the early days, and this same interest has made education one of the most cherished objects, so that in 1902 there are thirty-seven hundred names on the school rolls of Salem and Winston. Religion was greatly neglected in many sections in those early days, but from the time that the first house of worship was erected, in 1766, till 1902, the people have been a religious people. The community was important from the beginning, has

SALEM FOUNDED

continued to exert a power all through the succeeding years, and has a call to continue the work of solving certain problems in the development of the commonwealth. For these reasons a detailed account of the founding of Salem will be given. (See map of Wachovia.)

Near the centre of the tract of one hundred thousand acres there is a hillside, at the foot of which is a stream called on the first maps the Wach. At this point the Wach flows from east to west. A number of smaller streams empty into it, among them the Lech, which is a mile or more east of Salem, and about the same distance west is another small creek called on the map Petersbach. The present resident of Salem will at once recognize in the Wach, the Salem Creek; in the Lech, the Brushy Fork; and in the Petersbach, the Paper Mill, or Peters Creek. This body of land, bounded by the Wach, the Lech, and the Petersbach, is about three miles wide, and slopes upward from the Wach a distance of two miles before it reaches the elevation which the land has as it stretches northward toward Bethabara.

These creeks were larger in the earlier days than now, since the rains, falling upon the forest-covered land, filtered slowly through the covering of leaves upon the ground; while at the present day the rains fall upon the cleared hillsides, and rush down into the valleys in a freshet, and thus in a day an amount of water flows by which one hundred years ago would have slowly found its way down the same stream during the entire month.

This land was the centre of Wachovia, as we have already said; and when Frederick William de Marshall arrived for the purpose of selecting the site for the central town, he naturally turned his attention to this neighbourhood.

The first mention of a search for the place to locate the town was in November, 1764. Marshall, Frommel, Lash, and Ettwein went southward down the Petersbach to the general Friedberg neighbourhood. They speak of the falls of the Wach, which was no doubt some miles below Salem, at what was later called Laugenour's or Stafford's mill. On this first search they travelled as far south as the point where the south fork, middle fork (Wach), and the north fork unite before they empty into the Yadkin River. This selection was disapproved, as was also the one made a month later. A third place was found, and this was negatived. December 19 it was made known to them that the location was to be between the Petersbach and the Lech.

With the beginning of the new year, the search was continued, and all the possible sites along the Petersbach and the Lech were examined, but each selection was in turn disapproved by the lot. February 14 a place was found near the Wach, and about halfway between the Petersbach and the Lech. This was approved, which gave great happiness to the people. The text for the day was, "Let thine eyes be open toward this house night and day, even toward the place of which thou hast said my name shall be there." (1 Kings 8 : 29.) The decision was formally announced to the congregation in the evening service, and all united in singing : —

"Die Stadt soll werden
Dein Lob auf Erden."

We hear little of the project during the year 1765. Marshall returned to Pennsylvania. The name Salem (peace) was given by Count Zinzendorf before his death. With the beginning of 1766 the work was pushed rapidly forward.

FREDERICK WILLIAM DE MARSHALL

SALEM FOUNDED

Before taking up the events connected with the actual beginning of the town, we will glance at the life of the man who was in a special manner connected with the founding of Salem. A careful study of the one hundred and fifty years under review show us that, though many good, wise, and able men are found all through the years, certain men stand out as specially connected with periods of development. Spangenberg is the central figure connected with the beginning of Wachovia. Marshall's influence is felt from 1764 to 1802. Louis David de Schweinitz, Reichel, and Van Vleck were strong men in shaping affairs from 1800 to 1850. Then the names of Bahnson and E. A. de Schweinitz stand out prominently during the succeeding twenty-five years, and the present period of growth and progress has felt in a marked degree the personality of Rondthaler. Thus we recognize the leaders and their special work.

Frederick William de Marshall was born February 5, 1721. His father was the commander of the great fortress of Königstein on the river Elbe. Marshall received a military training, strict and severe, and was thus fitted for the hardships which he was later called upon to endure, and habits of punctuality and order were formed. Doubtless the spirit of the soldier was present when Marshall and Tryon, in 1771, stood as the central figures of the one hundred officers, and witnessed the evolutions of the three thousand soldiers on the hillside east of Bethabara. Marshall, when a young man, became acquainted with Zinzendorf, and joined the Moravian Church. He always took the part of a leader. He spent more than sixty years in the service of the church of his adoption, and was active till the day of his death, February 11, 1802.

The first act in the founding of the new town of Salem

took place January 6, 1766. A company of twelve men went from Bethabara to the site selected to clear the ground and build the first house. The weather was very cold. During the singing of a hymn the work was formally begun by the felling of the first tree on the lot at present belonging to the Shaffner estate, corner of Liberty and Shallowford streets. The house which they erected is still standing, being a part of the building used many years as a pottery. Immediately north of this was erected a small second house occupied by hired men. Their home was so far completed that February 19 the following persons moved to Salem, and thus made the beginning:—

From the Europeon party, Gottfried Praezel, Niels Peterson, Jens Schmidt, and John Birkhead.

From Bethabara, George Holder, Jacob Steiner, Michael Zigler, and Melchior Rasp.

To Peterson was given the special duty of writing the diary and caring for the home, and he and Praezel conducted the religious services. On the journey to Salem two deer were shot. Bagge went with them and spent the first night with the party. The wagons carried tiles and brick.

During the month Reuter was very busy surveying, and ran a straight line over the ridge, probably what is now Main Street. This was cleared the same year. At the middle of this line a square was laid out, probably between Bank and Academy streets, as this was the first selection of the open public square around which the large congregation houses were to be built. At the northwest corner they located the first church building, on the lot now occupied by Hampton's store. It is probably known to but few persons that the Salem square was originally one block farther north. The reason why it was moved south

SALEM FOUNDED

was that, after the place had been decided upon, it was found that the water from the springs (south of Calvary Church) could be led to the houses only at the lower end of the original square. The first church building had already been finished, and the above fact explains why it was so far north. April, 1766, the first or upper site for the square was chosen, and two years later, April, 1768, it was decided to locate it one block farther down. Thus the first place of worship was not on the public square, though according to the original plan it was so located.

Under date of April 12, 1766, the diary says, "furthermore on the northeast height, behind the outer street, the place for a graveyard was decided."

A careful examination of the original diary shows the order of the erection of the first houses to be as follows:—

January 6, 1766, first house, located on the lower corner of Liberty and Shallowford streets, still standing.

In 1766, a little later than the above date, a small house of logs, north of the first one, and probably the log building still standing.

June 6, 1766, first meeting hall, forming part of a dwelling house, later removed to make place for Fries' store, which in its turn was replaced by Hampton's store.

October, 1766, a dwelling house, later the property of Fries, now removed to Liberty Street, corner of Bank Street, and used as a tenement house.

After this the dwelling houses were built in rapid succession.

July 23, 1768, the lot was measured for the single brethren's house, the largest building undertaken, thus far, in the town. It was finished December 27, 1769, and was opened and occupied by sixteen single men and four boys. A very interesting and complete history of this house (now occupied as a home for the widows of the congregation) was written by Mr. J. A. Lineback, and appeared in the *Wachovia Moravian*, June, 1900, to February, 1901. In December, 1768, a site for a hotel was selected, and in 1769 the graveyard was enclosed by a fence.

Much is said in regard to the water-works, and this forms an interesting subject to be treated later. The first supply of water was obtained from the springs on the "reservation" near Calvary Church, and led to town through wood pipes.

At Easter, 1770, the corner-stone of the new congregation house was laid, and on November 13, 1771, the meeting hall in this building was consecrated. It faced the east side of the Salem square, and was the residence of the ministers, and contained the hall for religious meetings. The consecration services were solemn and impressive, and mark an epoch in the history of Salem, and it was at this time that the constitutional changes took place which made Wachovia an independent province.

On the day of the consecration services a large number of friends came together. At ten o'clock all the members gathered in the meeting hall. After singing a hymn they knelt down and Marshall offered the dedicatory prayer. The texts were: "The Lord is in his holy temple, let all the earth keep silence before him." "One is your Master, but ye are all brethren." In the afternoon the company that gathered was still larger, filling the large hall and the two small adjoining rooms, there being present more than three hundred persons. One of the features of the occasion was the baptism of the converted negro, who was named "John Samuel." After this they partook of the cup of covenant. During the service it was announced that the ministers called to the work in Salem were Mar-

Congregation House, Salem, 1771

SALEM FOUNDED

shall, Tiersch, Utley, and Graff. The latter was to continue as the head of the married people, but would reside at Bethabara. The day was a blessed one, and all returned to their homes happy and thankful.

The Synod of 1765, at Lititz, Pennsylvania, was the last American synod held under the old state of affairs. In 1770 Christian Gregor, John Loretz, and Hans Christian Alexander de Schweinitz were sent to America in order to settle the affairs which related to the property of the Unity and of the American congregations. In 1771 these commissioners visited Wachovia, and established a local administration, the centre of government having thus far been vested in the Bethlehem board. 1771 may therefore be looked upon as the birthday of the Southern Province, and also as the birthday of Salem, as an independent, self-governing congregation. This was a step of far-reaching importance. Wachovia was henceforward to be no longer an experiment. Heretofore it had been receiving help from Pennsylvania and from Europe, and it had had little voice in the government of its own affairs. Now it became self-supporting, gradually paying all its obligations to other provinces, and receiving its title to its own lands. This was opportune and providential; otherwise, the questions which arose during and after the Revolution would have caused great embarrassment and the possible confiscation of the property.

The time had now arrived when by natural evolution the common housekeeping would have to be discontinued. This had already been done in Bethania, also in part in Salem, and the three visitors arranged to have it dissolved in all the congregations.

The Bethania land difficulties were of long standing, and for a time fears were entertained that this congregation would become greatly disaffected, or even withdraw from the communion of the church. The affairs were happily adjusted by the purchase of the twenty-five hundred acres of land at $1.50 per acre.

Salem received a little more than three thousand acres of land for its portion.

The governing board, consisting of Marshall, Graff, Tiersch, and Utley, were to reside in Salem.

The title to the land in Salem was transferred to Marshall in 1778, and the actual purchase money paid to Lord Granville and those to whom he sold his rights. The total sum paid in rents and purchase money was $32,777.02. (See "Forsyth County," Fries, p. 44.)

One feature which cannot but cause a bit of regret in the mind is the virtual discontinuance of Bethabara as a village. It is true that the plan was not to make Bethabara a town. Still, we have learned to know it as a place in which had occurred many thrilling and interesting events; we have seen it populous with residents and refugees; we beheld it as a busy centre, with store and shop, farm and mill, tavern and trade, all busy and thriving; hence the mind unconsciously lost sight of the fact that this was all temporary, the very name Bethabara meaning "house of passage." Therefore, with a feeling akin to surprise, we read that after the dedication of the church hall and the location of the governing board in the new town the population of Bethabara was reduced to fifty by the removals to Salem. At the close of 1772 there were one hundred and twenty persons connected with the Salem congregation.

Reichel gives a list of some of the first settlers in Salem: —

| F. W. Marshall. | Daniel Schnepf. | Gottfried Aust. |
| Paul Tiersch. | George Holder. | Traugott Bagge. |

SALEM FOUNDED

Richard Utley.	Jacob Steiner.	C. G. Reuter.
John M. Graff.	Charles Holder.	Matthew Miksch.
Jacob Bonn.	Valentine Beck.	Jacob Meyer.
John B. Herbst.	Philip Meyer.	J. G. Stockberger.

Henceforth the history will centre around Salem, though, during the Revolution, the mill and store in Bethabara played an important part; and it is not till after the year 1783 that Bethabara drops into the background, and Salem assumes the position of leadership which it has ever since maintained.

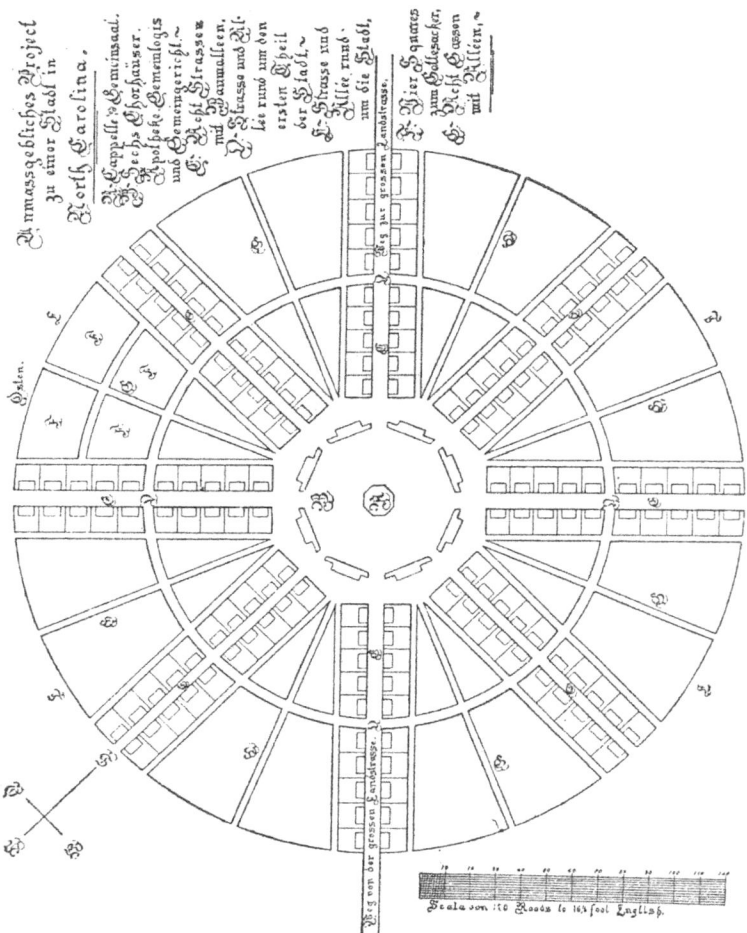

Plan for Salem made about 1750, or a little later, in Germany. The church forms the centre; the hotel, congregation houses, etc., around the church; the streets, with the dwelling houses, radiate from the central group. The ground was unsuited, hence this unique plan was not carried out.

CHAPTER X

TRYON, THE ROYAL GOVERNOR, MAKES TWO MEMORABLE VISITS TO WACHOVIA

1763–1773

THE events which appear in this chapter have remained buried in the yellow and time-stained leaves of the Bethabara diary for more than a century and a quarter. A brief allusion is made by Reichel to the second visit, but only six lines are devoted to the subject, and the first one is not even mentioned. Yet these visits brought the people of Wachovia into intimate relations with a very important event of North Carolina history, and witnessed the gathering of a larger number of distinguished North Carolinians than at any time previous to the meeting of the legislature in Salem at the close of the Revolution.

Governor Tryon has carried with him the bitter hatred of our people. It is not our intention to pass an opinion on his character, but the mention of a few events connected with his rule in the colony will lend interest to the record of his visits to Wachovia. He became royal governor upon the death of the aged Governor Dobbs. His wife and her sister were ladies of great culture and personal charms. At Newbern, the residence of the governor, there was established a miniature court. The legislature was under the influence of this charming social atmosphere, and voted $25,000 for the erection of a governor's palace. The house cost nearly $100,000 before it was completed. This was a very large sum for that period, and for a poor colony already groaning under the burden of taxes. The erection of the governor's palace was only a type of the other oppressions by the company of unscrupulous men who surrounded Tryon. From Fanning, the chief lawyer, down to the most ignorant tax-gatherer, it was a rule of injustice and oppression. One simple illustration will open the entire view of what the people were suffering. The tax-gatherers were accustomed to demand immediate payment, and if the money was not at once handed to them, any article within reach was taken and sold at any price. A collector calling at a home in Orange County found the father away. There was little in the house which could be converted into money, so the tax-collector required the mother of the family to change her dress, as she was wearing a new one, woven with her own hands. When she had given him the garment, he slapped her in the face, as he rode off, and told her to weave another one (Caruthers).

With these oppressions, from the governor down the entire list of officials, the temper of the people was aroused. An organization was formed for the purpose of righting the wrong, and the name "Regulator" was given to them. This body had among its members many good men, but it also contained many who were lawless. The worst feature was that they had miserable leaders and were misguided. Their chief, Herman Husbands, was entirely unfitted for such a position. These men were originally acting with a desire to correct the evils of the times, and they had just cause for complaint; but their methods were lawless, as bad as the outrages of the officials, and their acts led directly to the annihilation of law and order, which is anarchy.

The above statement is based upon the opinion of a

number of historians, all of whom admit that many good men were in the ranks of the Regulators, but who claim that leaders, methods, and results were wrong.

Waddell says, "The warmest apologist of the Regulators has never justified the lawless and cruel acts perpetrated by them — their gathering in arms to overawe the legislature, and rescue Husbands, who had been expelled from that body and afterwards imprisoned, and the various other acts leading up to the battle of Alamance."

Moore writes: "These misguided people, however much justified in their original movements, had become an intolerable nuisance — an impediment alike to legislation and the administration of public justice.... Brutal mobs ranged unchallenged from where Raleigh now stands, to Charlotte."

Caruthers, the ablest apologist of the Regulators, admits that their leader, Husbands, was not at that time in membership with the Quakers, although he had been.

Wiley, another apologist, says Husbands, "was not a character worthy of much commendation."

Waddell further says: "The conduct of the Regulators forced the issue between law and mob rule, and left no alternative to the authorities but the prompt suppression of them by force.... It was the plain duty of officers and citizens ... to suppress revolt ... which meant naked anarchy."

These opinions are cited to show the propriety of the position held by the people of Wachovia. They were friendly toward the Regulators, and succeeded in securing the release of some of their members while Tryon was in Bethabara. They were opposed to mob law in all forms, and hence could not either join the Regulators, or espouse their cause. Equally strongly did they condemn

Tryon's course, characterizing his sentences as being "inhuman obstinacy"; but as governor in office they paid due respect to him, and the narrative of his visits shows an admirable side to Tryon's character, which no writer has thus far brought out, and will therefore be of interest to the general student of North Carolina history. The facts are absolutely reliable and have never appeared in print.

We again take up the history of Wachovia. Marshall, Gammon, and others visited old Governor Dobbs at Brunswick and Newbern, and on these occasions met the new lieutenant governor, Tryon. In 1767 information was sent to Bethabara that Governor Tryon intended to pay them a visit. Preparations were made for a proper reception of his Excellency. Literature was sent from Bethlehem to present to their honoured guest, and among the books was the history of the Greenland missions. This publication had recently appeared, and it is stated that it created a stir in scientific circles, since it opened a hitherto unknown land. There were enough articles written about this book to fill a volume. In reading the Bethabara diary we must bear in mind that at this time Governor Tryon had not yet fallen into disfavour with the people, in fact, he did not win their bitter hatred till after the Regulator War; and it was during this struggle that he made his second visit to Wachovia, hence both occasions antedate the final popular condemnation, which followed his cruel and unwarranted sentences at Hillsboro, after he left Bethabara in 1771.

The diary says:—

"*Wednesday, September* 16, 1767.—From the information received we felt sure that Governor Tryon would arrive within a day or two. Men were sent to repair the road over which he would travel.

"*Thursday, September* 17, 1767. — Letters were received from Colonel Fanning informing us that the governor would arrive next day. A conference was held to discuss the question of the proper reception and entertainment of the governor and his party. We were greatly pleased by the willingness of our people to help in these preparations.

"*Friday, September* 18. — Warden Lash and Dr. Bonn went ten miles to meet the governor. Graff had been called to Bethania to conduct a funeral service. At one o'clock the party arrived. It consisted of the governor and Mrs. Tryon, the counsellor, McKellock, the colonels, Fanning, Frohock, and Banton, the English minister, Micklejohn, from Hillsboro, and others. As the company approached, our band of musicians with French horns and trumpets greeted them. Half an hour later they dined in the hall of the single brethren's house, the musicians furnishing music while they sat at table. At the conclusion of the repast the governor, accompanied by some of the gentlemen of the party, took a walk through the village, inspecting the property, the stables, and the farm. As it began to rain, they returned to their rooms. In the meantime, Mrs. Tryon was entertained by the ladies of the congregation, she conversing with them in a charming and lovely manner. [This remark bears out the statement so often made that Mrs. Tryon was possessed of unusual personal charms. The adjective used in the original diary is very expressive.] When comfortably seated in the room, the governor had a long and familiar conversation with Graff. He was greatly interested in our constitution and government. Graff presented him with the book, 'Acta Fratrum in Anglia.' Supper was served to our visitors in their rooms, though some of them gathered at the tavern. Thus the first day was concluded.

"*Saturday, September* 19. — The governor informed us that he had read 'Acta Fratrum in Anglia' till late in the night. This morning he was presented with a 'History of the Moravian Missions in Greenland,' the book having been sent to him by the missionary society at Bethlehem. After having breakfasted, the governor and his party went across the great meadow to Salem. He examined everything with interest. He was pleased with the regularity of the streets, and the care with which everything is laid out. When we returned to Bethabara, dinner was served, as yesterday, in the large hall, and later his Excellency examined the potter shop. The party then went to Bethania, spending some time at the mill. In the evening we were again in Bethabara, the governor having expressed himself as greatly pleased with what he saw. As he passed and greeted the young people, and saw them in front of the houses, he said the country would be blessed in these happy children. In the evening we had our usual service, and our visitors were present.

"*Sunday, September* 20. — The English minister from Hillsboro preached from the text, Hag. 2 : 6. The sermon of the Moravian minister was based on Gal. 5. The English minister then baptized the children of a number of members of his church, who lived in the neighbourhood of Wachovia. We had arranged for a quiet afternoon for our visitors, but Mrs. Tryon expressed a desire to play upon the organ, and as she played a number of the girls sang. This pleased her. She later requested Graff to perform on the organ, and he did so. By this time the governor became interested in the music, and came to the meeting hall from his room. An hour was pleasantly passed in this way. From the meeting hall Mrs. Tryon visited the room which specially belongs to the older girls, and she requested them to sing for her as they had done during the afternoon. While thus engaged, supper was announced, and the visitors seemed loath to have the little gathering broken up. Supper being over, a visit was paid to the home of the single men [one of the largest and most important buildings in the village]. At the usual hour the Sabbath evening service was held, a portion of the exercises consisting of responsive singing. Governor and Mrs. Tryon were present, and manifested a devout interest, being specially pleased with the antiphonal singing. After the service Mrs. Tryon was presented with a copy of the 'Berlin Sermons' preached by Count Zinzendorf. When the friends had gone to their rooms for the night, a number of the musicians gathered in front of the house and discoursed music as a pleasant way to express our 'good night.'

"*Monday, September* 21. — This morning his Excellency visited all the remaining houses of the village, and studied carefully all the business enterprises carried on in each. A number of questions were asked privately, and he seemed pleased and satisfied with the answers. He asked whether a man could retain his own property as an individual separate from the general economy, and we told him that he could. He studied with great care the methods of conducting the common housekeeping, the business enterprises, and all the affairs which differ from the customs elsewhere; and as a result of the study, he expressed himself as being impressed with the wisdom of the plans and methods. We gave him a catalogue, or business directory, which described each house and the occupation carried on therein. Our distinguished guest advised us to arrange to have a representative in the legislature. We told him we thought that a step of this kind would arouse the jealousy of our neighbours. He replied that our prosperous condition would arouse envy and jealousy even if we were not represented in the legislature. [These were prophetic words.] Later in the day the governor and his party began their return journey. They were profuse in their expressions of satisfaction at what they had seen, and were very grateful for the kindness shown them. A number of our members accompanied them some ten miles, and Lash went to Salisbury."

From this simple, clear, and interesting account we cannot but trace a genial and sympathetic line running through Tryon's nature; and on his memorable march from Alamance to Wachovia he sent in advance the request that the people of Bethabara should correct the erroneous opinion which many persons seemed to have of his "dreadful severity and cruelty."

According to an arrangement made with Governor Tryon while he was in Bethabara, they sent to him seven wagons loaded with goods, in order to open commercial relations with Brunswick on the Cape Fear River. Though Brunswick is now marked only by the interesting ruins of the old English church, it was then a busy centre, with vessels coming and going, and with crowds thronging the wharves. The following articles are mentioned in the invoice of goods: A windmill, 476 pounds of candles, 150 pounds of butter, 6 beehives, a new gun, 3 bushels of rye flour, and so on. All these things had been ordered by the governor. The contract was that the wagons should be in Brunswick by November 6, before the governor left. Bad roads and other causes delayed them, and they arrived after he had left Brunswick. This was unfortunate, since they did not receive proper consideration, and hence the venture was a financial failure. They received in cash $5 per hundred pounds for the flour, and 20 cents per pound for the butter. The other articles had to be exchanged for goods. The Brunswick charges were as high as the Bethabara selling prices, and this was the last trip made to Brunswick for commercial purposes. The governor later wrote to them and expressed regrets that he had been absent when the wagons arrived, stating that if he had been there at the time, the results would have been different.

The Bethabara diary is not written with the intention of picturing the course of history, either in the colony or the country at large; but the statements bearing upon current events are remarkably clear and correct, much more so than many made by historians who lived generations later, and who insert tradition as facts, and whose accounts will often bear a question mark. The writer of the Wachovia diary is very careful to say only what he knows to be true, and, as he lived contemporaneous with the events, he seldom makes a statement contrary to the general history of the colony. For that reason the account which follows concerning the Regulators and Governor Tryon is of great value to the state history because of its reliability.

Little is written of political events from 1767 to 1770. A note says that in 1768 the Regulators were at work in the neighbourhood of Pine Tree store. The same year there were sent from Bethabara two wagons loaded with "rusks" for the colonial troops. The governor wrote a courteous note of thanks. They speak of the governor's visit to Salisbury, and say that he returned to his home with an escort of men, and another item says that all "is quiet at Hillsboro." Evidently this remark is connected with the turmoils which beset the legislature, as well as Fanning and others, and which were the forerunners of the struggle at Alamance. In August, 1768, we find a note that the Regulator matter was becoming serious. About this time Chief Justice Howard visited Wachovia, and after examining all things, he said to the friends who entertained him that he considered the Moravians "a happy and blessed people." In 1769 a note states that an assault had been made in the neighbourhood upon a tax-collector by the Regulators.

In 1771 we find the people of Wachovia surrounded by circumstances which called upon them to definitely decide whether they would espouse the cause of the Regulators or remain neutral. Let us hear what the people in other parts of the colony thought, in order that we may judge of the wisdom of the decision. Waddell says, "The best men of the province were all on one side, and that was the side of law and legitimate rule." Tryon himself writes to Lord Hillsboro, "His Majesty's Presbyterian subjects showed themselves very loyal on this service, and I have a pleasure in acknowledging the utility that the Presbyterian ministers' letter to their brethren had upon the face of public affairs." In like manner a careful conference was held in Wachovia, and it was decided that their duty was to submit to the powers then in authority. They never acted in any other than a kind and friendly manner toward the Regulators, and the latter came and went with perfect freedom during these years; but the Moravians could not espouse their cause, since it was opposed to law and order. Having arrived at this conclusion, they awaited the development of events, and soon the cloud darkened and the storm burst. We copy a part of the diary which describes the days before and after the battle of Alamance.

"*May* 16, 1771. — Many Regulators pass through our town on their way to Guilford, where they are massing their forces to oppose Governor Tryon.

"*May* 17. — More Regulators march through. Some are friendly to us. One of them, a Mr. Allen, gave Mrs. Bagge a gold coin, with the request that if he did not escape in the battle, she should send it to his wife. Others are very bitter and hostile. Old man Jarvis is loud in his threats against the Moravians for their unwillingness to take up arms against the governor, and he declares that if the battle is decided in their favour, severe punishment will follow for Bethabara. On this same day a rumour reaches us that a battle has already been fought, and that many have been killed on both sides. Our informant says that when he left, a truce had been declared that both sides might bury their dead.

"*May* 18. — All during last night and during to-day Regulators continue to pass, and they tell us that when the governor began to fire upon the Regulators with his cannon, they were so terrified that they fled and left everything in the field.

"*May* 19. — A one-armed man by the name of Hughes came from the camp of the governor and confirmed the rumour that the Regulators were unable to withstand the cannonading by Tryon's troops.

"We had on this day a visit from an unknown man, who requested Dr. Bonn to go to the home of James

Hunter and assist in the care of the wounded Regulators. Hunter lives about five miles from the field of battle. He reported that more than twenty wounded men were there, and that the surgeon in charge did not have the proper instruments for his task. Bonn declined to go, stating that his duties to this section required him to remain at home.

"Old man Borg, a Regulator, was in town to-day, making wild and excited speeches, filled with lies, and trying to stir up our people to take part in the troubles.

"Armstrong and Hall passed through on their way to the governor.

"*May* 20. — Whitsuntide. Lanier visits us, and brings the startling news that the man who visited us yesterday was none other than Herman Husbands, the ringleader of the Regulators, and the man on whose head the governor had fixed a large reward. He had met Husbands as he was leaving our town, had talked with him, and knew him well personally. There is no mistake about his identity.

"While Husbands was in the tavern yesterday, a certain visitor was making his boasts that if he could get help, he would capture Husbands, deliver him to the governor, and receive the reward offered for his capture. The unknown stranger listened to the conversation, but said nothing.

"The man who had been boasting of his intentions to capture Husbands started home by way of Bethania. When a short distance beyond the town, he was attacked by five Regulators and shot. The bullet passed through his clothing, and made a flesh wound, but his horse wheeled and galloped back to Bethania, so he escaped. When he entered the town, he was pale as death, and was weeping from terror. It is supposed that Husbands himself made the attack on the man.

"The Regulators continue to pass in large numbers day and night. One of the men related his experiences. He said that in Thursday's fight the Regulators had withstood the first two volleys from the governor's troops. When he left the field nearly all the Regulators were fleeing. He had passed near a spring and had been accosted by a wounded man. He stopped and found that the poor fellow had a terrible bullet wound in his abdomen, and he exclaimed, 'For God's sake give me a little water!' He had dipped up some water with his hat and had given it to the wounded man. As he turned to continue his flight, he saw another man lying near by, with a portion of his skull shot away.

"A company of three men passed. They related how they had approached the home of James Hunter, where the wounded men lay. They were drawn to the house by a desire to see the wounded men. This was five miles from the scene of the battle. Before arriving at the spot they were discovered by the governor's troops and were fired upon. They fled, and in so doing they came within range of a company of Regulators, and they also opened fire. For a time they were surrounded by the utmost peril, but finally escaped.

"This conversation was evidently in the tavern, for the narrative continues, saying that the old man Borg upbraided them for their curiosity, at which the three Regulators became very angry, and replied to the old man, telling him he had no right to find fault with them, since he had not even been near the fighting. The discussion waxed so warm that we were afraid they would resort to violence. They related further that the leaders were the first to run from the battle-field, and the common people, after resisting for a time, also fled into the forest. The governor had hung some of his prisoners, and was now marching to Salisbury to join Waddell. He will remain in Orange County till quiet is restored, and after that he will come to Wachovia.

"Two wagons loaded with Regulators passed through Salem on the journey to Alamance. It is supposed that they were going to get their wounded comrades. Old man Borg was among them. He said that the people in Bethabara had given him good advice, and that he intended to follow it. Their advice was to surrender to the governor.

"*May* 22.— Old man Jarvis passed through to-day from the battle. When he was on his way to the struggle, some days ago, he was threatening and abusive. Now he was equally humble, and pleaded with Meyer to use his good influence with the governor when he came to Wachovia. Jarvis said the Regulators would never forget the kindness if the Moravians interceded for them.

"At this time the diary says the first court was held in Surry County, at the home of Gideon Wright, and the new charter was read. Bonn was sworn in as the first justice of the peace.

"*May* 24.— Two men came from the camp of the governor with letters for Lanier and Armstrong. They were already on their way to meet the governor, and the messengers had passed them without knowing it. We conversed with these men and received the following information:—

"The governor and his troops have arrived in the neighbourhood of Husbands and Hunter, and have utterly destroyed their property, both houses and crops. He has devastated other farms in the same manner, declaring the men themselves outlaws. His Excellency will spend some time in this section before returning to Newbern. He issued an ultimatum to the Regulators, and within a certain time they are to take an oath which he has prepared, and to promise the following: —

"1st, to be loyal to the government.

"2d, to pay all arrears of taxes.

"3d, to surrender their arms.

"The governor had quite a supply of arms which had already been surrendered, and which he intends to send to Newbern. It is further his intention to return them to the owners after a certain time.

"A pitiful incident was related by one of these messengers. A certain young man, a fine young fellow, had been captured, and when given the alternative of taking the oath, or of being hanged, he chose the latter. The governor wished to spare his life, and twice urged him to submit. But the young man refused. The messenger described how, with the rope around his neck, he was urged to yield, but refused, and the governor turned aside with tears in his eyes as the young man was swung into eternity. The diary, commenting on Tryon's part in this execution, says, 'this severity we call inhuman obstinacy!'

"*May 27.* — Two men report that the governor is detained by high water. The Regulators are in great confusion, since some have submitted and others have not, and between the dangers which threaten with the advance of the government troops, and the turmoils in their own ranks, no man's life is safe.

"The governor has made June 7th the limit when pardon can be obtained by submission. Those who fail to comply with the conditions of the proclamation will be considered outlaws.

"*June 1.* — Gideon Wright with two others came from

the camp of the Governor. They brought a copy of the proclamation [the original is in the possession of the Salem Historical Society], and also sent his greetings to his good friends, the Moravians. He requested the people of Wachovia to use their influence to correct the erroneous ideas which the Regulators have about his severity. Tryon had asked Wright how the inhabitants of Wachovia had acted during this time, and Wright gave a favourable account of our conduct. Among other things he told the governor that we had made ready the same room he had occupied on his former visit in 1767. This pleased him very much. He said further that among the various churches the Moravians were the only people who had without exception remained loyal to the existing authority. That if all men were like the United Brethren, the blessings of peace would be abroad in the land at all times.

"Governor Tryon made requisition of flour from us. He has with him three thousand troops and one hundred men of distinction. As soon as he has joined Waddell he will go to Hillsboro, to try a number of prisoners now with the army.

"Wright confided to Marshall the real object of his visit. He had come to try to arrange for the capture of Herman Husbands. He also gave an account of the battle of Alamance. He had counted thirteen dead Regulators. Many had taken refuge in the woods. [This doubtless refers to the wounded.] The governor ordered the woods to be set on fire, and thus the poor helpless fellows were roasted alive. Their charred corpses were found later. The governor had three men killed and twelve wounded.

"*Sunday, June* 2. — Copy of proclamation has been posted. Some men whose names are given on the proclamation were not included in the offer of amnesty, because of special offences in connection with the uprising. They are proclaimed outlaws.

"*June* 3.—The governor arrived at the farm of Merrill. [Merrill had been specially active in resisting the troops, and after the battle his son had made every effort to reach the governor in order to secure some consideration for his father. Merrill was captured before his son accomplished his task, and was later tried and hanged.] He was arrested in his house and his farm destroyed. It was here that Governor Tryon met Friedrich and Miller. He spent some length of time in questioning both, but especially Friedrich. The chief interest in this examination was to secure all the facts connected with the visit of Herman Husbands to Bethabara, May 19. When Tryon heard that Husbands had not been recognized, but had come and gone as any other stranger would have done, he was greatly pleased. He related in confidence how a proposition had been made by some of the officers of his staff to send a detachment of light cavalry to Bethabara to destroy the town with fire. He had not consented, since he did not believe the reports that the Moravians had aided and abetted Herman Husbands. Now he saw how wise had been his decision, and that all had turned out as he had expected. He said that he did not suspect the Moravians of being false to the established government. Governor Tryon sent two letters by Miller and Friedrich. The one was to Marshall, and in it he asked him to use every effort to have Husbands arrested, promising to the man who could secure him, $100 in money, and 1000 acres of land. The second letter was to Bonn, and was a requisition for 10,000 pounds of flour to be sent to his camp at Pough's place.

"Friedrich related that several women had fallen on their knees before the governor, and had besought him to pardon their husbands. Tryon replied that he could not do so. They would have to appear at Hillsboro for trial.

"Regulators exploded 150 pounds of powder at Pine Tree store, wrecking the building and destroying the goods. This was confused by some with the destruction of the Waddell powder train of wagons, by the so-called 'Black Boys.' Two of the latter were later captured and hanged.

"On this side of the Yadkin River, Miller and Friedrich saw Fanning with his corps of five hundred soldiers, and conversed with him. He refused to make known his destination.

"*June 4.*— Yesterday Adam Lash was at Reedy Creek camp, and came early with the news that his Excellency would arrive in Wachovia that same evening. Holder and Mushback went from Salem to meet him, and as he approached Bethabara, he was met by Marshall and Bonn, who escorted him to the same rooms he had occupied four years before. After a short delay he rode with the brethren and a number of his officers to inspect the fields on the Bethania road, and having chosen a site, he announced his intention of remaining four days, and during this time to appropriately celebrate the birthday of King George III. Even on the day of his arrival a number of Regulators came, with their prayers for pardon. After returning to the village, and a brief season of rest, the governor dined in the brethren's house, having with him only his counsellor and secretary, together with Marshall and Bonn. His staff consisted of thirty people. In the evening one company after the other, under Waddell, arrived, and took up camp in the field. The number of horses was three hundred, and they were placed in the large meadow and were carefully guarded. Forty prisoners came with the soldiers, bound together, two and two [at another place the diary says with chains], and this indeed furnished a pitiful sight. Hardly were the troops in camp when a thunder-storm broke upon them, but they appeared to be accustomed to such things. A guard was placed over the tavern, bakery, kitchen, and wash house, as the village was filled with soldiers. Notwithstanding these precautions they complained so much of hunger that our people gave them all the provisions they had.

"*June* 5. — Many Regulators came to-day. One hundred and thirty-five took the oath. Among these were some Southfork people, who brought their requisition of eight hundred pounds of flour and six oxen. Bethania furnished bread and mutton. This supplied the most pressing needs of the soldiers. Utley came from Salem to pay his respects to the governor, and had a friendly talk with him. His Excellency shows on all occasions his kindly feelings toward the people. We referred certain parish affairs to Tryon, but he said these matters would have to go through the hands of the counsellor, De Rosette, the brother-in-law of the speaker of the assembly. To-day about thirty more prisoners were brought in, among them Sam Jones, of Yadkin, who, though outlawed, had given himself up. His Excellency heard that he was a good, honest, simple man, and had had little to do with the recent trouble. Marshall made a strong appeal for Jones. The former was approached by a great many persons who implored him to intercede for them, but he told them that his influence with the governor in political matters was not great, though socially there seemed to be a strong bond of friendship.

"In the evening his Excellency attended the song service in the church, and he requested us to repeat the sweet singing which he had heard on his previous visit. It was an hour of harmony, but it was also an hour of strange impressions, with the chief executive in the audience, with the room filled with colonial officers, with the door guarded by sentinels, and with the village and the surrounding country filled with soldiers. At ten o'clock there was another severe thunder-storm, but by midnight the sky was again clear.

"*June 6.* — We had a conference early this morning in order to discuss the question of sending a formal address to the governor, to express our submission to the existing government, and we felt that the occasion of the king's birthday would be a fitting time. The governor had not required us to take the oath of allegiance. Having decided to send the address, we consulted the secretary, Mr. Edwards, and he referred the matter to the governor. The latter was much pleased with the idea, and appointed as the time the close of the review of the troops.

"The celebration of the king's birthday was after the following manner: —

"At ten o'clock in the morning all the troops came out of their camp by companies. Our musicians furnished the music for the review. The soldiers marched to the field beyond the barn. [This was on the slope of the hill in front of the Bethabara church, and can be seen in the picture to the left.] The army was drilled for several hours, and the manœuvres of the battle of Alamance were repeated. Volley after volley was fired, both from the musketry and the artillery, until the houses in the village trembled and shook. This display of an army of 3000 men, under the command of select officers, was a grand

TRYON'S TWO VISITS TO WACHOVIA

and imposing sight. At two o'clock the manœuvres were finished and the army marched back to its quarters.

"Meanwhile the governor's tent had been erected in the public square. [This was just north of the present church. See map.] After returning from the drill ground he entered his tent with a number of his more distinguished officers. Then Marshall, Graff, Utley, and Bagge were received in the tent by the governor and his staff, and Marshall read the formal address. At the mention of 'His Majesty' or 'His Excellency' they made a low obeisance.

"'To His Excellency Willm Tryon, Esqur, *Captain General and Governor in Chief in and over the Province of North Carolina.*

"'May it please your Excellency.

"'Upon this most solemn Occasion the celebration of the Birthday of our most gracious King, the United Brethren in Wachovia inviolably attached to his Majesty's Government, esteem themselves particularly favoured by the presence of this Representative of the Province in the person of your Excellency. With hearts full of the warmest sentiments of allegiance, give us leave, Sir, to lay before your Excellency our most fervent Wishes to the Lord, by whom Princes rule, to pour down his choicest Blessings upon the sacred person of our Sovereign, King George III and all his Royal Family, and to establish his Kingdom to the latest posterity over the British Empire.

"'May the Troubles which have of late unhappily torn this Province, be the last that shall ever give any Uneasiness to the paternal Breast of the best of Princes, and may this very Day be the blessed period from which this Province shall date her future happiness through the good success of your Excellency's measures, as well as in the

Reward of the Dangers your precious life was eminently exposed to in his Majesty's Service. The kind protection this Settlement has enjoyed during your Excellency's happy Administration will ever leave the deepest impression of gratitude in the minds of the thankful people and combine their prayers with all well wishers of this Province for your Excellency's prosperity in your future Government.'

"After this address had been communicated the governor graciously read his answer, and then handed it to Marshall.

"'To THE MINISTERS AND CONGREGATION OF THE UNITED BRETHREN IN WACHOVIA.

"'*Gentlemen:*— I return thanks for your loyal and dutiful address. I have already had the pleasure to acquaint his Majesty of the Zeal and Attachment which his Subjects of Wachovia have on all occasions shown to his Government, and the laws of this Province.

"'I am obliged to you for your congratulation on the success with which it has pleased Almighty God to bless the Army under my command, and cordially wish with you that it may lay the foundation of peace and stability to this country.

"'Your affectionate Regard for my Particular Welfare I gratefully receive.

"'WM. TRYON.

"'MORAVIAN CAMPE,
"'BETHABARA, June 6, 1771.'

"During the reading of these papers it was noticed that there was special attention and a sympathetic feeling displayed by the governor. This was spoken of by the officers later. The four who presented the address to the governor were invited to dine with him, and all accepted the invitation except Utley, who was unable to remain. There were several toasts during the dinner, and to each of the toasts the response was a loud:—

"'Hurrah! Hurrah!'

"Our musicians furnished music while the dinner was in progress. The last toast was

"'For the prosperity of the United Brethren in Wachovia!'

"The governor was specially gracious to Marshall and placed him at his right hand during the meal. Next to Marshall sat Graff.

"The remainder of the day was spent in a happy and cheerful manner. As soon as it was dark there was a display of fireworks in front of the governor's tent, by order of his Excellency, and the houses around the square were brilliantly illuminated.

"*June 7*. — His Excellency had conference the entire morning, in the hall of the brethren's house, which could only be made ready for dinner after the close of the conference. The governor dined in his tent. Meanwhile his time was occupied with the examination of Regulators, and other matters. James Klan was released, but Adam Cresson remained in irons. He cried like a child whenever he saw one of our number, and begged us to intercede for him. We told him that we had done all that we could, and advised him to address himself to the honest old counsellor, De Rosette, as others had done, and with success.

"At noon the great army marched away. [The governor did not accompany the main body of the army.] It was pleasant to see how mutually pleased the officers and the people were with each other.

"*June 8*. — Several notes are made with regard to the visit of the army.

"There was great confusion and loss in connection with

the laundry work of the officers, but they did not lay the blame upon the people of the village, but upon the carelessness of their own messengers who took the linen back and forth. The bills were paid without protest.

"From the tavern many articles were borrowed by the officers. A record was kept, and when the bill was presented to the proper authority the only remark was that the bill was too small.

"For the governor's entertainment we declined to take any compensation, insisting that he should be considered our guest.

"The governor gave strict orders to his soldiers before they arrived at Bethabara that no damage dare be done to property, under penalty of severe punishment. This order was carefully observed, and we feel grateful to his Excellency for his interest in the matter.

"Governor Tryon dined in his tent, at three o'clock, and afterward walked up the hill to the graveyard. He passed the place where a number of the sisters of the congregation were engaged in domestic duties. He stopped and exchanged a number of pleasantries with them. Many of the officers of the army had very strange ideas in regard to our customs. They thought our ladies were shut up in a prison-like nunnery, and had other similar absurd conceptions. The ladies were equal to the task of defending themselves against these erroneous ideas.

"*Sunday, June* 9. — Our wagons returning from Charleston some days ago fell into the hands of the Regulators, but they spared the goods.

"The governor has issued a second proclamation to the effect that no pardon will be given to those who blew up Waddell's powder wagons.

"The poor prisoners were confined in our barn.

"At nine o'clock the governor left. One of his attendants told us that he seemed as reluctant to leave Bethabara as if it was his own home. As it was Sunday, he requested us to commend him to Almighty God in our united prayers.

"Soon after leaving, a Mr. Walker, a captain, was brought back to us, as he had suddenly become very ill, and they wished Dr. Bonn to attend to the case. De Rosette, his brother-in-law, brought him to us.

"The governor went to Salem and met Rutherford. Von der Merk and Holder were made justices of the peace.

"*June* 10, 1771. — The five wagons arrived safely from Charleston.

"We received £75 sterling for hay used by the horses of the army. All our bills were paid in coin, but the bills of other people were paid in paper money. This caused some bitter feelings against us on the part of our neighbours.

"The new proclamation extended the time of swearing allegiance to July, but no mercy will be shown those who blew up the powder."

There are more items scattered through the diary of the succeeding days, but we will not add to the length of the extract which we have already given. From the several histories of North Carolina we learn that Tryon returned to Hillsboro, and went through the form of a trial with the poor prisoners whom he had guarded in the Bethabara barn, and in whose behalf the people of Wachovia did all they could. It is the universal judgment of all writers that there was no justification for the criminal severity which the governor and his court used. Tryon's injustice had stirred up these poor misguided men, and though it was necessary to check this lawlessness, when he had accomplished that, he should have gone no farther. As it was, Tryon had one poor half-witted fellow executed, because he had uttered some wild expressions about the person of the governor. Six other prisoners were hanged, in the presence of the governor and his entire army. This absolutely inexcusable act was a crime against justice and mercy, and has been designated a "butchery." This deed, more than anything else, has caused the name of William Tryon to be odious to the people of North Carolina. Still, we must admit that, aside from the crime already described, he was an able soldier and leader, a polished gentleman, with magnetic personal powers.

After the battle of Alamance Tryon was appointed governor of New York, and in a few weeks left North Carolina for that colony.

He was succeeded by Josiah Martin, who pursued a quite different course. He was conciliatory, travelled among his people, made right their wrongs, and while on his journeys came to Salem, Bethabara, and Bethania, August 11–13, 1772. He was very cordial, and expressed himself as being greatly interested and pleased with his visit.

And this brings us to a different era — an era in which violence is again abroad in the land; but this time the American is the central figure, and he uses the right and proper methods — methods in harmony with law and order, even though revolutionary in their nature. The students of North Carolina history tell us that the Regulator and the American patriot of the Revolution are not the same. We leave the Regulator and enter a new period, one which has a record of events more momentous than any other in the history of our country — the period of the American Revolution.

SALEM GRAVEYARD.

CHAPTER XI

WACHOVIA DURING THE REVOLUTION

1773-1783

THE third decade of the thirty years under discussion introduces experiences which differ widely from the other periods. The perplexities were multiplied, the difficulties increased, the dangers far greater. The history of Wachovia during the Revolution is not easy to relate, because the experiences follow each other in rapid succession, in reality blend and interlace, so that only a careful study will bring order out of the apparent chaos of events. Still, the narrative is filled with thrilling interest, and in order to assist in making clear the story of these years we will devote a brief chapter to a general view of the situation.

The Moravians of that day had conscientious scruples against bearing arms and taking an oath.

When they refused to bear arms, it was not from cowardice, for they were brave and able men, and did much to protect the lives of the inhabitants of western Carolina. They defended their own people, and they defended their neighbours, from Indians, from wandering bands of Tories, and from stragglers who followed in the wake of the troops. The people of Wachovia were not cowards, but they would have emigrated to the other side of the world rather than enlist as soldiers.

When they refused to take an oath, it was with them a matter of conscience, as with the Quakers and some other bodies of Christians. They were willing to affirm, and their affirmation was worth more than the oath of many another. But at the particular time under discussion any one refusing to take the ordinary oath of allegiance to the new Republic was at once brought under suspicion.

When we study this portion of the history of Wachovia, we must never doubt the patriotism of the people. They would not become soldiers, but they supported the government by equally valuable methods.

They would not take the prescribed oath, as the form was against conscience; but they made an equally solemn affirmation that they would support the state, lend no aid to the enemy, and deliver up to speedy justice any one who was untrue to the government.

A strong example of their loyalty is shown by the action taken in August, 1776. Previous to that time the church litany was the same used by the Moravian Church in England. August 6 they received official news that in Philadelphia a declaration of independence had been made. Three days later they sent notice to each church in the Province that they should discontinue the prayer "for his Majesty, King George III," and replace this petition with the one "for the authorities of our land who have rule over us."

To fully appreciate the situation, we should understand who were their enemies, and who were their friends.

Their enemies were divided into four classes :—

First, the desperadoes who always flourish in a time of public confusion.

Second, a class of envious, shiftless people who felt that if by some political tangle the Moravians were banished, they could enter claims for the mills, the trades, the homes, the well-cultivated farms. Therefore their enmity was based upon the prospect of material gain.

WACHOVIA DURING THE REVOLUTION 123

Third, a number of "hotheads" who laid undue stress on some fancied personal wrong. For example, the refusal of store or hotel to receive a doubtful piece of money.

Fourth, honest men who misunderstood them, because of lack of information. This class of enemies frequently became their warmest friends.

Those who were friendly toward the Moravians were divided into three classes: —

First, those who represented them in the legislature, in Congress, or in the courts. Such men were Armstrong, Lanier, Williams, and others. Their friendship and support never wavered for an hour.

Second, the officials who studied them and their actions. Among them we mention the Committee of Safety, and the legislature, after its meetings in Salem.

Third, the army officers. We have the record of friendly visits from Washington and Cornwallis, from Tryon, Waddell, Rutherford, and others.

When we contemplate the situation of Bethabara, surrounded by large bands of hostile Indians, in 1759, we recognize the divine protection as the only power that could save them from destruction. The study of the time of the Revolution calls forth the same acknowledgment of special divine guidance, for during these years they were threatened with every form of danger, from the vicious prowler to the great armies of Greene and Cornwallis; from the petty envy of the county magistrate to the animosity of the full meeting of the legislature in 1778.

In the end they were successful in carrying out their honest plans. They had a pure religion, they cared for education, they were honest and thrifty, they lived in the midst of the world, but were not of the world. They understood men and things, but were themselves not understood. They had burdens placed upon them that would have crushed almost any other colony. They were beset with dangers which often made them feel that sudden destruction was sweeping down upon them, yet they were always mercifully preserved.

CHAPTER XII

FRIEND AND FOE

1773-1783

THE year 1776 was ushered in by the movements of soldiers hither and thither, in rapid succession, and the passing of refugees, fleeing from either the royal power or the continental authority. North Carolina entered an early protest against English oppression. The Mecklenburg Declaration of Independence was formally made before the Philadelphia paper was signed; the tea had been thrown into the Cape Fear River as was done in the Boston harbour, because the people hated the Stamp Act; the colonial dames met at Edenton and refused to drink tea sent to them from the mother country; the Regulators, misguided and lawless as they were, entered their protest at Alamance; and from one end of the North State to the other there was unrest and excitement. The presence of the soldiers of both parties in the field led to the greatest confusion. The Tories claimed that the Moravians were in sympathy with the continental forces. The Committee of Safety accused them of secretly aiding the royal party. At one time a troop called expecting to find the governor concealed in the town, and determined to capture him if found. At another time an agent of the government waited upon them, to investigate certain charges. The result of these conflicting flying rumours was that threats were made to destroy the fortifications (see map, p. 39) at Bethabara and burn the town. These threats were made by the lawless element, and were not sanctioned by authority. We have already said that the people in Wachovia were peaceful, but they were not cowards, and any attempt upon their lives and property by these miserable prowlers would have been a dear experiment for the attacking party. A special decision in a conference required each house to be prepared with heavy cudgels; in case of an attack by a band of marauders the church bell was to be rung, special watchmen were placed on duty, and every precaution for defence taken. In speaking of the various and conflicting rumours which filled the land, the writer of the diary says, "The stories abroad seem to point to the fact that all men are liars."

Certain people from the general neighbourhood of Wachovia joined the army collecting at Fayetteville to resist the forces of the king. While there they saw a number of the Bethabara wagons enter the town and depart again. The object of this visit was to secure salt; but these hostile neighbours spread the report that they carried both arms and ammunition concealed beneath the merchandise. Hence, after the battle of Moore's Creek, in which the Tory forces were defeated, the Committee of Safety, from Salisbury, decided to formally investigate the charges. In February they came to Bethabara, and having assembled the principal men of the town, the Committee of Safety informed them that they were present to find out whether it was true —

1. That they were accustomed to hold secret meetings, or that they were cognizant of such meetings;

2. That they had arms and ammunition concealed for the use of the king's soldiers;

3. That they refused to receive continental money as freely as the old money.

FRIEND AND FOE

There were sundry other minor charges which the enemies had gathered, and the record says, "we resolved to talk less in the future."

The investigation showed that all the charges were false, and after having visited Bethabara, Bethania, and Salem, the committee were not only satisfied that there was no cause for censure, but on the other hand that the communities deserved the full protection of the law. The following papers (never before printed) will show how fully they understood each other, and how friendly they were at parting. The first paper was given to the Committee of Safety, and is as follows: —

"We, the Subscribers, Inhabitants of the towns of Salem, Bethabara and Bethany, in the Parish of Dobbs, for ourselves and our fellow Inhabitants of said towns, hereby solemnly promise and declare, that, in the present calamitous circumstances of North America, which we heartily pray to God Almighty in his Mercy soon to avert, we intend to demean ourselves as hitherto, as quiet People, who wish the welfare of the County and Province, and that we, nor either of us, will not at any time intermeddle in political affairs, and that we will cheerfully assist and support the county, along with our other fellow Inhabitants, in paying of Taxes and anything else that is not against our conscience and the privileges upon which we have settled here, and that we in no case whatever shall or will be anything that shall be detrimental to the good Province we inhabit.

"SALEM, the 15th Day of February, 1776."

Then follow seven signatures from Salem, four from Bethabara, and seven from Bethania. The paper was attested by Graff. The people of Wachovia, in their turn, received the following :—

"I hereby certify that agreeable to the Direction of the Council of Safety, dated February 8, 1776, directed to Captain John Armstrong and Captain Jesse Wallon, together with myself, by Order of the Committee for the County of Surry, waited on the gentlemen of the towns of Salem, Bethabara and Bethany, and after a mature deliberation on the Cause of Our Meeting received full satisfaction.

"I hereby require and charge all persons whatsoever to take notice that as far as cognizable by me, the said Gentlemen, together with the rest of their Brethren in the aforesaid towns, have a right to protection both of their persons and their properties, and that no person molest them who has not a proper authority and show just cause for his so doing. Given under my hand this 15th Day of February, 1776.

"COL. ARMSTRONG, COL. OF S. R.
"A true copy,
"JOH. MICHAEL GRAFF."

This closed the episode of the "salt wagon charges," and although one or another company of overzealous patriots from time to time demanded an explanation of floating rumours, the paper from the Committee of Safety satisfied every one.

An incident which produces a smile in the midst of the serious events of these days was the result of a summons to Salisbury in March, 1776. Graff and Bagge responded to the summons. The object was to deliver to them a package which was regarded as suspicious, and they were required to open the same in the presence of the officials.

The ominous budget was untied, and found to contain magazines with the church news. The officials had no further interest in the matter, and no doubt the astonishment of the inquisitors brought a smile to the travellers as they journeyed over the score and a half miles homeward.

Indian troubles caused great uneasiness. The Tories had enlisted the Indians against the American sympathizers, and preparations were made for a vigorous campaign. Notice was sent to Wachovia that they should enlist or furnish substitutes, or each pay £10 fine. The officer who issued the order was hastily summoned elsewhere, and the demand was never enforced. Great fears for the safety of the place were entertained, but the army sent against the Indians was successful and peace was again restored.

The disturbed state of the country is illustrated by an occurrence in July, 1776. Four desperadoes entered the home of the single men in Salem and made a murderous assault, seriously, almost fatally, wounding one, and injuring a number of others. They terrorized the town for a time, and then continued northward. Later they were arrested by the Moravians from Salem, and taken to the Salisbury jail.

Every effort was made to show to the world that the people of Wachovia were law-abiding citizens. Taxes were paid promptly; they were willing to sign another paper similar to the one given the year before; still the situation was critical, and Mr. Lanier, their representative in the legislature, advised them to be very discreet in their conversation, since enemies and spies were all around them. 1777 closed with enmities increasing rather than diminishing.

The paymaster of the soldiers came to Wachovia, at times, and this was a signal for turmoil. There was much drinking and fighting, broken heads in some cases, and on one occasion the hostility to the town began to crystallize, and they trembled for their safety. Fortunately for them, disputes arose among the soldiers themselves, which diverted their minds, and gradually the crowds dispersed.

Not less alarming was the nature of the companies which gathered at the hotel, made up of Tories and patriots. They came to hear and talk over the news. The battles were discussed, and the note is made that on one occasion information was brought that Washington had crossed over the Delaware, on the ice, and that he had captured a large number of Hessians. In the midst of the heated discussions now and then a voice would call out "Hurrah for King George!" or "Hurrah for Washington!" and a conflict was imminent.

Among the other items which came to them was that of the imprisonment of some members in Pennsylvania, for refusing to take the oath. The facts on which these rumours were based is thus stated by Hamilton:—

"April 1, 1778, twelve members of the Emmaus congregation were imprisoned at Easton, and were kept on bread and water till the 29th, because they refused to take the oath; and in September thirteen others repeated the experience. . . . Conscientious scruples in respect to military service called for further pecuniary sacrifices. . . . The fines thus imposed upon seven amounted to £294. At another time eight men were mulcted to the sum of £401."

In these days conference was held by the Wachovia officials with the Pennsylvania members, and they gained comfort and wisdom. The Pennsylvania Moravians had

FRIEND AND FOE

the opportunity of conferring with the national authorities and the state officials at Philadelphia. They frequently received advice and aid from friends, among the most prominent in the affairs of the country, such as Henry Laurens, John Hancock, Samuel Adams, and George Washington.

Among the members themselves there were differing views which led to unwise discussions, and remarks were frequently picked up by unfriendly visitors for future use against the towns. The diary says, "Several of our brethren were taken to task for incautious remarks about the condition of the country, but if they will not listen they must suffer." Again, "We reproved two boys for unwise enthusiasm, the one hurrahing loudly for Washington, the other responding in an equally enthusiastic manner for King George!"

Strict orders for "general muster," or heavy fines in lieu thereof, were issued. The fines were paid. The taxes were doubled, and finally a triple tax was imposed. The state collected the full amount, and from time to time borrowed money from Wachovia, and still the enmities continued. About the middle of this period we find a paragraph which contains the key-note of the final result. The statement is made that the number of friends are increasing, but that henceforth still greater caution is necessary.

A pleasing experience it was which won for them a larger number of friends than any other single event. It was after one of the bloody battles of those days that a number of wounded soldiers were brought to Salem. Here they remained several months, receiving tender nursing and the most skilful surgical care. In fact, the work of Dr. Bonn is said to have effected some marvellous results in the case of the severely wounded soldiers. Some of these men were Virginians, and some North Carolinians. They left Salem, and reported to those in authority how kindly they were treated, and that the skill of the physician had saved their lives; the diary says from that time forth "we never lacked friends among those high in authority."

CHAPTER XIII

WITH THE LEGISLATURE

1773–1783

A MORE difficult and perplexing question probably never presented itself to a community than that which confronted the governing board of Wachovia in its dealings with the legislature. We have already seen how hostile were many persons, and this enmity would have been a burden in peaceful times. When we consider all the circumstances, it is marvellous that they escaped voluntary or forced banishment. We must not judge them by our standards, for their unwillingness to take an oath or bear arms was a matter of conscience, and they were ready to endure any loss or hardship rather than act against conscience. Therefore the complications which met them were the following. The title to the land had been made to Hutton, *in trust*, for the Moravians in North Carolina, hence it escaped the Confiscation Act which was passed upon land held by the non-resident English; this saving clause (in trust) was not known to all, and hence the popular belief and desire was that the Moravians should go, and at one time the shiftless class of neighbours had preëmpted the mills, stores, houses, and lands. Again, the legislators could not understand the motives which caused them to refuse to take the oath. It appeared to be lack of loyalty, while in reality there were no truer patriots in the land. The officials construed their unwillingness to bear arms as indicating a predisposition toward King George, or cowardice, while in reality the Moravians did as much, if not more, for the cause of American independence than any similar number of men in any portion of the state. Still, when the condition of their remaining in North Carolina depended upon the task of securing from the same hostile legislature an official indorsement of these very principles which were the prime cause of the difficulties, the task indeed seemed to be a hopeless one.

Already, in 1777, information was brought by their representative, Mr. Lanier, and also by Colonel Armstrong, that the attitude of the legislature was hostile. The statutes were very severe; in one instance there was a fine of £100 and a ban which forbade association with other men. At last, in 1778, they determined to send official representatives to Hillsboro, where the legislature was in session, and work earnestly to change public opinion, and gain legislation which would make their future secure. It was necessary that some action should be taken. A few of the younger men were willing to take the state oath. All were willing to affirm their loyalty to the state. But the majority were unwilling to forswear the king, under whom they might have to serve in the mission fields, and furthermore, they were not willing to join the army. Banishment would be welcome when compared with acting against conscience. These facts were known to others, and some eager settlers had already moved upon Wachovia lands, believing that within a few weeks the Moravians would be driven into exile.

The visit of the two representatives from Salem to the legislature in Hillsboro, August, 1778, is given in full in the records, and aside from its being the pivotal point on which the affairs of Wachovia turned, it also gives us a good view of the methods of work pursued by the lawgivers of that day.

Bagge and Blum were the men chosen to bear the petition to the legislature. The petition itself is a strong and dignified paper. A careful perusal shows the true ring of the patriot, the honest citizen, the law-abiding member of the commonwealth. But all through the paper we notice that the gauntlet is thrown down, and that in a dignified manner they claim that, if freedom of conscience is assailed, the same spirit which drove the great Comenius out of Bohemia, and caused the Georgia colony to forsake their homes, will influence the Moravians to emigrate from North Carolina and settle in the midst of a people who would allow freedom of conscience. There is not a breath of hostility in the paper; they were observing every law of the land, they were paying the triple tax, they were feeding and sheltering the soldiers, and nursing the wounded, their broad acres were cultivated for the benefit of the army, their shops and mills furnished supplies for troops, they never aided the enemy by word or deed, every effort was put forth to support the powers ruling over them; but freedom of conscience had been promised them, and this they would have, at any cost. This is the spirit of the petition, which we give in full:—

"To the honourable House of the Senators and the honourable House of Commons in the State of North Carolina, gathered now together for the General Assembly, is presented this petition of the United Brethren in this State, who live in Bethabara, Bethania, Salem and the adjoining sections of Wachovia:—

"We respectfully declare unto your honourable body, that the ancient Episcopal Church, called the Unitas

Fratrum, or Unity of Brethren, having heard of the great religious liberty in America, sent representatives, chiefly from the country of Moravia, to preach the gospel to the Indians of the Colony of Georgia, and to establish settlements where a place of refuge could be found by those who were being persecuted and banished from lands in which the blessings of freedom and religious liberty could not be enjoyed. After these settlements in Georgia had been established, the war with the Spaniards, of Florida, began. Although we had received full assurance that our conscientious scruples against bearing arms would be respected, the authorities of that colony were not true to their promises to the Moravians, and oppressions and persecutions followed. Realizing the great injustice of the position taken by the authorities who had invited them to settle in this Colony, under the above mentioned conditions, and had then refused to allow them the very freedom which had caused them to forsake home and fatherland, and cross the ocean, the Georgia colony removed to Pennsylvania where they were assured religious liberty and freedom of conscience. They settled in the wilderness in the forks of the Delaware river. Here they found the liberty which had been denied them in their first home in America, and they lived in peace with God and their fellow men. Their industry and success attracted the attention of many people. During the thirty years that followed they received invitations from many sections of the British possessions to establish settlements. Especially urgent was the call to begin a colony in North Carolina. The reply to this invitation was to the effect that if the church began a colony in North Carolina the new effort must be under the same conditions, and for the same objects which had governed the settlement in Georgia.

WITH THE LEGISLATURE 137

To make this firm and sure, our deputy appeared before King George and the English Parliament, and petitioned his Majesty to assure to the new settlement the same rights which had been given to them in Pennsylvania, New York, Maryland and other colonies. These rights included the privileges of affirming instead of taking an oath, and also included exemption from bearing arms, or serving as a soldier in time of peace or war. Parliament examined very carefully and thoroughly into the affairs of the Unitas Fratrum, its history, its doctrine, its daily life and customs, and its discipline. Being fully satisfied that it was an ancient Episcopal Church, that its doctrine was pure and its discipline correct, an act was passed encouraging them to settle in the English Provinces in America, and assuring them forever these rights and privileges. All this is set forth in the copy of the above named Act of Parliament, the original of which is herewith submitted to your honourable body. The present duly elected Governor of the state of North Carolina has examined this document, has confirmed it, and has declared that it is binding upon the new government of North Carolina.

"This act held out strong inducements, and encouraged by the prospects they came to America, to enjoy freedom of conscience for themselves and their posterity. This desire for freedom was not a mere sentiment; many had suffered persecutions for the sake of the Gospel. They forsook houses and land; they left homes and loved ones; they gave up material possessions, but they did all this cheerfully for the sake of their religious liberty and freedom of conscience which they expected to find in North Carolina. For a quarter of a century these privileges have been enjoyed, and our people have lived in Wachovia quiet, happy and useful lives.

"Then the war broke out, and the developments which followed began to encroach upon those rights which we deem the very foundation condition of our settlement in Wachovia. We should not be considered as other than loyal subjects of the present government. We are willing to bear our full share of the burdens of the war. But liberty of conscience in the matter of bearing arms and taking the oath, we believe to be consistent with loyalty to the government, and the fulfilment of our duties.

"Not long since an act of the legislature imposed upon us military duties, or in default thereof a heavy fine. Again an Act of your honourable body has ordered us to attend the general musters, and if we do not appear, men are to be drafted for service and the cost therefor to be paid by the people of Wachovia. From the Constitution of this state and the Act of Parliament, already referred to and which has been endorsed by the present authorities of North Carolina, we feel that we can justly claim the privileges which induced us to come to North Carolina, and that we are justified in humbly petitioning your honourable body to abolish these oppressions, which petition we do herewith respectfully present.

"Furthermore, there has been placed upon us by an Act of the Assembly the necessity of taking a prescribed oath of allegiance to the United States of America, and the State of North Carolina, and of forswearing allegiance to Great Britain, to King George III, and to his posterity forever. The penalty attached to the violation of this act is either banishment, or the loss of all protection of the law.

"Concerning this Act of the legislature, we beg to say, that with our whole heart we promise allegiance to the state. But the forswearing of Great Britain is against our conscience for the following weighty reasons. We are

WITH THE LEGISLATURE 139

intimately connected with the Unitas Fratrum in all parts of the world. According to our general church government our people stand ready to respond to the call of the church to labour in whatever field is assigned. Hence, within the next years, without doubt, a number who are now called upon to forswear King George III will be sent to serve the church in England, or as missionaries in English provinces. One of the objects of this settlement in North Carolina was to create a training school for missionaries. How can these men who expect with reasonable certainty sooner or later to labour on English soil, forswear the King? We esteem an oath too solemn a matter to thus forswear the King with the lips but with the heart repudiate the words of the lips.

" As the greater part of the United Brethren do not wish to take the prescribed oath, since it is against our conscience, we humbly petition your honourable body not to take from us the right of affirming. We furthermore humbly petition you to still accord to us the blessings of the protection of the laws, so that we may not suffer violence of person and property at the hands of evil men. We feel that this protection is due us, unless we are found guilty of treacherous actions against our own or other states, and this, by the grace of God shall never be.

"We will be bound by conscience to seek the best interests of the land where we dwell, and to discharge our duties in an honourable and honest manner. Not one of us will hesitate to solemnly affirm 'that he will not undertake or do anything that will injure the United States, or the state of North Carolina, that he will not furnish news, help or assistance to the British, at war with this or other states.' In case an individual proves faithless to his affirmation, let him be punished as an individual. We will give all possible assistance to bring such an one to justice, but our humble prayer is that you will accord protection to our persons and possessions against all violence and injustice and that you will allow us the full benefit of the law.

"Permit us to remain in peace and quiet in the homes in which Providence has placed us. These homes are consecrated to the furtherance of Christianity and the promotion of the fear of God and virtue. We have demonstrated by our manner of life that the Moravians are industrious members of society. Give to us permission to serve the public in our daily callings; enable us to show to our fellow members in this country and in Europe, that the new government insures to us the same liberty which we enjoyed under the late rule; if the same generous treatment is given by this government, then many worthy men and women will gladly come to North Carolina to enjoy the blessings of freedom, and will build up the interests of the new commonwealth.

"We have no implements of war. We do not wish to use violence against this or any other power, as has been falsely charged against us. We do not covet positions of honour, nor lucrative offices. We have paid our taxes promptly, and no obligations to the state have ever had to be collected by process of law.

"The officials of our church who reside in Pennsylvania, New Jersey and Maryland have presented to the national government, on our behalf, as well as on their behalf, a petition similar to this one, which we now respectfully bring before your honourable body. We are not without hope that it will be granted, since this hope is based upon a letter from General Washington, a copy of which is added to this petition.

"Should any members of your honourable body fail to fully agree with us in your opinions as individuals, we will crave your sympathy in your official capacity. Our common Lord and Master has said, 'Blessed are the merciful, for they shall obtain mercy.'

"We the undersigned beg leave to submit this petition and respectful presentation of our case to your gracious and earnest consideration, and pray you to give to us and our brethren such help as you are able to give consistently with leniency and justice. We remain your obedient petitioners."

On the 4th of August Bagge and Blum began their journey to Hillsboro, to appear before the legislature and present the petition. We will let them tell the story of the succeeding days.

When we arrived at Lindsey's, we learned that a conspiracy to assassinate General Rutherford had been discovered. The conspirators were scattered through Rowan, Surry, and Guilford counties. We stopped with Councilman Strudwick, and there we were informed that the intention to present the petition was already known, and had met with much opposition, even thus far in advance. Strudwick also informed us that a party of ladies and gentlemen from Hillsboro were especially active in promoting ill will against us, because last year they had visited Wachovia, and received some fancied slight. He predicted that our petition would meet with strong opposition. At noon, on the 7th of August, we rode into Hillsboro. As soon as we had dismounted, we were told that the conspirators in the plot to assassinate General Rutherford had declared under oath that the Moravians were cognizant of, and party to, the plot. We were at once questioned on this point. August 8th we began our work of preparing the way to present the petition to the legislature. We worked in and out among the people, here and there, making them acquainted with our affairs, and distributing copies of the pamphlet which contained our church history. This publication was read with great interest. We found some persons who had been in Bethabara with Governor Tryon, and they were very friendly. Still matters were by no means in a satisfactory position.

The House of Commons met in the afternoon. Their sessions are held in the church, and the Senators meet near by in a small house. During the oath taking, a man called down from the gallery, asking whether we were implicated in the recent plot. We gave an emphatic denial, adding that if any individual member of our church was connected with it we would use our utmost endeavour to bring him to justice. A merchant of Cross Creek, a Mr. Patterson, formerly a resident of Santa Cruz, testified to the excellence of the Moravians as a people. August 9th, as his Excellency Governor Caswell went to church to-day, Bagge introduced himself and was received in a polite and courteous manner. We met many people and conversed at length with two gentlemen of prominence who seemed to be favourably disposed; but in another quarter the reception was anything but friendly. The leader (Fuhrer) soon became our friend. On the 10th the preliminary work was begun, and our documents were examined. We continued to work in and out among the people and the officials. The governor told us that the evening would be the most favourable time for an interview with him, but when we called he was engaged and could not see us. We left our papers for him to examine. A certain lawyer, of great influence, was approached, but he

WITH THE LEGISLATURE

answered shortly and gave little hope. Another leading lawyer made an appointment, but when we called he slipped away. General Parsons arrived to-day, and is very friendly toward us. He has already examined the petition. During the night of the 10th and till noon of the 11th a very severe storm prevailed. Great damage was done, and it was difficult to secure the attention of any one. On this day Bagge had half an hour's interview with the governor, who handed him back his papers. He promised to aid him all he could, but said he was afraid he could not do us much good. He expressed himself very warmly toward the Moravians. There was no session of the legislature to-day as the storm had injured the church, and the documents were wet. Bagge handed our papers to Colonel Alexander Martin, and he promised to carefully examine them. On the 12th it became apparent that it was time to have our petition formally presented to the legislature, and Mr. Brooks promised to do so next day. August 13th, being our special festival day, we were in spirit with the congregations in Wachovia. In the afternoon there seemed to be an opportunity for presenting our petition. When Mr. Brooks arose he became entangled in a discussion in regard to some unpopular measure, and when he recognized the antagonism which he aroused, his judgment told him he could now do us no good. He therefore requested the leader, Hawkins, to take in hand our matters, and he agreed to do so. A man, by name Whiteaker, asked for our petition. He read it during the evening, and became our friend. The historical pamphlets continued to circulate, and many persons asked for them.

A company of people called the Nickolites were petitioning the legislature for certain privileges, and Bagge and Blum, as well as their friends, were desirous of keeping the affairs of the Moravians separated from these people, as their record was in some respects unsavoury.

On the 14th of August, Mr. Hawkins presented our petition. It was read by the under clerk. Usually there was so much disturbance in the house that the voice of the reading clerk could not be heard. But when it was announced that the petition of the United Brethren would be communicated, an impressive stillness came over the assembly, and in a clear voice, with marked attention on the part of every one present, the clerk read our paper. When he had finished, on motion it was referred to the proper committee. We then proceeded to the Senate, and the petition was read to this body, and in like manner referred to a committee.

The next morning before breakfast the joint committee met in a large room. There were at least one hundred visitors present. Among them were the Speaker of the House of Commons and the President of the Senate. The committee organized by electing General Rutherford chairman. From the Senate the members were Carr, Battle, Stone, Alexander Martin, and a few others. From the House of Commons, Generals Parsons and Bryan, and Whiteaker, Hawkins, and Brooks. Abner Nash was to have come, but failed to appear. The papers were read. Bagge was requested to address the committee, and produced a printed copy of the Act of Parliament, which made a good impression on the members of the committee. This Act of Parliament was unknown to any of the committee men. Carr and Bryan were particularly interested in our case, and we trust the Lord will reward them for thus endeavouring to further his cause. All save two or three, who remained silent, indorsed our cause. Colonel Martin made himself special guardian of the Act of Parliament, lest harm should come to it, as it was passed from one to the other. After full discussion the following favourable report was adopted : —

"The joint committee selected to consider the petition of the United Brethren who live in the settlements of Bethabara, Bethania, Salem and the neighbouring sections of Wachovia, met and elected General Rutherford chairman. The committee begs to submit the following report. We find that the religious society which is called Moravian, have received by an Act of Parliament their full rights and liberties as free citizens. We find further that by industry and frugality they have improved the commercial and manufacturing interests, as well as trade and agriculture; that their peaceful and orderly behaviour has won the respect of all good men; that on all proper occasions they have contributed their quota for the public needs, and have assisted in the support of the public weal in as far as their religious scruples will allow. It has further been represented to your committee, that the Moravians in North Carolina have an organic connection with the Moravian Church in all parts of the world, and that their members in this State are often called to mission fields, in many lands and among many peoples. In view of this fact petition has been made to the honourable Assembly that the following words be omitted from the form of their affirmation of allegiance, to wit: 'And I renounce all allegiance toward the present King of Great Britain, his heirs and successors.'

"Therefore, I, Griffith Rutherford, chairman of the joint committee, in behalf of the committee, do recommend to the honourable legislature that the members of the Unitas Fratrum or Moravian Church be allowed to omit the above clause from their affirmation of allegiance.

"I further recommend in behalf of the committee that the members of the above religious society be allowed to pay a regular tax, or a money equivalent, in lieu of military service, in militia drill, or actual warfare. The above-named tax to be used for the need of the general government, and to replace the fines heretofore imposed, said fines having been applied to the payment of substitutes.

"The report is approved by the committee and is respectfully submitted to your honourable body.

"August 15, 1778." "GRIFFITH RUTHERFORD, *Chairman.*

The committee seemed to feel very kindly toward the Moravians, and before the report was handed in it was shown to Bagge, and he was asked whether he desired to add to the paper or alter anything.

Already at breakfast we received an intimation that the report would not be accepted.

The morning passed and there were no developments. At noon we heard that the Speaker of the Assembly was unfriendly. After dinner Bagge spoke to him, and he admitted that there was truth in the rumour, but added that in his capacity as a public official he would use every effort to deal fairly with the question without allowing his private opinions to unduly influence him. A number of senators were interviewed. The majority were friendly to our cause. The chairman of the committee, General Rutherford, was a senator, and he presented the report to the Senate in the afternoon. Immediately the lawyer, spoken of by Strudwick, arose. This was one of the party whom he said we had in some way offended last year when he visited our place. This lawyer addressed the senators and painted us in dark colours. He said that we did not treat visitors with proper hospitality; that we refused the current money, receiving only gold coin; that we boasted about our improvements, and of the great value to the state of our commerce; the only object of this boasting was to throw dust in the eyes of the honourable senators; that the improvements were nothing more than a tavern and a few houses; that the wonderful commerce consisted in the stronger wresting money from the weaker, and sending it, no one knew where; that we formed a dangerous, independent little state within the commonwealth of North Carolina; that if we were not willing to live as other people, the sooner we cleared out of the country the better.

Mr. Carr and Colonel Martin spoke in our favour, and presented true statements.

Mr. Shepherd advocated freedom from military service, but did not consent to the affirmation.

General Rutherford agreed with Shepherd, and made a powerful speech.

We sat in the midst of all this with calmness of feeling, and thought of the evil which had been spoken against our divine Master, and felt that if he suffered thus the members should also be willing to endure persecution.

The abusive lawyer repeated his remarks several times with great vehemence.

When the vote was taken it resulted as follows:—

In favour of the report, 11.

Against the report, 13.

Thus the report was voted down.

Colonel Martin at once arose and introduced a bill which he had already prepared. In this bill he suggested to the House that the matter be compromised by allowing the forswearing of the king to cover only such time as they are citizens of the United States. This was sent to the House. It was already dusk, and according to the rule the lower House could not consider the measure until Monday.

Sunday was passed quietly, but we noticed that the enemy was busy. Some strongly advocated a refusal to further consider the matter, or to allow it to again be introduced. We quietly continued to disseminate information about our people and our communities.

Monday morning the message from the Senate was read in the House. The suggestion was approved, but the House added the condition that we take the form of the oath as all others do; hence the only benefit we seem to have gained by all our work is the introduction of a clause making the forswearing of the king binding only while we reside in the United States; the taking of the prescribed oath and the bearing of arms, the very things we came here to have removed, are imposed in a more emphatic manner. Parsons, Hawkins, Brooks, and even Gilbert spoke in our favour. A lawyer, one Williams, abused us shamefully. In the midst of the harangue he was called to order by the Speaker, and thus the matter closed, in a worse condition than when we came.

Already, before we knew how the matter would be received by the House of Commons, we had determined to take our case to the courts, and endeavour to secure from them the protection which the legislature declined to give us, and thus await the gathering of the next legislature. In the evening Colonel Armstrong called upon us and advised us to make no further attempt to secure legislation. That the members wished to adjourn speedily, that during these times of war they were not in a condition to look at such questions in an unbiassed manner, and we could expect nothing further at this time. He promised to

WITH THE LEGISLATURE 149

secure for us all possible protection for life and property.

Early Tuesday morning, August 18, Colonel Armstrong came to inform us that the preceding evening Lanier had received a startling piece of information. It was to the effect that the Surry court had decided to enforce the law of banishment from the county, within sixty days, in the case of all who refused to take the prescribed oath. Armstrong advised us to make a determined effort to have some act drawn up which would afford us temporary protection, and offset this action of the Surry court. Bagge hastened to Lanier and found it even as Armstrong had represented.

The situation, as it stood on that critical day, was as follows : —

The legislature declined to free them from the oath, or to allow them to affirm instead of taking the oath; it also declined to permit them exemption from bearing arms.

The court of Surry County had decided that they must leave the county in sixty days, if they failed to take the prescribed oath.

The Moravians would have forsaken homes and lands rather than have acted against their conscience.

Hence, as matters stood on the morning of Tuesday, August 18, 1778, the voluntary removal of the Moravian colony from North Carolina, because of unjust legislation, seemed to be one of the strong probabilities, and if no change in the situation could be effected, it appeared to be inevitable. But it is the darkest hour which always precedes the dawn.

Bagge and Lanier went at once to Mr. Hooper. He drew up a bill which would allow us to affirm instead of taking the oath, and his plan was to attach this as an amendment to some act which was about to pass the final reading. All now appeared to desire the passage of a bill which would counteract the work of the Surry court; they felt that it would be to the detriment of the commonwealth to drive out so large a body of honest, thrifty citizens. The loss of a thousand and more of the best people of the thinly populated state was no small consideration, and the legislators seemed to at last have realized that it was trivial and belittling to refuse the request of these good and honest people. The amendment was first attached to a bill which had no manner of connection with the subject in hand; illogical as was the amendment, it passed the House of Commons, but in the Senate it was defeated, because their rules allowed no amendment to be attached to a bill which came up for its third reading.

It was now no longer a question in the minds of the representatives. They felt that they must save this colony from banishment, hence the following bill was drawn up and passed in the Senate, with only three dissenting votes, and in the evening it passed the House of Commons: —

"Resolved in the General Assembly, this 18th day of August, 1778, that all Moravians . . . who before the next session of the General Assembly will take the affirmation of allegiance prescribed by law, shall be admitted to the full rights and privileges of citizenship."

We received a copy of this resolution on the evening of the 18th. At five o'clock of August 19, when the Assembly convened for the last time, this was the first bill which the speaker signed. Thus they gained their object,

WITH THE LEGISLATURE

at least in part, and their position was made secure for the present. At seven o'clock the same morning, Bagge and Blum began the return journey, and on the evening of the 20th of August they were once more at home.

The neighbours around Wachovia still firmly believed that the people would leave their homes rather than submit to the laws which deprived them of freedom of conscience. They continued to preëmpt the land at the rate of fifty shillings per hundred acres, and even the town plots of Salem, Bethania, and Bethabara, as well as the land on which stood the mills, were entered by speculative neighbours, they erroneously thinking that no lawful deeds existed (Reichel).

In the midst of this state of affairs the alarm of the Moravians may be imagined when the legislation in January, 1779, placed the position in a more dangerous shape than at any time before. (See Fries, "Forsyth County," and the Laws of North Carolina, printed in 1821.)

Without quoting the exact words of the various preambles and the acts, we give the substance of the same. The law enacted, that because certain persons who came under the Confiscation Act of 1777 had failed to appear before the present legislature, in order to show just cause why the act should not apply to them, therefore their lands shall be forfeited to the state. That three commissioners shall be appointed by each county court, in each county; that these commissioners shall give bond to the amount of £250,000, and take a prescribed oath; the commissioners shall take charge of all confiscated lands, etc., and shall have the power to summon all the citizens to appear before them, in the several counties, to give an account of forfeited property. It was the duty of the commissioners to report to the county court, and the court had the right to stay execution if the justice of the action appeared to be in doubt. In October, 1779, this law of January, 1779, was repealed, but was replaced by one which was in effect the same.

This was adding fuel to the fire of their difficulties, and two representatives were at once sent from Wachovia to Halifax, where the legislature was in session. The task was not as difficult as last year. The petition was favourably received, and the act which was passed is as follows : —

"An Act to prescribe the Affirmation of Allegiance and Fidelity to this State to be taken by the Unitas Fratrum, or Moravians, . . . and granting them certain Indulgences therein mentioned and other Purposes.

"I. In order to quiet the Consciences and indulge the religious Scruples of the Unitas Fratrum, or Moravians;

"II. Be it enacted by the General Assembly of the State of North Carolina and by and with the Authority of the same, that the Affirmation of Allegiance and Fidelity to this State shall hereafter be taken by all the above People, in the Form Following, viz: [here follows the form]. Which said Affirmation being taken before any Justice of the Peace, in the County where they reside, at or before the first day of May next, shall entitle them to all those Rights, Privileges and Immunities, they heretofore respectively enjoyed, any Law to the contrary notwithstanding, the Assessment and Payment of Taxes only excepted.

"III. And be it further enacted by the Authority aforesaid, that all and every of the said People, upon taking and subscribing the Affirmation of Allegiance and Fidelity to this State as aforesaid, before the Entry-Taker of the County, may reënter all their Lands formerly made in Earl

Granville's Office, or Public-Land Office, or any Lands they or either of them, have had the prior Occupancy of, or may enter a Caveat or Claim against any Person or Persons who may have entered or surveyed the same, provided such Entry, Caveat or Claim, be made on or before the first day of May next after the passing of this Act, and shall be entitled in Preference of all others to obtain a Grant for the same, according to the Rules of the Act of the Assembly for establishing Offices for receiving Entries of Claims for Lands, etc.

"IV. And whereas many ignorant though good subjects of this State have not taken the Oath of Allegiance owing to the Neglect of the Justices of the Peace in many Counties; Be it therefore enacted by the Authority aforesaid, that all Residents of this State, who have not been inimical, or heretofore refused to take the Oath when particularly called upon, and who shall take the Oath of Allegiance to this State prescribed by Law before the first day of May next, or who have taken the said Oath since the Time prescribed by the said Law, shall be admitted to all the Rights, Immunities, and Privileges of Citizens, hereby granted to the Moravians; any Law to the contrary notwithstanding.

"HALIFAX, January 19, 1779."

The diary says that Praezel and Heckewelder, whose visit secured the above legislation, had been sent to Halifax after hope had failed, and the property was being seized and occupied. When they returned all was changed, and from that time forth there was no serious fear of the loss of their homes and land.

In the month of February, Justice Dobson met the men of the several towns, and they gathered in the church, forming a half-circle about the magistrate. The latter read the form of the affirmation, the men repeated it after him.

"I, A. B., do solemnly and sincerely declare and affirm, in the Presence of Almighty God, that I will truly and faithfully demean myself as a peaceable Subject of the independent State of North Carolina, and will be subject to the Powers and Authorities that are or may be established for the good Government thereof, and not inconsistent with the Constitution, by yielding either an active or passive Obedience thereto; and that I will not abet or join the Subjects or forces of the King of Great Britain, or other enemies of this State, by any Means, in any Conspiracy whatsoever, against the said State, or the United States of America; and that I will make known to the Governor, or some Member of the Council of State, Judge of the Supreme Court, or Justice of the Peace, all Treasons, Conspiracies, or Attempts, Committed or Intended against the same, which shall come to my Knowledge."

At the end of this formula Dobson said, "so help ye God." He then gave each one the written certificate. This closed forever the question of their liberty in the matter of affirming. They were likewise relieved of further anxiety regarding military duty by the imposition of a triple tax. This tax was paid until 1783.

There seemed still to have been some who annoyed the people of Wachovia in regard to their land, and hence, to settle any legal complications, in May, 1780, the legislature in Newbern, Abner Nash, governor, passed the following: —

"An act for the relief of the People called Moravians, . . . within this State.

"I. Whereas by an Act of the General Assembly of this State, entitled an Act to amend an Act for declaring what crimes and practices against the State shall be treason, and what shall be misprision of treason, and providing punishments adequate to the crimes of both classes, and preventing the dangers which may arise from persons disaffected to the State, all persons within the State are requested to take an oath, or an affirmation to the State, and in case of refusal are either to be sent out of the State, or to be deprived of the benefit and protection of the laws of said State, and disabled from prosecuting or defending any suit either in law or equity: and whereas numbers of persons under pretence that the people called Moravians, . . . have not taken an affirmation to the State have entered and taken up the lands which the said denomination of people have remained in quiet possession of for many years: for remedy whereof, and to prevent such abuses for the future,

"II. Be it enacted etc., That from and after the passing of this Act, when it shall appear that any of the people of the said denomination within this State, . . . shall have been lawfully possessed of any lands within the said State, either by patent, deed, or otherwise, whereon any other person hath heretofore made entry, and under the above said pretence, all such entries and the proceedings thereon shall be deemed null and void; and in case any entries shall hereafter be made on any of the lands of said people, such entries shall also be void and of no effect.

"Read three times and ratified in General Assembly, the tenth day of May, A.D. 1780.

"ALEXANDER MARTIN, S.S.
"THOMAS BENBURY, S.C."

When Marshall took the deeds which had been received from England, to Salisbury, in 1780, to have them recorded, the recorder declined to accept them at that time. These were the deeds made by Hutton, of London, to Marshall. Hutton had received the deeds from Lord Granville, the original proprietor, and he had held the land in trust for the church. He, in his turn, transferred them to Marshall, as proprietor. Soon after Marshall's visit to Salisbury, he and Bagge were summoned to appear before the commission which had in charge the affairs of confiscated estates. The interview between the members of the commission and the Moravians was fairly satisfactory to the latter. When the legislature gathered in Salem, in 1781 and 1782, their affairs were fully studied and finally understood by the legislators. It became apparent that there had never been any just cause for doubt in regard to the title; hence, to settle the question beyond the possibility of any further complications which might arise as a result of plots against the people of Wachovia, Marshall appeared before the legislature in April, 1782, and the following act was passed, thus ending the years of unjust persecution: —

"I. Whereas, Frederick William Marshall, esquire, of Salem in Surry County, hath made it appear to this General Assembly that all the tracts of land in this State belonging to the lord advocate, the chancellor and the agent of the Unitas Fratrum, or United Brethren, have been transferred to him from the former possessors, in trust for the Unitas Fratrum, or United Brethren; and as doubts have arisen whether the said tracts do not come within the description of the Confiscation Act; and to quiet the minds of those to whom conveyances have

WITH THE LEGISLATURE

been made, or are to be made, of any part or parts thereof;

"II. Be it therefore enacted by the General Assembly of the State of North Carolina, and it is hereby enacted by authority of the same, that a certain deed of lease and release, dated the twenty-seventh and twenty-eighth of October, one thousand seven hundred and seventy-eight, from James Hutton, conveying the tract of Wachovia, in Surry County, to said Frederick William Marshall, be hereby declared valid in law, and to be admitted to probate in the County of Surry, and registered in the Register's office thereof, agreeable to the testimonials thereunto pertaining; and that all lands which by deed of bargain and sale of the twentieth of April, one thousand seven hundred and sixty-four, between William Churton and Charles Metcalf, registered in the County of Orange in book number one, page one hundred and six, and in Rowan County, in book E, number five, page four hundred and fifty-two, etc., were then conveyed to said Charles Metcalf, be hereby vested in the said William Marshall in trust as aforesaid; and all conveyances of the above mentioned lands, or any one of them, made, or which shall be made, by the said Frederick William Marshall, shall be as good and valid to all intents and purposes as if the Confiscation Act had never passed.

"III. And be it further enacted by the authority aforesaid, that the power of Attorney of Christian Frederick Cossart, dated the third of November, one thousand seven hundred and seventy-two, empowering said Frederick William Marshall to sell his lands, be admitted to probate and registry in the County of Wilkes, and be as good and valid in law as it could or might have been, had the Act of Confiscation never passed."

The proprietors of the Wachovia tract were and are the following: —

1. James Hutton, of London, Aug. 7, 1753 — Oct. 28, 1778. Title transferred by deed to
2. Frederick William Marshall, of Salem, N. C., 1778 — Feb. 11, 1802. Transferred by will to
3. Christian Louis Benzien, of Salem, 1802 — Nov. 13, 1811. Transferred by will to
4. John Gebhard Cunow, of Bethlehem, Pa., 1811 — March 28, 1822. Transferred by deed to
5. Lewis David de Schweinitz, of Bethlehem, Pa., 1822 — Feb. 8, 1834. Transferred by will to
6. William Henry Van Vleck, of New York City, 1834 — Aug. 7, 1844. Transferred by deed to
7. Charles F. Kluge, of Salem, N. C., 1844 — April 19, 1853. Transferred by deed to
8. Emil A. de Schweinitz, of Salem, 1853 — Dec. 1, 1877. Transferred by deed to
9. The Board of Provincial Elders of the Southern Province of the Moravian Church.

In 1781 the legislature appointed Salem as the place for meeting. The time was November. On the 8th of the month Governor Alexander Martin arrived, and also two companies of soldiers. Ex-Governor Caswell came, and sixty-three members of the Senate and the House. Twenty-eight members of the House were absent, and ten members of the Senate. On the night of November 24 the alarming news was received that a large body of Tories was near the town, and intended to make an attack for the purpose of seizing the person of the governor. Governor Martin had his room in the Brethren's House, corner of Main and Academy streets. It was a cold November night, rain was falling, and all night long the two com-

Cedar Avenue. Salem

WITH THE LEGISLATURE

panies patrolled the streets. No attack was made, and at 9 o'clock in the morning, the tired, cold, and wet soldiers retired to their quarters.

On the 27th of November it was decided to adjourn. Several meetings were held, but no business was transacted. The utmost cordiality existed between the people and the officials. Homes were engaged for the next meeting, and with this kindly feeling the members departed.

Governor Martin again arrived in Salem January 25, 1782, and with him the Speaker, and a number of the members of the legislature. Among the representatives present on this second occasion were many who were not present the first time, and thus nearly all the representatives were in Salem, either in 1781 or 1782. On the 30th of the month Governor Burke unexpectedly arrived. He had been a prisoner in the hands of the British, and his sudden appearance was a source of so much joy that a number of thanksgiving hymns were sung in the evening service. Colonel Steward was present to officially represent General Greene's army, and Major Taylor was sent from the Virginia legislature. Several sessions were held, but a quorum not being present, no business was transacted. Some were in favour of waiting a week, but it was suddenly decided to separate, which was done at once, a number leaving the same evening, the remainder the next day.

While it is true that no executive business was transacted either in 1781 or 1782, the legislature was present and was represented by almost all the members on the two occasions. The first time they were in the town three weeks, the second time two weeks. The great benefit resulting from these meetings was that the leading men of the state became acquainted with the people of Wachovia, and not only did all unkind feeling toward the Moravians disappear, but we read on many occasions of the social visits and the fraternal exchange of courtesies. Hence the close of the decade finds the Province of Wachovia like a vessel in the harbour after a stormy voyage. Many times it seemed that the ship could not weather the tempest, but when the great Peace Jubilee was celebrated to commemorate the close of the struggle between England and the United States, the Moravians could also rejoice over the complete defeat of all their enemies, and rest in the benefits arising from the friendly legislation which assured to them and their posterity that freedom to secure which they forsook home and fatherland, and which was to them a most precious treasure.

CHAPTER XIV

"IN THE VERY THEATRE OF THE WAR"

1773-1783

"In the very theatre of the war" are the words used by the writer of a century and a quarter ago. He was fully justified in using this description, for although actual fighting did not occur in Wachovia, the horrors of the struggle were all about them, the hardships were many, and their part was none the less meritorious, even though they did not engage in the battles. The years 1780 and 1781 formed a dark and trying period for North Carolina, as well as its neighbour, South Carolina. There were bloody battles, defeats and victories, doubts and uncertainties. The interest in Wachovia's part is divided between the actual scenes in this Province, and the relation which the events bear to the general history of the Revolution.

In 1780 a large number of soldiers gathered at Fayetteville, ten thousand or more, to resist the English, who were invading the states from the south. After the harvests had been gathered, a company of men from General Gates's army came to Wachovia and impressed horses, wagons, and men to carry provisions to Camden. This place is about one hundred and twenty-five miles from Wachovia in a direct line. At Camden a bloody battle was fought August 16, and in this struggle the American forces were totally defeated, with two thousand killed, wounded, or prisoners. The visit of General Gates's troops to Wachovia, the preparation of the army supplies, the trip to Camden, the terrible battle, the loss of the horses and wagons belonging to the Moravians, — these were the things which brought them into contact with the actual warfare of that period. Though they lost property, no lives were sacrificed in the South Carolina battle.

After the defeat of the American army at Camden the Tories became very bold. They gathered in large numbers all around Wachovia, and committed many depredations. The experiences connected with this uprising show very plainly that the sympathies of Wachovia were not with those who were arrayed against the government. At one time the Tories were one thousand strong in this neighbourhood, and the military officials detailed three hundred Virginia soldiers to "chastise" them. The methods of these troops were not as severe as those employed in other sections, but what they did had the desired effect. Arriving at Bethabara in August, the troops established their headquarters in the town, and sent out small detachments to arrest and bring in the Tories. They were in Bethabara three weeks. The first company of prisoners numbered twelve. Then another and another scouting party brought in the suspected men and confined them in the Brethren's House, the same building in which Governor Tryon was entertained. The trial took place as soon as the prisoners arrived, some were discharged, some were whipped, and one man received more than one hundred lashes. At the end of three weeks this company withdrew, but the town was not left long in peace.

A detachment of Georgia soldiers, under Pickens, five hundred in number, arrived about this time, at Bethabara, and remained several days. It was a time of terror, though we are not told in this instance what form the danger assumed. Plundering was common, houses were entered at will, and we infer that they threatened to destroy the town, as it is stated that it was a time of the greatest peril. The soldiers, among other depredations, broke into the mill, stole the flour belonging to the villagers, and then went to the houses and requested the people to exchange bread for their flour. When Pickens's troops retired, the town was nearly ruined.

In October of the same year, 1780, the battle of King's Mountain was fought. The British officer, Ferguson, had taken a position on top of the mountain, and he considered his position so strong that he declared impiously that "God Almighty could not drive him out." The attack was made by the American soldiers, and the British were completely defeated. Two hundred of the British were killed, one hundred and fifteen were wounded, and six hundred were taken prisoners. The Americans had fifty killed. Three hundred of the prisoners and a number of the wounded were hurried northward, and arrived at Wachovia a few days after the battle. Fifty British regulars were taken to Salem, two hundred and fifty British militia were assigned to Bethabara, while the wounded were sent to Bethania. They remained in Wachovia about three weeks, till all the provisions had been consumed, and then troops and prisoners moved on.

At this time General Greene was placed in command of the American forces, his task being to check or crush the British in their invasion from the south. In view of the losses already sustained, and the demoralized condition of the army, he had a difficult task. But he was a brave man, an able soldier, and a strict disciplinarian. A detachment of Greene's soldiers, was stationed in Salem, and remained during the month of January, 1781. Their object is not stated in the diary of Salem, but it was no doubt to establish a base of supplies for the army. These soldiers, together with the church officials, determined to establish what they term barracks. It was a building twenty-four by thirty feet, and was built west of the hotel, outside the edge of the town. The first effort was to cover the expense by private subscriptions, and use it as a shelter for indigent travellers who could not pay the hotel charges. They thought that it could also be used for soldiers passing through the town, for military supplies, and in case of need as a hospital. The private subscription plan failed, but the military authorities took up the matter, and the building was erected, and used as a commissary and for other purposes. The developments of the next days were such that Greene's soldiers and wagons had to leave, to escape the approaching British, and February 5, 1781, Greene's men withdrew, and removed the supplies. We hear nothing further of the barrack-building. A hospital was established in the two-story building, corner of Main and Bank streets, the same house which contained the first meeting hall.

By this time, January, 1782, the American forces under Greene were beginning to rally; Morgan and William Washington were sent to the border line of South Carolina to dispute the progress of Cornwallis and Tarleton. The battle of "Cowpens" followed, and the British were defeated. This stung the pride of Cornwallis, and he determined to make a bold dash and capture Morgan, and then crush Greene. He knew that the hopes of the Americans in this section depended on these two men. Then began the wild chase which became famous in the history of the Revolution, and which brought Cornwallis and his whole army into Wachovia. The chase covered a distance of two hundred miles, and the pursuit of the Americans, under Greene, by the British, under Cornwallis, was so

"IN THE VERY THEATRE OF THE WAR" 165

energetic that often the armies were within sight of one another, and the bugles of one army could be heard by the soldiers of the other; and frequently the British would arrive at one side of a river only to see the rear-guard of the Americans hastening up the bank on the other side of the stream. In the end Greene outgeneralled Cornwallis, as the history of the Revolution shows.

It was in the midst of this famous retreat and pursuit that, on the 9th of February, the British army of seven thousand men marched into Wachovia, under the personal command of Cornwallis. The soldiers encamped just outside Bethania, and took entire possession of the village and the surrounding country. Cornwallis had his headquarters in the house now occupied by Professor A. I. Butner, north of the church. Fires were kindled in the streets and yards, to feed which all fences and outhouses were demolished. The ladies of the town were required to spend the entire night in baking and cooking for the soldiers. The younger people were all gathered in the house of the pastor. The soldiers foraged all through the neighbouring country, and found several still-houses. Liquor was freely consumed. Caruthers is responsible for the statement that during the night there was so much drunkenness that five hundred American troops could have captured the entire army. The people were alarmed lest the numerous fires would start a conflagration in the village. During the night rain began to fall, and this danger was averted. The next morning, when the army marched away, a scene of desolation was presented: fences and many buildings gone; all their poultry taken; cattle killed and perhaps only half consumed, the remainder lying untouched. The little village lost thirty head of cattle and twenty-three horses. Cornwallis says in his despatches that while passing through Wachovia he had no trouble to find supplies for his army. Requisition for bread, meal, flour, and spirits was sent to Bethabara and Salem. The people in the latter place had a difficult time to protect themselves against the Tories, who had become very bold in the presence of the British army.

The next day, February 10, the army passed through Bethabara. It required six hours, from eight o'clock in the morning till two o'clock in the afternoon. Guards were stationed at many points in order to prevent depredations. Cornwallis dismounted at the hotel, and he was respectfully addressed by a delegation of citizens, to whom he replied in a friendly and pleasant manner.

Continuing the march, the army passed through Salem and encamped once more in Wachovia, this time near Friedland. Here the soldiers scattered all through the country, and committed much violence on their foraging expeditions. Heintzman was surrounded by a company of eight British soldiers, and demands were made for food. The poor man did not have it, so he could not comply with their demands. This enraged them, and with bayonets at his breast they were about to run him through, when a company of people approached, and he escaped. All supplies were seized, and when the British troops passed on, there was a feeling of great relief that Wachovia had escaped complete destruction.

One incident threatened serious consequences. The depredations of Tories, freebooters, and straggling bands of soldiers were so burdensome that it was decided to send a deputation to General Greene to solicit protection. At that time it was not known that the British were so near. Bewighausen and Holder went to Greene's camp. They returned only an hour or two before Cornwallis entered

Salem. Had they been a little later, and their visit discovered, it would no doubt have appeared to the British as if information had been sent to Greene, and would probably have cost the two men their lives, and possibly the destruction of the entire town. It was a narrow escape from a serious trouble.

Hardly had the British army of Lord Cornwallis disappeared when new and even greater troubles swept down upon them. Different bodies of troops followed in the wake of the English. Major Dickens, of Mecklenburg, came with a detachment; Pickens arrived with another company; freebooters came with no commanders. They were not friendly, and could not understand the Moravian position of neutrality in the matter of hostilities. No doubt they were anxious to find an excuse which would enable them to plunder without restraint. Accordingly, in every form of question and imputation they endeavoured to force from the people the acknowledgment that they were Tories. This they could not do, as they were stanch and loyal adherents of the new government, and dreaded the Tories. We find no notice anywhere in the diary that they were on friendly terms with the Tories, or were ever associated with them. They always dreaded these men, who lived in North Carolina but were not true to the home land.

With the arrival of the Wilkes militia matters grew worse. No doubt this was a company of rude mountaineers, and they wrought great injury to Wachovia. The soldiers from Mecklenburg and from Georgia, reënforced by the freebooters, still retained the semblance of responsibility to their commanders, but when the Wilkes militia arrived, the last barrier was broken down and riot ran amuck. Homes were entered and plundered. Property was seized and destroyed. Men were dragged into the streets, and, with loaded muskets placed against the breast, demands were made with which it was impossible to comply. This state of affairs seemed to be as bad as it possibly could be, but the next day, February 17, was the darkest and most dreadful day of the war. Just as in legislative matters August 18, 1778, was the darkest day, so in military matters February 17, 1781, was the time when the highest point of danger and terror was reached. On that day seven hundred men, rough, wild, and hostile, were in Salem. They were plundering and destroying, threatening and unrestrained. On this day, when mob rule was abroad and the citizens had lost all hope, they found the Scripture portion in the text-book was:—

"Thou hast been a strength to the poor, a strength to the needy in his distress, a refuge from the storm, a shadow from the heat, when the blast of the terrible one is as a storm against the wall."

The last marked event in the history of the movement of the soldiers took place in connection with the battle of Guilford Court-house. The scene of this battle is near the present city of Greensboro, and about a score of miles eastward from Salem. Some of the soldiers alluded to in a preceding paragraph were on their way to this struggle, which every one knew must come, but where it would occur could not then be calculated. When Cornwallis failed to catch Greene, he retired to Hillsboro. Terrible cruelties were going on all over the state by bands of Whigs and Tories, and so many lives were being sacrificed by these bands that Greene declared North Carolina would be depopulated if a stop were not put to these things. Hence he returned to North Carolina, determined to decide the matter. The armies met at Guilford Court-

"IN THE VERY THEATRE OF THE WAR" 169

house. The Americans retired before the British veterans, and although Cornwallis was left in possession of the field, he had lost more than five hundred men, and among the dead officers was the brave and daring Colonel Webster, personally so dear to Lord Cornwallis. Even American writers declare that Cornwallis and his troops fought like heroes on that day. But it was of no avail. The American troops began to recognize the first faint streaks of the dawn of victory in the campaign. Though they had retired from the field of battle, they returned and pursued the retreating British army, driving it before them, to Wilmington and out of the state.

After the battle, troops again began to pass through Wachovia. They were accustomed to violence and bloodshed. The Wilkes militia had expressed their determination to finish the destruction which they had begun when first in Wachovia. Hence, when news reached Salem that the Wilkes militia were returning, an appeal was made to Campbell with his sixty Virginia soldiers, and to Colonel Armstrong, their tried and true friend, and these two officers, with their companies, placed themselves in an attitude of defence, ready to give battle to the Wilkes militia, whose duty it should have been to defend instead of destroy. By these means the needed protection was given and the crisis was passed. No further overwhelming dangers came nigh them. Many soldiers passed; large burdens were laid upon the people; but they were in the end able to say with the good man of old: —

"He shall deliver thee in six troubles; yea, in seven there shall no evil touch thee."

We will in conclusion mention two points in connection with these turbulent times.

The first was the care given to the wounded brought to

Salem from the battle-field of Guilford Court-house. They were cared for in the hospital by Bonn, and tenderly nursed by the people of the place. When they had all recovered at the end of some months, these men spoke far and wide of the true kindness of the Moravians, and this, more than anything else, won the friendship of the general public.

The second point is the remarkable amount of provisions supplied from the time the wagons went to Camden battle-field, till the last stragglers left after the battle of Guilford Court-house. The amount of the requisitions is often given, and these, added to the supplies which are not enumerated, makes the matter a marvel to us as we read the account.

The preliminaries of peace were signed in Paris, January 20, 1783, and February 4 they were ratified. July 4, 1783, was appointed as a day of rejoicing for the return of peace. September 3, 1783, the treaty of peace between Great Britain and the United States was signed, and November 23, 1783, official notice of this final act in the great war drama was received in Wachovia.

The celebration of the Peace Jubilee, July 4, 1783, was like the bright awaking of the morning after a night of darkness and storm. The governor issued a proclamation, calling upon all good people to fittingly celebrate the event. All of the congregations complied with the proclamation. The people of Salem were awakened on that morning by appropriate trombone music. In the morning meeting the "Te Deum Laudamus" was chanted with trombone accompaniment. Benzien preached the sermon, taking as his text the scripture portion for the day when the preliminaries were signed, "The Lord of Hosts is with us, the God of Jacob is our refuge."

He spoke of the blessings of peace, and urged his hearers to seek the peace of heart which is to the individual as blessed as is the peace we are now celebrating to the entire land. At the end of the sermon the choir sang "Glory to God in the Highest."

At two o'clock all gathered for a happy love-feast, on which occasion a specially composed ode was sung. This paper is still in the possession of the Salem archives. The title to the composition is "A Psalm of Joy of the Congregation in Salem, for the Peace Jubilee, July 4, 1783." The first choir hymn begins with the line,

"Peace is with us! Peace is with us!"

At eight o'clock the congregation gathered in the church and engaged in singing several special hymns. They then proceeded to the front of the congregation house, and with two choirs, each discoursing vocal and instrumental music, the entire procession moved reverently and solemnly along the main streets of the town. The houses were illuminated, and after the line of march had been completed, all returned to the church and were dismissed with the blessing of the Lord. It was a deeply solemn occasion, the very stillness of the atmosphere being in harmony with the hush which came over the large congregation in this evening hour.

CHAPTER XV

PROVINCIAL AFFAIRS

1773-1783

MUCH of the history of this period has already been given, but, in addition to what the narrative has shown us, there were some experiences which were connected more directly with the church life, and these we will gather together in a brief closing chapter.

Marshall's visit to Europe separated him from his people for five years, at a time when his presence was specially needed. He left Salem to attend the General Synod in Germany, and because of the unsettled condition of travel was unable to return until 1779. In 1774, Tiersch, the first minister of Salem, died. The following year Utley, the English pastor, was called to his eternal home, after a life of unusual success, not only as a worker in Wachovia, but as an evangelist in this entire portion of the state. The large concourse of people gathered from far and near attested the deep love which all felt for this good man.

In 1774 an effort was made to again begin work in Georgia. Miller and Wagner went to Knoxboro, and in 1775 Broesing left Wachovia to join them, and to begin work on the estate of Silkhope. Miller died of fever, and when the Revolution broke out, the conditions placed upon the others were such that the second effort in Georgia was abandoned. The authorities gave the two Moravians the choice of four things. First, to enlist in the army, which was against their conscience; second, pay a tax of £7 per month, which was impossible, as they had no means wherewith to pay it; third, go to jail, which was decidedly disagreeable, since they had committed no breach of propriety; fourth, leave the country, which they did. Miller went back to Europe, and Broesing to North Carolina.

One of the severe trials of the period, and that which added untold sufferings to the war troubles, was the prevalence of smallpox. This dread disease was introduced by the soldiers, and spread rapidly all through Wachovia. Preceding the movements of the soldiers and following the season of unrest, the diary says the sufferings were indescribable.

It is noted in the diary that early in the period they had helped to pay the debt of the Unity by contributions.

In Salem the strangers' burying-ground was fenced, and improved in 1775, and in the same year in Bethabara a new tavern was built.

The pottery interest is specially mentioned in 1777, and when the ware was taken from the kilns great crowds gathered to purchase.

In 1778 mention is made of the beginning of the infant school.

Rather amusing as well as interesting is a little local experience which took place in 1778. A number of young men resided in the single brethren's house. They pursued various trades, received a regular salary, took their meals in the common dining hall, and paid a fixed price for board. In view of the increased cost of living they requested a larger salary, and expressed a willingness to pay more for their meals. The proper authorities increased the salaries and fixed the price for the meals. The scale did not please the young men. In an evening conference they were admonished to consider these matters in a correct and proper light. A young man spoke rather freely on the subject, and he was advised to seek a wider field in which to use his talents. When the young men returned to the Brethren's House the smouldering fires of discontent broke out, and the next morning they left their work, hoping that the day labourers would follow. The latter did not do so. Some of the young men went from Salem to Bethabara, others went into the woods, and thus they passed the day. In the evening all were satisfied with the length of the "one day strike," and returned, humbly asking pardon for their insubordination, and realizing that they had become the laughing stock of the town.

An important event in this period was the visit of Bishop J. F. Reichel in 1780. He was a man of keen insight into affairs, and he seemed to intuitively recognize the needs of the times. He laboured zealously to harmonize the conflicting political views; he explained clearly to the congregations their duties in view of the changed state of affairs; when he left, it was found that his visit had been signally blessed by the Lord.

One special work which Bishop Reichel performed in Wachovia was the inauguration of the "ministers' conference," which he established September 15, 1780. This consists of a gathering of the ministers of the Province, in Salem, the first Thursday morning of each month. In this meeting the affairs of each congregation are discussed in a friendly manner, though the conference has no executive powers. The welfare of the congregations is promoted, and plans for the new month are discussed. Much good is done in this respect, and still, probably one of the best features of the conference is the fraternal feeling which this contact of the ministers, one with the other, promotes. For one hundred and seventeen years this ministers' conference has been held in the Southern Province.

CHAPTER XVI

THE CLOSE OF THE CENTURY

1784–1799

WITH the close of the Revolution the history of Wachovia passes into an entirely new and different development. For generations they enjoyed the blessings of peace; they were free from the dangers of warfare, and even the enmities of their neighbours ceased. In 1783 Bagge became a member of the legislature, the first citizen of Wachovia to take a seat in that body. There was no further trouble with the lawgivers of that state. In 1792 both the state legislature and the Congress of the United States granted them full liberty to abstain from taking an oath, and to have perfect freedom from bearing arms. In this connection we will add that with the passing years the community voluntarily renounced both these rights, and in the Civil War of 1861–1865 no braver men went to the field than those from Forsyth County.

The results of the Revolution were very hard for the people in the western portion of the state. As we have already stated, many settlers were shiftless and improvident. This class of people were compelled to begin anew, and with nothing to aid them. The diary states that famine was abroad in the land, many subsisting on roots and berries till the wheat harvest. Scarcity and suffering continued several years. As was the case in every pre-

THE CLOSE OF THE CENTURY 177

ceding trouble, the Moravians shared their scanty store of provisions with those who were in an even worse condition.

Frequent mention is made of the sympathy which they felt for their fellow-members in various parts of the world. It was in this period that the country of France passed through the horrors of its bloody revolution. And with the rise of the Napoleonic power, and with the whole of Europe filled with the war which followed, a number of our congregations were brought into the greatest peril, especially those of Neuwied, on the Rhine, and of Zeist, in Holland. It will be remembered that from the latter congregation much aid had been given in the founding of Wachovia.

In 1793 the news of a terrible hurricane in the West Indies reached them, and called forth additional sympathy. At this time and all through the succeeding years we find the people of Wachovia sending aid to afflicted brethren, not only to their neighbours in the West Indies, but even to those living in distant Russian Sarepta.

In the year 1783 a party began the journey to America, and were twenty weeks on the stormy ocean. The successive storms prevented the ship from entering the port of New York, hence they sailed southward, and were finally shipwrecked on the West Indies. Here they were treated kindly, and later they set sail for Philadelphia, in a passing vessel. Among the members of the party were Bishop Koehler, the pastor for Salem, and Bishop John de Watteville and his wife Benigna. Bishop de Watteville was on an official visitation to the churches of America. On the occasion of this visit, which extended from 1785 to 1786, the governing board, which had existed since 1772, was formally recognized as the Provincial Elders'

Conference of the Southern Province, and consisted of Marshall, Koehler, Praezel, and Benzien.

Benzien went to the General Synod in 1778.

Spangenberg died in 1792, after a service of sixty years.

Hans Christian de Schweinitz, and his son, Frederick Christian, came on a visit in 1796. The former had been in North Carolina twenty-five years before, and the latter remained in Wachovia.

At this time the prospects for beginning a work in South Carolina appeared to be very bright. Henry Laurens, formerly President of Congress, and one of the commissioners for the United States at the peace of Paris, had long been well acquainted with the Moravians at Bethlehem.

"He invited the Moravian Church to begin work in South Carolina, and offered a gift of two thousand acres of land in the district Ninety-Six. This district embraced a section of western South Carolina, and it derived its name from the military fort built in the Indian wars, about ninety-six miles from Orangeburg. On its site now (1855) stands Cambridge, in Abbeville district.

"The church in Wachovia was very anxious to begin work among the coloured people, hence they looked favourably upon the offer. Marshall and Benzien undertook a journey to this wild and unsettled region in November and December, 1790.

"They visited Mr. Laurens at his rice plantation on the Cooper Run, nine miles from Monk's Corner. They then proceeded to his partner, John Lewis Gervais, in Charleston, by whose assistance they were conveyed to the agent in the Abbeville district, Major Bowie. After a difficult journey over almost impassable roads they reached, on December 10, the wilds of Long Cane Creek and Reedy Branch, where Major Bowie assisted them to select, from

THE CLOSE OF THE CENTURY 179

the five thousand acres belonging to Mr. Laurens, a tract of two thousand acres which seemed well adapted for a settlement, distant about twenty-five miles from the Savannah River. As the season was already far advanced, the survey could not at the time be made. They thereupon returned home; Major Bowie promised them, as soon as practicable, to have the survey made. Before this was accomplished Mr. Laurens died. By his last will and testament all his property was bequeathed to a grandchild, without any provision being therein made for the proposed grant, hence the whole plan had to be abandoned" (Reichel).

In the final negotiations in connection with the South Carolina effort, another gentleman offered a tract on the Santee River, but this project also in the end failed.

The work among the Indians was not begun until in the new century. The first prospecting tour was by Schneider, in 1784. He met with encouragement, having visited the Cherokees on the Tennessee River. The chief, Tayhill, promised to communicate the proposition to the council, but the times were so unsettled that nothing could be done. Again, in 1799, Abraham Steiner and Frederick Christian de Schweinitz visited the same tribe. The journey was begun October 28, and they travelled three hundred miles, visiting Knoxville and Tellico Blockhouse. Friends interested themselves in the visit, and though many Indians were away hunting, the journey was attended with encouraging experiences. They returned December 28.

The health record speaks of the prevalence of smallpox in 1786, when the citizens of the towns were inoculated. The good physician Bonn died in 1781, after his faithful attendance upon the wounded soldiers. It was not until 1784 that Dr. Lewis arrived. Measles were abroad in the towns in 1784, but the most serious visitation was what the diary calls "hitzige Hals Krankheit." Reichel translates this "scarlet fever"; this is no doubt an error. It was a malignant form of diphtheria which attacked adults as well as children, and which is described by writers of that day as having occurred in this state and also in Virginia. The disease was given various local names, such as black sore throat, etc., and mortification began before life was extinct. Tradition has come down to our day, as well as the record which we have just given, describing the terrible disease, as well as the great mortality in their village. The disease was so dreaded by others that no visitors approached the place during its prevalence.

In the great flood of 1796 William Hall was drowned. An account of this sad occurrence is given in the *Wachovia Moravian*.

An accident happened to Matthew Stach, in 1782, and he suffered from the effects of the fall until his death in 1787. Stach is well known in history as the first missionary to Greenland. He laboured in that land many years before any results appeared, and presents to the world one of the heroic characters of history, defying discouragements, trusting in the Lord, and in the end seeing the fruits of his faith and works. January 19, 1783, he visited Salem on the occasion of the semicentennial jubilee, and gave an animated account of his experiences in the missionary service. In the Bethabara graveyard a granite shaft marks the resting-place of this great and good man.

The building operations of this period were on an extensive scale, and some of our well-known structures date back to the closing years of the century. The hotel was burned in 1784, and rebuilt the same year. The single sisters' house was begun in 1785, and finished in 1786.

BETHABARA CHURCH, 1788

THE CLOSE OF THE CENTURY 181

Bishop de Watteville preached the first sermon in the chapel, and the next year a special thanksgiving service was held. (See article, *Wachovia Moravian*, December, 1900.) The schoolhouse for the boys (now the Wachovia Historical Society building) was erected in 1794.

The new church in Bethabara was begun and finished in 1788. This building still stands, and is in a good state of preservation, as the picture given in this volume shows. April 8, 1788 the Provincial Elders' Conference with many other members went to Bethabara to witness the laying of the corner-stone. By 9 o'clock a large congregation had assembled. Koehler preached the sermon. The inscription and lists were read. With the trombone choir leading, the congregation went to the church site and formed a circle. The corner-stone was laid with the usual ceremony, in the northeast corner, and then walled up. Koehler stepped on the stone and offered an earnest prayer. After the singing of a hymn the masons began their work, and the congregation dispersed. November 28, the same year, a large number of people again gathered in Bethabara, this time to take part in the dedication of the church. The following Sunday, November 30, the first public services were held, six hundred persons being present. Koehler preached in German and Fritz in English. The Spirit of God was manifested in a special manner on this occasion.

The erection of the large Salem church was decided upon in April, 1797. The corner-stone was laid June 12, 1798, and by the close of the year 1799 the church was under roof. Bachman came from Lititz to build the organ.

In 1785 two fire-engines were brought from Europe.

An addition to the Brethren's House was built in 1786,

and during the construction one of the workmen, Kremser by name, lost his life.

In 1792 the sycamore trees, forming the avenue from the hotel to the bridge, were planted.

The graveyard was enlarged in 1795.

An embankment, forming the approach to the bridge over the Salem Creek, was built in 1798.

The number of people in Wachovia at the close of the Revolution exceeded one thousand.

The society for propagating the Gospel was founded in 1788.

In 1790 English preaching was arranged for one Sunday in each month.

A post-office was established in 1792, with Gottlob Shober as postmaster.

In 1792 mention is made that the question is frequently asked why a girls' school, like the one at Bethlehem, was not established. Applications have been made to place pupils with us. There were difficulties in the way, especially in securing teachers, and for various reasons the matter was deferred.

This year, 1792, the early morning Easter service was conducted in the graveyard, the disorder and confusion accompanying these occasions during the previous years having led to their being discontinued.

One of the pleasing events of this period, the account of which will close our history of the century, was the visit of President Washington to Wachovia, May 31 to June 2, 1791. The President, with his secretary, Mr. Jackson, came from Salisbury, and with him a number of servants. Marshall, Benzien, and Koehler went to meet him. As he approached he was welcomed with music. He descended from his coach, in front of the hotel, and greeted the assembled company in a friendly manner, being especially happy to see the bright faces of the children. He conversed with some of the citizens, who acted as a committee, and was then escorted to his room, on the second floor, northeast corner of the building.

He intended to continue his journey next day, but when informed that Governor Martin would meet him here, he decided to remain another day. During the evening meal, music was furnished for his entertainment.

The next day Washington, Jackson, and a number of the citizens visited the places of business and the manufacturing establishments. The President expressed himself as pleased with all these things, especially with the system of water supply for the town.

At two o'clock a formal address of welcome was presented to President Washington. At that hour Marshall, accompanied by several others, read the address, which is as follows: —

"TO THE PRESIDENT OF THE UNITED STATES: —

"Happy in sharing the honour of a visit from the illustrious President of the Union to the Southern States, the Brethren of Wachovia humbly beg leave, upon this joyful occasion, to express their highest esteem, duty, and affection for the great patriot of this country.

"Deeply impressed as we are with gratitude to the great Author of our being for his unbounded mercies, we cannot but particularly acknowledge his gracious providence over the temporal and political prosperity of the country, in the peace whereof we do find peace, and wherein none can take a warmer interest than ourselves, in particular when we consider that the same Lord who preserved your precious person in so many imminent dangers has made you in a conspicuous manner an instrument in his hands to forward that happy constitution, together with these improvements whereby our United States begin to flourish, over which you preside with the applause of a thankful nation.

"Whenever, therefore, we solicit the protection of the Father of Mercies over this favoured country, we cannot but fervently implore his kindness for your preservation, which is so intimately connected therewith.

"May this gracious Lord vouchsafe to prolong your valuable life as a further blessing, and an ornament of the constitution, that by your worthy example the regard for religion be increased, and the improvements of civil society encouraged.

"The settlements of the United Brethren, though small, will always make it their study to contribute as much as in them lies to the peace and improvement of the United States, and all the particular parts they live in, joining their ardent prayers to the best wishes of this whole continent that your personal as well as domestic happiness may abound, and a series of successes may crown your labours for the prosperity of our times and an example to future ages, until the glorious reward of a faithful servant shall be your portion.

"Signed, in behalf of the United Brethren in Wachovia,
"FREDERICK WILLIAM MARSHALL,
"JOHN DANIEL KOEHLER,
"CHRISTIAN LEWIS BENZIEN.

"SALEM, the 1st of June, 1791."

The President was pleased to return the following answer : —

THE CLOSE OF THE CENTURY

"To the United Brethren of Wachovia:—

"*Gentlemen:* I am greatly indebted to your respectful and affectionate expression of personal regard, and I am not less obliged by the patriotic sentiment contained in your address.

"From a society whose governing principles are industry and the love of order, much may be expected toward the improvement and prosperity of the country in which their settlements are formed, and experience authorizes the belief that much will be obtained.

"Thanking you with grateful sincerity for your prayers in my behalf, I desire to assure you of my best wishes for your social and individual happiness.

"G. Washington."

Six of our citizens were invited to dine with President Washington, and the meal was enlivened with enjoyable music.

Many people came from all the surrounding country to greet the President.

Late in the afternoon Governor Martin arrived from his home, forty miles distant. Washington, Martin, and Jackson attended the evening service, which was liturgical, the choir and congregation engaging in the singing. Late in the evening our distinguished visitors were serenaded by a number of our musicians.

A history of the church and also a copy of "Idea Fidei Fratrum" were presented to the Secretary, and he was pleased with the gift.

At four o'clock the next morning the presidential party left, Marshall and Benzien accompanying them to the borders of Wachovia.

CHAPTER XVII

SALEM CHURCH BUILT

1800

MARSHALL had been the guiding spirit during the closing years of the old century, and he lived long enough to see the fruit of his own labours and that of his coadjutors. There is seldom found a conjunction of circumstances presenting a more attractive picture than the history of these years. The close of the old century and the beginning of the new; the culmination of the labours of half a century in Wachovia; the results of the previous years of preparation, viz. the erection of the large Salem church, the founding of Salem Female Academy, and the beginning of the mission work among the Cherokee Indians; the presence of at least a few of the veterans of fourscore years (Marshall in Salem, and Grube and Ettwein in Bethlehem), who were closely identified with the bright and dark days of the previous fifty years, and who were permitted to see the happy opening of the new century; the peaceful, triumphant end of these fathers in Israel, after they had witnessed the final success of their labours,— these things make the first years of the nineteenth century a bright and happy period in the history of Wachovia.

The erection of the Salem church was an undertaking of great magnitude one hundred years ago, and would be no small task in our day. The picture of this building is

SALEM CHURCH BUILT

given elsewhere. April, 1797, the decision to erect this church was made. The corner-stone was laid June 12, 1798, and by the close of 1799 the building was under roof. The dedication services were held November, 1800.

The erection of this church marks an epoch in the history of Salem and of Wachovia. What impresses us is the character and size of the structure. The walls are three feet in thickness, and the timbers in the framework for the roof are remarkably heavy. The plan of the auditorium is pleasing and symmetrical. The organ finished in 1800 is still in use, and has furnished music for generations of worshippers. The organ covers a floor space of ten by ten feet, and is fifteen feet high. It has two manuals, eighteen stops, and eight hundred pipes. The clock was built even before the church, and has marked the passing hours during all these years. The material and workmanship were such that the walls, the timbers, the organ, the clock, the architecture, the iron work, all have served the congregation well, and few buildings of half its age are as perfectly preserved.

The Salem church was one of the most pretentious structures in this section of the state at that day. Its capacity is about one thousand. November 9, 1800, was the day appointed for the consecration. The event had been announced all through Wachovia and the surrounding country. The company which assembled numbered fully two thousand. A full account of the services of the day is given in the diary, and we will use the substance of this account to show to our readers a bright and happy scene, one which will form a companion picture to the centennial celebration in 1900.

Shortly before nine o'clock, the members and friends

assembled on the open grounds, the men alongside of the boys' schoolhouse, the women before the old chapel. Between these two companies were the musicians. As the clock struck nine the members of the Provincial Elders' Conference, with some visiting ministers, came from the congregation house. The musicians led the procession into the new church, playing the choral, —

"God bless our going out, and bless our coming in."

When the first company of musicians were inside the auditorium, they ceased playing, and a second band, stationed in the gallery, took up the strain.

As the procession passed into the church, the full choir sang, —
"This is the day the Lord hath made."

Then the following prayer was offered, from the church litany, the pastor leading, the congregation responding : —

"Lord God, our Father in Heaven !
Hallowed be Thy name.
Lord God, Son, thou Saviour of the world !
Be gracious unto us.
Lord God, Holy Ghost !
Abide with us forever."

After the New Testament blessing was sung,

"The Grace of our Lord Jesus Christ,
And the Love of God,
And the Communion of the Holy Ghost,
Be with us all, Amen,"

the double choir sang the hymn beginning, —

"The Saviour's blood and righteousness."

Benzien made an opening address in which he congratulated the congregation upon the completion of the great work, which, by the blessing of the Lord, had been accomplished without accident, and which has in large part been paid by the earnest efforts of the congregation. He alluded to the fact that the consecration of the church is in the same month in which the first settlers arrived in Wachovia, forty-seven years ago, as well as the consecration of the first meeting hall twenty-nine years ago. He said it was our custom to present such an house to the Lord, and for this purpose the large congregation had assembled. The dedicatory prayer was then offered by Benzien, after which the pastor of the Hope congregation, Samuel Kramsch, preached the English sermon. The music at this service, as in all the meetings of the day, was inspiring, and in the afternoon love-feast a specially prepared English ode was sung. One thousand buns had been prepared for the love-feast, yet on account of the number of the people it was necessary to cut these buns into two pieces in order that all might be served.

The feeling of reverence was very great; not the slightest disorder marred the occasion. Some declared that the presence of God had been revealed in such a remarkable manner that children's children would recall the day with pleasure, a prediction which was fulfilled November 9, 1900, when a reverent congregation gathered in the same church, heard the story of the blessings of that day, and rejoiced.

A festival service was celebrated in the evening, and this closed the first happy dedication day.

The second in the series of consecration services was November 13, when all the members of the Wachovia churches were invited to join in a union Communion. The weather was fine, and all the members of the Province were present except the sick. The festal service was held at nine o'clock, and the pastor, Benzien, addressed the congregation on the subject of the special event which makes November 13 a festival day in our church throughout the world. This was followed by smaller meetings for the men, for the women, and for the children of the church, the members of each class consecrating themselves anew to the service of the Lord.

All gathered together in the love-feast, and this was followed by the Holy Communion, in the celebration of which there was a persuasive sense of the gracious presence of the Lord, and the members were drawn closely one to the other in the union which comes from the merits of Jesus' sufferings and death.

The writer of the diary of one hundred years ago gives the account of the impressions of the day and of the evening service, and is inspired to close the account with the words:—

"Glory be to Him in the church which waiteth for Him, and in that which is around Him, from eternity to eternity, Amen.

"Amen, hallelujah, hallelujah! Amen. Hallelujah!"

On November 17 the last of the dedication services were held, this being an enthusiastic missionary meeting. The mission spirit was always strong in Wachovia, but the way had not been open for independent action. Several efforts had been made to begin preaching among the coloured people of Georgia and South Carolina, and preliminary steps had been taken to inaugurate work among the Indians. But not till the year 1800 were these efforts crowned with success. In the third of the three enthusiastic consecration services was begun the independent mission work by the church in Wachovia.

CHAPTER XVIII

SALEM FEMALE ACADEMY

1802

THE present year (1902) completes the century of the history of this school. There are many interesting features connected with the uninterrupted work of a hundred years. The school has never been closed since its founding in 1802. It is the third school in the United States, in point of age, for the higher education of young women. Its patronage is drawn from every portion of the land, and the register shows an attendance of ten thousand pupils, or an average of one hundred new names each year all through the century. It is non-sectarian in its principles, but deeply religious in its methods of work. State universities are identified with their particular states. Denominational schools are associated especially with the churches to which they belong. Salem Female Academy is looked upon as the school of the South which has done a work of great usefulness for the promotion of true womanhood. It stood alone for half a century, and now, at the end of a hundred years, in the period of general educational interest, it continues to do its work with zeal and energy.

To appreciate the influences which have given this long and uninterrupted history to Salem Female Academy, it is necessary to understand the relation of the Moravian Church to education. More than four hundred years ago, in the old home lands of Moravia and Bohemia, the seed was sown which has borne fruit all through the succeeding generations. The ancient Moravian Church had its well-known schools of higher learning, which numbered among their leaders men like the great pioneer of modern education, the Moravian Bishop John Amos Comenius. It also had schools in every parish in Moravia, Bohemia, and Poland, which in excellence and numbers resembled the modern common school system.

When the church was renewed nearly two centuries ago, after it had passed through the fires of persecution, it felt called upon to undertake any special work which the Lord would assign to it. The members believed that there was some particular task for it to perform. The wonderful preservation of the "hidden seed" and the not less wonderful renewal, in another land, indicated this. In time the special work was pointed out, and consisted, on the one hand, in beginning the great modern movement of foreign missions. On the other hand, the special work was education. These two fields of usefulness may not at first appear to be connected, but they are closely related. On the foreign mission fields the schoolhouse is often erected before the church. An unusual conjunction of circumstances inaugurated our boarding-school system. The care of the children of the missionaries became a serious question. It was decided to organize schools in the home lands, where everything would be planned as nearly as possible after the model of the home, so that, while the parents were in Greenland or Labrador, Ceylon or South Africa, the children would be under the care of consecrated men and women. In other words the Moravian schools, as planned a century and a half ago, in the renewed church, were in reality *home* schools in an especial and particular sense.

SALEM FEMALE ACADEMY

This plan of work soon attracted the attention of others. Parents felt that what was good in the case of missionaries would be equally good for their children. Therefore applications for admission into the Moravian schools were made by many outside friends, and the church found that a second great work was the training of young people in the higher and nobler form of education. Schools increased in Germany, in Switzerland, in Holland, in England, and as early as 1749 the first Moravian boarding school was founded in Bethlehem, Pennsylvania.

Before the close of the century the question was frequently asked by visitors why the church authorities of Wachovia did not establish schools similar to those of Pennsylvania and European countries. One and another applied for a place in the school if it were begun. One circumstance and another deferred the actual organization.

October 31, 1802, the Rev. Samuel Kramsch was called to be the first principal, and soon after assumed his duties, the school being held in the congregation house. The following year active measures were inaugurated to erect a school building. In February, 1803, a conference was held, which resulted in the decision that the new building should be placed between the congregation house and the sisters' house. The building was to be two stories and to have accommodations for sixty pupils. It was further decided that, if boarding pupils arrived before the building was finished, a dozen could be accommodated in the congregation house. The decision was also made that with the utmost zeal the work of construction be pushed forward.

The corner-stone of this first school building was laid October 6, 1803. A complete account of the ceremonies is given in a paper in the Wachovia Historical Society, including an abstract of the addresses and prayers. At 9 o'clock in the morning the congregation gathered in the church, and an appropriate sermon was preached, followed by prayer. Bishop Reichel then read the lists which were to be deposited in the corner-stone, and among them one contained the names of the forty-two girls in the congregation, twenty-three of whom were pupils of Salem Female Academy. The inscription which was deposited with these papers is interesting, and is as follows: —

"In the name of God, the Father, and the Son, and the Holy Ghost, in the year after the birth of our Lord and Saviour Jesus Christ one thousand eight hundred and three, on the sixth day of October, in the twenty-seventh year of the Independence of the United States of America, when Thomas Jefferson was President of them, in the fiftieth year after the settling of the first members of the church of the United Brethren in North Carolina, and the beginning of building Bethabara, in the thirty-eighth year since the beginning of building Salem, the foundation stone of this house for a boarding school of girls was laid in a solemn manner, in the presence of the whole congregation, with fervent prayer to our Lord, that by this school, to be established in this house, his name may be glorified, his kingdom of grace be enlarged in this country, and the salvation of souls of those who shall be educated therein be promoted."

The daily word was: "Believe on the Lord Jesus Christ, and thou shalt be saved, and thy house." (Acts 16:31.)

> "A dying risen Jesus,
> Seen by the eye of faith,
> At once from danger frees us,
> And saves the soul from death."

The doctrinal text was "He had done no violence, neither was any deceit in his mouth." (Isaiah 53:9.)

> "May our minds and whole behaviour
> Bear resemblance to our Saviour,
> And his sanctifying merit
> Hallow body, soul, and spirit."

The box was then closed and returned to the presiding minister. Kramsch carried it as the procession moved to the site of the new building. The very order of the procession and the disposition of the different portions of the congregation are given in the paper referred to. With the solemn words, "In the name of the Father, the Son, and Holy Ghost, we lay the corner-stone of this girls' school," the box was placed in position. The stone was then struck three times by each of the ministers, and Bishop Reichel, stepping upon the stone, offered the prayer. It was then walled in, hence it is not visible, which custom differs from that of the present day.

The first boarding pupils arrived May 16, 1804. Four were in the first company, and four came later, and to these eight were added two pupils from town. The following is the list of these ten boarding pupils:—

Elizabeth Strudwick, Hillsboro, N.C.
Ann Kirkland, Hillsboro, N.C.
Elizabeth Kirkland, Hillsboro, N.C.
Mary Philips, Tarboro, N.C.
Anna Norfleet, Scotland Neck, N.C.
Felicia Norfleet, Gates County, N.C.
Anna Staiert, Fayetteville, N.C.
Rebecca Carter, Caswell County, N.C.
Anna Pauline Shober, Salem, N.C.
Mary Steiner, Salem, N.C.

The teachers were Sophia Dorothea Reichel, Maria Salome Meinung, and Johanna Elizabeth Praezel. The day scholars, a score or more in number, added to these, formed three classes.

Another paper in the archives gives an account of the dedication of the new house, July 16, 1805. The day was made a festal occasion in which the entire congregation joined.

At 7 o'clock in the morning the trombone music greeted the village, and in this way announced the special nature of the day.

At one o'clock those connected with the school gathered in the chapel of the congregation house. In the company were the trustees and visiting ministers, the teachers and pupils, both day scholars and boarders. Half an hour later they formed a procession, and accompanied by music, rendered by a special choir, left the house which had thus far been their school home, and entered the new school building. In the large upper room parents and friends had already gathered, and when the procession entered there was a special programme of song, including such hymns as " Peace be to this habitation."

Bishop Reichel offered an earnest prayer, consecrating the building to the use and service of the Lord. At the conclusion of the prayer, they sang the New Testament benediction.

A love-feast followed, during the serving of which a special ode was sung. The voices of the young people were particularly sweet and beautiful during this service.

In the evening the entire congregation, as well as the school and visitors, gathered in the church, and an address was made by Benzien, with special reference to the occasion.

The close of this meeting was an open-air service. The procession passed from the church to the square, in front of the new school. The buildings were illuminated, and the friends and pupils were arranged in two semicircles.

First Building of Salem Female Academy, 1805

With song and prayer, in a most pleasing yet solemn manner, the exercises of the day were concluded.

The building which was dedicated on this day, in the manner described, and which is shown in the accompanying picture, was in use for more than half a century, until in 1873 two stories were added, and it assumed the shape which it now has, under the name of South Hall.

In the teachers' conference, held the next morning, at which the members of the Provincial Elders' Conference were present, Bishop Reichel, as president of the board, exhorted the teachers to remember the great object of our school work — to train the heart as well as the mind, and to inculcate a true and pure religion.

CHAPTER XIX

HALF A CENTURY

1800–1850

WE will now advance fifty years in our narrative. The time from 1800 to 1850 witnessed no marked changes, either in Wachovia, or in any other portion of the church. There were many good and faithful men, and their work was done with earnestness and success. The missions in heathen lands continued to spread, and in the home lands liberal gifts were made both by members and friends. But the policy of the church in these years in Wachovia, and we may say all through the Unity, was conservative, even exclusive. At the end of the half century the mission work had greatly increased, in numbers and in importance. We thus advance fifty years and place ourselves at the middle of the century. As one topic after the other comes up for consideration, we will look backward over the field in order to gather up the historical threads, and avoid any break in the continuity of the story. But before so doing let us glance briefly at some of the events which took place, in order to at least outline the history of these years.

In Salem the business interests were strengthened and enlarged, and the foundation was laid for some enterprises which have continued to the present day.

In the neighbouring congregations Salem's example was followed, and new and improved churches were erected. Bethania built its large church in 1807. Friedberg built a new church in 1827, Friedland in 1847. Philadelphia and Macedonia date their organization as congregations to the close of the period.

The Sunday-school work, under the influence of the American Sunday-school Union, assumed large proportions from 1825 to 1840. The Salem members and ministers were active, and there were county gatherings of six hundred and more young people, in addition to the many friends who were present. These gatherings were at times held in the Salem square, on the anniversary days.

Then there were festivals, and celebrations of special events. The jubilee of the founding of Salem was celebrated in 1816, with an elaborate programme and with appropriate ceremonies. The consecration of the church buildings were interesting and impressive days, and there were many other events which called the members of the entire Province together.

The Academy had its changing experiences, as will be shown in the lists and in the autobiography of the Principals. Sometimes the attendance fell below fifty, and at other times it approached two hundred. There were times of sickness and epidemics, but the good work went on, and the blessing of the Lord rested upon the labourers who had the school in charge.

The details connected with these and other events will be gathered as we proceed, hence we will now consider ourselves as standing in the middle of the nineteenth century, ready to go forward into new fields of study, or to look backward for events which have a bearing upon the later history of Wachovia.

CHAPTER XX

MISSION WORK AMONG THE CHEROKEE INDIANS

WE have already seen the attitude of the Indians of this tribe. At times it was hostile, again it was friendly. Many were hospitably entertained in Bethabara, and yet they surrounded the town intent on its destruction. Later we find that the chiefs as well as the warriors invite the Moravians to send missionaries to their tribe. It was not unusual to have visits in Wachovia by Cherokee chiefs on their way to Washington, the national capital.

Journeys had been made to the Indians in several sections at earlier dates, but the work of evangelization was not begun until 1801. In that year the missionaries Steiner and Byhan settled at a place called "the springs," hence the name Springplace was given to the station. One of the veterans of this work was John Gambold, who spent almost all the time from 1805 to 1827 as a missionary among them. He died at Oo-yu-ge-lo-gee. Many other faithful workers went from Salem, and their descendants now reside in Wachovia. Reichel gives the list from 1801 to 1855, which is as follows:—

Abraham Steiner, 1801.
Gottlob Byhan, 1801–1812; 1827–1832.
Jacob Wohlfart, 1802–1805.
John Gambold, 1805–1827.
John R. Schmidt, 1820–1828; 1838–1839.
George Proske, 1822–1826.
Francis Eder, 1828–1829.

H. G. Clauder, 1828–1837.
Miles Vogler, 1837–1844; 1852–1854.
Gilbert Bishop, 1841.
D. Z. Smith, 1841–1849.
Edward Mock, 1847.
Alanson Welfare, 1847–1855.
Samuel Warner.

AMONG THE CHEROKEE INDIANS

Since 1855 they have been served by a number of brethren, among whom we mention Ward, Wesley Spaugh, Theodore Rights, Benjamin Lineback, and Herman Beck.

The story of this work is worthy of being written as a separate history. The letters and the papers in the archives furnish ample material, and the hardships and difficulties equal those in many of the mission fields, the histories of which are eagerly read and studied.

The location of the mission was in the section of country where North Carolina, Tennessee, and Georgia join. The Cherokees were the first tribe to take steps toward civilization, yet they were utterly averse to the message of the Gospel. They respected the good people who came to them, but it was five years before the first Indian embraced Christianity. This convert was Margaret Van, the widow of James Van, one of their earliest and best friends. Three years later Charles Hicks, an influential man in his tribe, was baptized, and in time a congregation of faithful converts was gathered together, though the work was discouraging and surrounded with hardships.

The government gave small grants of money, from time to time, for school purposes, and at a critical juncture, when the whites were engaged in hostilities against the Indians and their teachers, the only thing that saved the mission property was the fact that it was a government post-office.

At the same time that the work was being carried on among the Cherokees, Peterson and Burkhardt began a similar mission among the Creeks. This was surrounded with even more difficulties. From the accounts given in the diary, it was apparently not safe to openly proclaim themselves missionaries. Hence they came into the country, living as ordinary settlers, and made friends with the Indians who came to visit them as they were at work in their shop or in their garden. Occasionally they held religious services, and Indians were present. After a time the missionaries were stricken with fever, and for weeks and months were prostrated. They had a warm friend in Colonel Hawkins, the Indian agent, who supplied them with a home, and at times also supplied them with necessary provisions, as their sickness made it impossible to secure support. So great was their suffering that the Salem physician, Shuman, made the journey to their station, and spent some time with them, attending to their wants. Notwithstanding all this effort and suffering the breaking out of a struggle between the Indians and the whites compelled them to leave that section, and abandon the mission.

The same causes which occasioned the failure of the mission among the Creeks completely revolutionized the work among the Cherokees. In 1838 Springplace and Oo-yu-ge-lo-gee were abandoned, and the Indians moved from Georgia. They tarried a time in Tennessee, and then continued westward to the Mississippi River, and thence onward to what is now the Indian Territory. Here the Cherokees were gathered, and the new stations received the names New Springplace and Caanan.

During the war of 1861–1865 there was great suffering in the mission. It was during this time that Missionary Ward was murdered. The Indians were divided among themselves, and the sorrows were very great.

Bishop Herman visited this mission in 1854, and after this long and fatiguing trip was taken ill with a malignant fever and died. This was on the return journey, at McCullah's farm, Green County, Missouri, eleven hundred miles from home. On this visitation he was accompanied

AMONG THE CHEROKEE INDIANS 203

by Augustus Fogle, and the latter brought the sad news to the relatives in Salem. Fogle later returned to Missouri, and brought the remains of Bishop Herman to Salem, making the long journey in a private conveyance. The labour of love involved difficulties which none save the brother himself ever fully realized, and to his end he never ceased to speak of this journey.

Another sad incident was the death of the visitor, C. L. Rights, who represented the Provincial Elders' Conference. This was a generation later. After spending some weeks pleasantly with his son, who was in charge of the mission, illness seized the brother, and he died after a brief period of suffering. His body was brought to Kernersville, to the congregation which he had so faithfully served for many years, and there laid to rest.

The mission had a checkered and uncertain existence during the latter years of its history. The authorities of Wachovia continued faithfully to care for this mission, amid discouragements, until the year 1890, when the supervision was transferred to the Northern Province.

CHAPTER XXI

HOME MISSION WORK

THE interest in home missions was always strong in Wachovia, as is shown by the work of Utley and Soelle in the last century. Their efforts were always of the most disinterested nature, but they were hampered by European ideas, to the detriment of the work here in America. When the converted people naturally expressed a desire to join the Moravian Church, they were referred to other churches, and were considered as "diaspora," that is, as a society ministered to by Moravian pastors, but not actual members. This state of affairs was not pleasing to the people, and they sought a church home in other denominations. Hence, during the first century of the church's history no congregations were organized outside of Wachovia. This policy has been changed, and within the half century following, a number of new congregations have been founded, and especially during the last twenty-five years has the church extended her borders.

In the year 1847 Mr. Alberti, a friend living in Florida, came to Wachovia. He had, previous to this time, sent a number of requests to the Moravians to begin a mission on his great estate at Woodstock, in Florida. On the occasion of his visit in February a call was made to the congregation, for some one to enter the work. Jacob Siewers responded. He, together with his wife and their three sons, journeyed to Florida. Their three daughters remained in Salem. A church and parsonage had already been built, the proprietor of the estate assured them a support, and the work was begun. Siewers had been ordained a deacon. The first converts were baptized in 1848. The difficulties which surrounded this particular work among the coloured people were different from those connected with other undertakings, but were inseparable from the conditions of slavery on a great estate. Siewers was allowed entire freedom to do religious work among the slaves, but his influence was limited in all other respects. The overseers were often harsh and cruel, and the minister was powerless to interfere. These and other circumstances caused Siewers to withdraw, after a three years' service.

Friebele spent two years more in the work, but it was finally decided to abandon the mission.

About the same time a special desire to bring the message of salvation to the mountaineers of Virginia and North Carolina filled the heart of Van N. Zevely. He had assisted in the erection of the large Salem church, and this connection with the material interests led him to study the spiritual work. He heard of the destitute and forsaken regions of the Blue Ridge, where, in the hovels and cabins, intemperance and profanity, Sabbath-breaking and ignorance, gambling and vice, reigned supreme. In 1839 Zevely made a visit to this section, and was welcomed by some, but persecuted by others. No interest had hitherto been taken in their spiritual life, hence it was but natural that he should be ridiculed and hooted at by the very persons whose welfare he was seeking. In time he won their affections, their hearts were softened, and he saw the fruits of his labours.

In Salem, November 11, 1835, an organization was effected which bore the name, "The United Brethren's

Home Mission Society of North Carolina." This society increased during the succeeding years, until it reached the number of two hundred or more members, and they commissioned Zevely to be their representative, with special reference to the prosecution of the work south of Salem, and in the mountains of Virginia.

The mountaineers erected a log meeting-house, which served a number of years. Zevely was assisted by members of the Salem congregation, John Vogler being specially active and interested. When the people desired to have their children baptized, Zevely, not being an ordained minister, was unable to comply with the request. Accordingly, a special visitation was arranged for Bishop Van Vleck, and he was accompanied by Vogler and Zevely. Several weeks were spent in this visitation, with preaching, baptizing, exhorting, encouraging, and distributing religious tracts. By this time the feeling of the people was greatly changed, and the party was received with marked kindness.

As years passed this section was served by the ministers Rights, Ruede, and Hagen. A strong desire arose for the erection of a church, where regular services could be held, and the sacraments be administered. A location was finally selected at Ward's Gap, nine miles north of Mt. Airy, and fifty miles from Salem. This church was consecrated, November 24, 1852. A congregation numbering thirty-seven was organized, and the name Mt. Bethel was given to it. A Sunday-school was also established.

Jacob Siewers had returned from his work in Florida, and he was called to take charge of Mt. Bethel in 1854. He and his family found temporary shelter in the church building, but soon moved into the mission house, erected at the foot of Blue Ridge.

The work has been continued through all the succeeding

HOME MISSION WORK

years, chiefly by ministers from Salem, but no resident minister has been stationed at Mt. Bethel for many years. In recent time interest has increased, and a new station was begun by McCuiston at Willow Hill, Virginia. Members of the Female Missionary Society of Salem have made visits on several occasions, holding normal classes to prepare the teachers for more efficient Sunday-school work, and arranging for the special celebration of the Christmas festival. The number connected with Mt. Bethel and Willow Hill at the present time (1902) is three hundred and thirty-six.

The work among the coloured people in Salem dates back to 1822. In that year the "Salem Female Missionary Society" was organized, with Susannah E. Kramsch as president, Mary Steiner, treasurer, Louisa E. Kramsch, Susan E. Peterson, Hedwig E. Shober, Rebecca Holder, and Sarah Steiner, collectors. This society has continued to exist and do its quiet but important work all through the eighty years which have followed. Through its efforts a separate congregation was organized for the coloured people, March 24, 1822, and in 1823 a church was erected at the lower end of Church Street, near the old parish graveyard. This church served for many years, and in 1861 a large brick building was erected. This house has been improved and enlarged in recent years.

The little congregation of coloured people has always remained faithful to its church, but with the abolition of slavery, nearly forty years ago, a change came over the condition of things. The manufactories attracted many negroes to Winston-Salem, but they were drawn to churches presided over by ministers of their own race. The Moravian Sunday-school was in charge of earnest and able workers, and as the instruction was superior to that of other coloured churches, large numbers of children and grown people attended this Sunday-school, the roll sometimes showing from three to four hundred. In time the day schools for coloured people improved, and hence the teaching in their Sunday-schools also improved. As a result the situation is again changing, making the question of the present work of the Moravian Church among the negroes a difficult problem.

After the war of 1861–1865, the home mission cause assumed a different phase, and the consideration of these changed conditions and their results will appear in our study of that period.

CHAPTER XXII

WINSTON FOUNDED

1849

STOKES COUNTY was divided in 1849. The new county of Forsyth[1] embraced the original tract of Wachovia, and about an equal amount of territory in addition. The legislature appointed five county commissioners. May 12, 1849, they purchased thirty-one acres of land from the Moravian Church, and this amount was later increased to fifty-one and one-fourth acres, the price being $5 per acre, a total of $256.25 for the entire county town site of that day. This lies in its extreme limit between First and Seventh streets, Winston, and is bounded east and west by Church and Trade streets. The plot was then divided into seventy-one lots, one square being reserved for the court-house. These lots were sold at public auction for $8833.50, which was a profitable investment. Robert Gray bought lot No. 41, south of court-house square, for which he paid $465. This was the most expensive lot. Thomas J. Wilson lived on lot No. 45, corner Main and Second streets.

The evolution of the corporations of Salem and Winston is admirably shown by a plot given in "Forsyth County," which we reproduce on the opposite page.

When Salem was incorporated, in 1856, it was bounded

---

[1] For a complete record of the evolution of this county, see "Forsyth County," Fries, 1898.

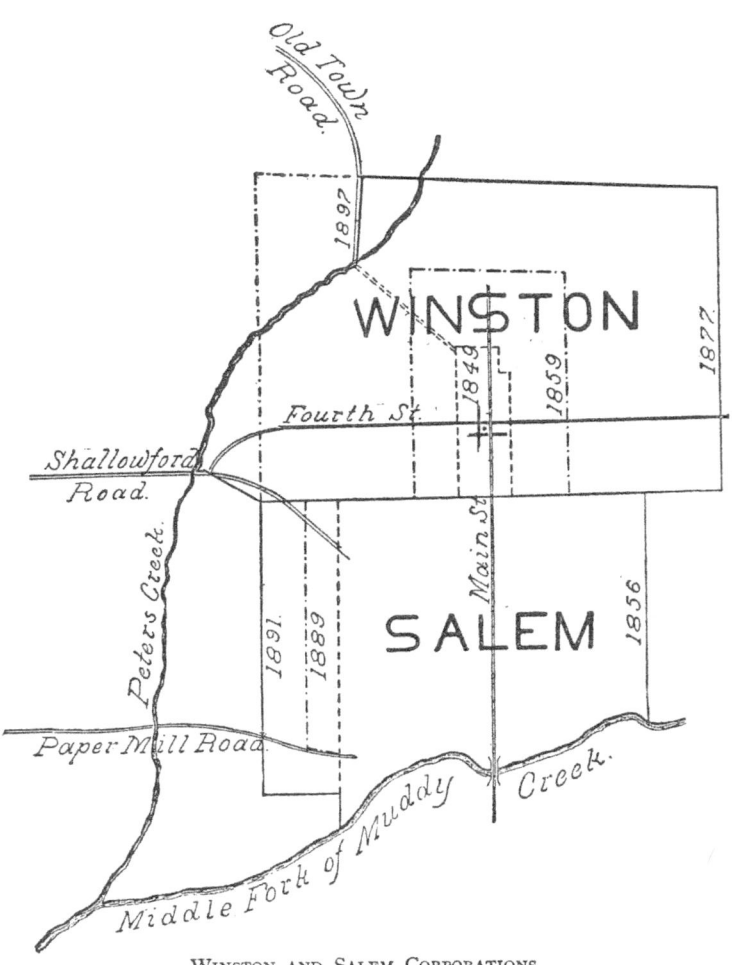

WINSTON AND SALEM CORPORATIONS

WINSTON FOUNDED

on the south side by the middle fork of Muddy Creek (Salem Creek), on the north by the Winston line, and extended half a mile east and west from Main Street. The other additions are shown in the plan.

This original purchase of fifty-one and one-fourth acres for the county town is shown under date of 1849, and the size at the date of its incorporation in 1859 was very much larger, as were the succeeding additions in 1877 and 1897.

The area of the two towns within the corporate limits in 1900 was one and a half by two miles, but with the suburbs the towns cover a much larger space.

The naming of the county town was the next step, and an attempt was made to have this done by a popular vote. The plan was to hold an election and take the name which had the largest number of votes. This plan failed, and January 15, 1851, the legislature passed an act which declared that "hereafter the county town of Forsyth County shall be styled and known by the name of Winston." This name was given in honour of Major Joseph Winston, a prominent North Carolinian, who figured in the War of the Revolution, and was also active in the political development, both state and national. Major Winston was born June 17, 1766, in Virginia, and died in Germanton, North Carolina, April 21, 1815.

The courts of Forsyth were first held in the concert hall, Main Street, Salem, which stood on the lot now occupied by the home of Dr. J. F. Shaffner. The stipulation was made that the whipping-post should not be within the limits of the town of Salem. One of the cases tried in the concert hall was noted in the memorabilia of 1850. It was that of a certain McBride, of Ohio, who had been distributing literature calculated to incite an uprising among the negroes. The people remembered the untold horrors of

FIRST COURT-HOUSE IN WINSTON

the Turner uprising in Virginia, in 1831, when the cruelties of the slaves went to the extreme of not only ruthlessly murdering men and women, but even of impaling infants; and we do not wonder that men who would incite an insurrection among the coloured people were adjudged guilty of one of the most dangerous of all crimes. McBride was placed on trial for his life; he was given the very best counsel for his defence, and still was found guilty. The sentence imposed was that he should be placed in the stocks one hour, receive twenty lashes at the whipping-post, and be imprisoned one year. He appealed to a higher court, gave a one-thousand-dollar bond, and when released he fled from the state nevermore to return.

The new court-house was so near completion that December 16, 1850, it was formally opened with religious ceremonies. It was a two-story building, forty-four by sixty feet, facing south. As will be seen from the accompanying illustration, the roof of the portico was supported by four pillars. These pillars were each thirty feet high. The court-room was on the second floor. The total cost of the building was $9083.38. The profit on the sale of the land was sufficient to pay all of this expense except $359.49. In other words, the last-named sum is all that the county had to raise to pay for town site, court-house site, and for the first court-house. The bill before Congress in 1902, having in view the purchase of the new court-house building, estimates the value of the square on which it stands at $40,000. This will illustrate the difference in value in 1850 and in 1900. During a period of nearly fifty years, the first court-house stood in the centre of the town and witnessed the gradual growth of Winston. At first this was slow, but later it became more rapid, and eventually from the village was evolved the city. Around the old building could be woven an interesting history, for within its walls were held, not only the courts of justice, but the gatherings within the old court-room were of every kind and description. Church organizations were formed; literary lectures were given; there were political meetings, and the waiting crowds heard election returns; there were war speeches and patriotic Fourth of July orations. Varied indeed were the gatherings held in this old court-house between the dates which mark Winston the village and Winston the city.

The march of time does not take into consideration sentiment or historical associations; hence the old court-house began to appear strange and incongruous when compared with the more modern blocks of business houses going up about it, and it fell into decided disrepute when the increased business of a growing and populous county had to be transacted in its now too small court-room and its cramped offices. Accordingly, plans were made to provide means for a new building. It was not quite as easy a task to secure the money for the second court-house, as it was for the first. There was opposition to the movement on the part of many voters in the county, but eventually bonds were issued to the amount of $55,000, and the new structure which is shown in the illustration was built. The committee in charge were successful in carrying out their plans at a reasonable cost, and the people of Winston-Salem are justly proud of the results. At the time that this book is printed a bill is before Congress providing for the purchase of the court-house as a government building. Whether the new court-house remains a court-house, or whether it becomes a United States government building, the following description of a recent writer is true:—

SECOND COURT-HOUSE IN WINSTON

"Standing on a slight eminence in the heart of a busy little city, this handsome structure of granite, buff brick, and brownstone is as great a contrast to the modest building whose place it took as is the present county seat with its widespread suburbs to the three streets and handful of houses of the county town of 1849, and both speak eloquently of the great strides that Forsyth County has made during the fifty years of her existence."

CHAPTER XXIII

TRANSITION PERIOD

1850-1860

ONE hundred years had passed since the beginning of Wachovia. The Moravian Church had adhered firmly to the principles laid down at the outset, and the strict adherence to these had resulted in two things. The one was beneficial, because it enabled them to use the well-tried European methods in this new and undeveloped land. The other was not beneficial, because this conservative adherence to customs not suited to a new and growing republic caused them to miss many fine opportunities. The fact that changes were necessary became apparent to many of the best minds in Wachovia, and was universally recognized by the younger people. With the usual careful, methodical, and earnest manner in which all things were done, this matter of a transition was taken up, and the decade of 1850–1860 witnessed some important modifications in the affairs of Wachovia. The movement was not confined to Wachovia, but is seen in the church history all through the Unity.

The General Synod, at which representatives were present from all parts of the world, met at Herrnhut, in Saxony, in 1857. In this synod there were important constitutional changes. These are not of interest to the general reader; suffice it to say that the result was greater independence for the American church in particular, and the abolition of those rules which had practically enforced

TRANSITION PERIOD

the principles of exclusiveness. There were also important financial measures which tended to place the control of all remaining property in America into the hands of the American provinces, and to separate the local affairs more and more fully from the affairs of the Unity in general.

One of the first results of this transition influence was to abolish the control of the trades and industries. The several boards of the church corresponded to the later municipal boards. These church committees planned for the proper care and improvement of the town, and supervised its interests. In the affairs of the community this patriarchal supervision started with the idea that the church and town formed a family, and that the interests of each individual must be guarded. They supervised the organization of business enterprises, and if the field was not large enough to support two of a kind, only one could be started. If two stores could flourish, and not three, then two were allowed, but the third was prohibited. Up to a certain point this was good, but there came a time when the principle was no longer necessary, nay, it even blocked the wheels of progress; hence after this time the business of Salem was no longer retained under the control of the church, but was thrown open to the individual, and to the world, with all the attendant advantages and disadvantages of competition in trade.

A second important change which came into this transition time from 1850 to 1860 was the abolition of the lease system. The object of the lease system was to retain control of the community so that its identity as a Moravian town should not be lost. To insure this as a permanent thing, land was not sold to the members, but leased, under certain conditions, and in this way no one could secure property in Salem without the consent of the church boards. The plan of retaining control of the ground is not an uncommon thing, but is found in the so-called "ground rents," of Philadelphia, Pennsylvania, and other cities, and in any form of lease at the present day. Nor was the supervision of the trades and industries by the boards at that time far removed from the license system, in general vogue, the object being to protect one class over against others who might have an undue advantage. Both the supervision system and the lease system have their modified counterparts in any well-regulated city of our day. Still, the systems were detrimental to the growth and general interest of the town, and hence the former was abolished in 1849, the latter in 1856.

Another change in this transition period was replacing the German by the English language. There was no surrounding population to support the use of the German language, and all the business transactions, as well as the social intercourse with neighbouring people, had to be in English. The English language had been in use to some extent from the very beginning, and there was always an English-speaking pastor resident in Wachovia; but during seventy-five years the German predominated, and at this time English was formally adopted as the language of church and town. German services were thenceforth held only at intervals. The records were written in English after 1855.

To the above points should be added the fact that the town was incorporated in 1856, with Charles Brietz as the first mayor, the board of commissioners being R. L. Patterson, F. Fries, A. Butner, J. R. Crist, E. Belo, T. F. Keehln, and Solomon Mickey.

Of this transition period we may say in general that it

In the Park, Salem Academy and College

TRANSITION PERIOD

was a natural evolution. The previous plans had been good for a certain time and for certain ends. But the time had expired, and the ends had been gained. Later history shows us that new fields were opening and that the circumstances were changing. The building of the county town of Winston as a near neighbour brought with it new obligations and responsibilities. The changed conditions which followed the Civil War were approaching, and opportunities for enlarged spiritual work in the last quarter of a century were to meet the church. All these things, together with weighty business responsibilities which the future had in store for individual members, rested on the proper outcome of this transition in the affairs of the church and town. The right position was taken; Salem became aggressive in principle, both in its town affairs and in its church matters, but the aggressive spirit was tempered with a conservatism which was calculated to produce the highest and best results.

CHAPTER XXIV

SALEM FEMALE ACADEMY AFTER FIFTY YEARS

THE experiment of founding a school in North Carolina was wise. During these early years there were no similar schools for girls and young women in any portion of the South, and very few in the North. On the other hand there was growing up in the South an aristocracy, accumulating wealth, with minds broadened by travel, refined by the experience of their well-known hospitality, only awaiting the founding of a proper school to embrace the opportunity of placing their children under its care. The study of the register shows that from the beginning the patronage extended beyond the borders of North Carolina, and not only were the neighbouring states of Virginia, Tennessee, and South Carolina represented, but, as the years passed, all the southern and southwestern states sent pupils; and even from the North and West they came, and during the century almost every state in the Union, and even foreign countries, have been represented.

There are many features connected with the school life of the first half of the century which impress us as being interesting and strange. The question of how to reach Salem was not an easy one to answer. When a patron living in Tennessee wished to place his daughter in the Academy, his first duty was to provide horses and a conveyance, using this more comfortable method of travel as long as it was possible to do so. Then the carriage was abandoned, and the party proceeded on horseback, with

MAIN HALL

the aid of trusty guides, and in this manner the difficulties and even perils of the mountains were passed. When Salem was at last reached, the horses used by the pupils were sold, and a special room was provided in the school for the saddles which would be needed for the return journey when the school days were over. From some sections the patrons were more favoured, and could make the entire journey in the handsome family coaches, and the wealthy planters would drive up to the well-known Salem hostlery in a style befitting the nobility of the Old World. While these were frequent scenes all during the year, at commencement time the interest was increased by virtue of the numbers. Then it was that the yard was filled with the coaches, the stables with the horses, the rooms with guests, and the gentry of the land took possession of the usually quiet town, and the days were marked with stir and excitement.

The friends of the school love to describe the successful lives of very many of these pupils, who by birth were entitled to prominence, and who were specially prepared within the school to ably fill their responsible positions. These writers point to the fact that many of the most successful men of the South have been blessed with noble wives, and are proud to claim that these same wives were once Salem pupils. They point us to the homes of statesmen, of foreign ministers, of distinguished professional men, of eminent financiers, of great generals, of governors, yes, they even point to the White House in more than one administration, and say that the ladies in these homes received their early training in Salem. It is a well-known fact that southern hospitality is proverbial; these same friends argue that hospitality depends largely on the culture and nobility of the mother, the wife, the sister, and

The Dell

the daughter. As this hospitality never appeared brighter and clearer than in ante-bellum days, and as so many of the ladies of the best families of those years were educated in Salem, this school, they say, should be given its due credit for the part it took in aiding to bring about this admirable picture of the noble type of womanhood found in the ante-bellum southern home. The claim of the alumnæ seems to be borne out by the words of a distinguished governor of one of the southern states which has sent scores, even hundreds, of pupils to Salem. This chief executive of the state in which he lives recently wrote to the president of the Alumnæ Association, "I know just enough of the history of Salem Academy to know that there is no institution on this continent which has done more for the education and elevation of southern womanhood than it has, and if official duty and Providence permit, it will be a pleasure and a privilege to be with you on the interesting occasion of the one hundredth anniversary of the school."

In a recent chapter treating of the founding of the school we noted the completion of the first school building. This was in 1805. As years passed, this house was filled, and the congregation house, just north, was occupied, room after room, till the school had taken entire possession. The principal's house had been finished in 1810, and the school continued to expand till it temporarily drove the boys out of their school building, and some room companies were placed in the widows' house, and even in private houses in town.

This state of affairs peremptorily called for enlarged accommodations, and on a generous scale. Thereupon it was decided to remove the congregation house and erect a new building in its place. It was removed in 1854,

A Favourite Retreat

and the corner-stone of Main Hall laid the same year. March 24, 1856, the school moved into its new home.

Main Hall was planned by Francis Fries, who also gave the construction his able personal supervision. The description given by Robert de Schweinitz, the principal, will convey an idea of the dimensions.

"The dimensions of the main building are one hundred feet front by fifty-two deep, with a wing at the north seventy feet in length and thirty-four feet in depth, and another one at the south seventy-seven by forty-four feet. The main building, as well as the north wing, is four stories on the front, and at the rear, on account of the descent of the ground, five stories. The fronts of the houses are of pressed brick, expressly manufactured for our building, and are probably some of the first of the kind made in the state.

"The front is ornamented by a large Doric portico, fifty feet in length, and thirteen feet in width. It has four Doric columns, with two pilasters resting against the house. The height of the whole, including bases, columns, and entablatures, is between thirty and forty feet, the cornice of the entablature extending three feet above the sills of the third-story windows. The whole is built strictly in accordance with the classical Doric order of architecture. The columns are of brick, stuccoed with hydraulic cement in imitation of brown sandstone, as is also the rest of the portico, excepting the bases and steps, which are of hewn granite."

Main Hall, with its north and south wings, forms an imposing pile, and east of this is the park. This park is a special gift of nature. It has been improved by walks and pavilions, bridges and fountains, but the natural beau-

The Spring

ties eclipse all the artificial additions. It is the pride of the school. The accompanying etchings will give a hint of the real attractions. The one view shows the campus as seen from Main Hall. In the foreground are the majestic trees, while the lights and shadows play in and out on the scene, giving glimpses of gravelled walks or a granite memorial, the whole reminding one of an Italian view.

The etching which shows us the long walk, with the trees of the primeval forest on either side, suggests the rambles which the pupils love to take in their free hours. The pavilion on the hill is a favourite retreat, where, on any pleasant day, in spring or autumn, groups of girls can be seen, reading some interesting book, doing a bit of fancy work, resting and chatting, with perchance something tempting from the confectioner, or perhaps with a Latin or geometry book.

Then there is the spring, the spot familiar to every pupil. We do not know whether the coin is thrown into the limpid pool, as is done in the Fountain of Trevi, in Rome, but we do believe that every pupil wishes to return, to visit the old spring and taste its sweet waters.

On the hillside, where is shown the rustic bridge, the romantic groups gather and recline on the soft grass, or promenade for exercise and the fresh air. From this point a view of the hillside beyond the brook is a delight to every lover of nature.

One of the daily recreations in fair weather is a stroll through the town or into the neighbouring country. Less than a five minutes' walk from the school is the famous cedar avenue, which is shown elsewhere. All pupils love to walk up and down the smooth white path, with the velvety grass growing on either side, while the double rows

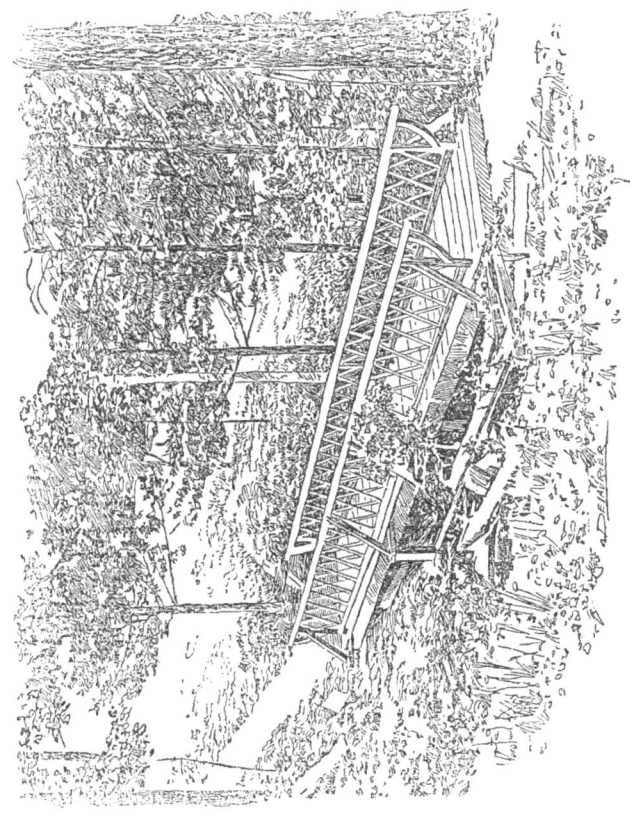

On the Hillside

A Peaceful Spot

SALEM ACADEMY AFTER FIFTY YEARS 231

of gigantic cedars gracefully droop their branches over them. They love, too, to visit the graveyard near by, because of the spirit of peace inspired by the sacred spot.

Finally, we will suppose that the afternoon stroll is over, and the group of girls is returning. As they enter the square in front of the school, and pass the fountain, before them is the view represented by the last in this series of etchings. This shows us the old Salem church, the corner of Main Hall, and the corner of the principal's house.

These views may not convey to the mind of a stranger the beauties of the park and the avenue, yet the former pupil who reads this chapter will no doubt find pleasure in glancing at these pictures of the old school haunts.

The course of instruction has been good from the earliest days. Specialists have often given their lives and talents for the good of the school. A regular graduation diploma was not presented to the graduates until within the past quarter of a century. Connected with the graduation is associated the cap and gown, and in the "sweet girl graduate," shown in this group of pictures, is introduced a member of a recent class. Only the seniors wear the cap and gown, and they prize very highly the distinction which draws a broad line between them and the other pupils.

As we leave the subject of the Academy, with its busy young people, coming and going, that which impresses us most, is not the age of the school, nor is it the fact that thousands of pupils have attended Salem, nor is it the size of the buildings, nor the beauty of the park; but it is the standard set before the girls. Music in all its forms is studied; art traces symmetrical lines, and blends beautiful colours; the class room strengthens the mind; the gymnasium develops the body. All these things are good and

A Graduate

SALEM ACADEMY AFTER FIFTY YEARS

aid in gaining successes in life; but that on which the Academy prides itself, more than all else, is the earnest effort which it makes to inculcate a high and noble standard of Christian womanhood.

This ideal it is which attracted the attention of parents from all sections of the Southland during the fifty years of which we speak, and filled the school so that one building after the other had to be added; and if we cast the glance forward a half a century, we will find that this same ideal it is which is drawing the alumnæ from North and South, from East and West, to rejoice in the celebration of a century's work in the history of their Alma Mater.

A Corner in Salem Square

CHAPTER XXV

THE TIME OF THE CIVIL WAR

1861-1865

THE records of the latter years of what we have termed a transition period are filled with forebodings of the coming Civil War. The conflict seemed to be inevitable, and though one compromise after the other was attempted, they had no further effect than to cover up and temporarily smother the flames of war. The inhabitants of Wachovia felt that the third time within the century of their history the Province was approaching the dark days of strife and bloodshed, and dread and anxiety filled their minds.

In 1831 the opposition to bearing arms had so far disappeared that a military company was organized in Salem, on July 4, and the officers were chosen from among the Moravians, the company making its own rules.

It is not our intention to discuss the questions relating to the causes and results of the Civil War. Forty years have passed, yet many of the participants of this great struggle are still living, and the growing generations hear the story of the war from the lips of those who were in the active service.

A new generation, North and South, has grown up since those dark days, and in business relations, social ties, and in true patriotism the dividing lines between North and South have been broken down. The immense volume of capital flowing into southern enterprises proves the first; the palatial trains bearing the visitors south to the genial climes of Florida, or North to the great centres, shows the second to be true; the way in which both the North and the South responded and stood side by side in the late Spanish War makes clear the third. Hence it is not our desire to comment on questions long since settled, but to describe the experiences of Wachovia in its relation to these dark days of sorrow and suffering.

South Carolina seceded December 20, 1860; North Carolina, May 21, 1861. North Carolina sent more than one hundred thousand men to the field, and, as in the days of the Revolution, the latter portion of the war saw many troops moving through the state and through Wachovia.

Early in 1861 a day of humiliation and prayer was observed throughout the entire South, and the services in Salem were solemn and impressive. Though no actual battles took place in Wachovia, this Province was so intimately connected with the terrible conflicts, that a paragraph from the memorabilia of 1861 will bring their feelings vividly before us.

"In some respects the year 1861 has been a year unexampled in the experiences of us all. Notwithstanding the apprehensions of the public danger, which rested like a gloomy cloud upon the minds of the thoughtful and observant, at the beginning of the year, the nature and extent of our national troubles probably exceeded our worst anticipations. The present year has witnessed the commencement of a fearful and calamitous war, between two different sections of our once united and prosperous country. When and how the strife will end is known only to God. Preparations on a gigantic scale have been made by both parties for the contest, which betoken an obstinate prosecution of the war on the one part, and an energetic and determined

THE TIME OF THE CIVIL WAR 237

resistance on the other. Already some of the fairest portions of our country have been ravaged by the destructions of war; fields have been laid waste, homes demolished, villages consumed, and districts that smiled as the garden of the Lord have been trampled down and made desolate by the footsteps of contending hosts. Battles have been fought and victories won, but sad and numerous have been the instances of individual suffering and distress, few of which have ever been published, and some of which cannot easily be imagined. Heart-sickening it is to contemplate, even in imagination, the horrors of the battle-field: the groans of the dying, wounds long left bleeding and undressed, loss of limbs, maimed and mangled bodies. Then there are the days and nights of loneliness and suffering in the crowded hospitals, or amid the yet greater privations of the camp. Mournful beyond expression is the loss of precious lives, every one of which is of inestimable value to at least some loving hearts, though the loss may not sensibly affect the public. How many families have been shrouded in mourning and gloom, how many hearts left desolate, now weeping over loved ones they will greet no more on earth."

These were the thoughts that filled the minds of the Salem congregation as it gathered in the church at the close of the year.

During the first months of the year 1861 the men of Salem and Winston and the surrounding country were gathered and organized, drilled and prepared for service. The white tents of the encampments gave a martial appearance to the towns. Companies from other sections began to pass as early as May, and in June three companies left Salem to join the army assembling in Virginia.

It was a pleasant June morning, Monday, the 17th, when two of the companies marched to the Salem square, and were drawn up in line in front of the Academy. Bishop Bahnson and the Rev. Mr. Doub, a minister of the Methodist church, occupied positions on the portico of Main Hall, and each delivered a short address, after which Bishop Bahnson offered a fervent prayer. The large concourse of people then sang the New Testament benediction, "The Grace of our Lord Jesus Christ." A multitude had gathered to bid them farewell, and the parting scenes were most painful and affecting. Some of the friends accompanied the soldiers as far as the Salem Creek. The entire scene was a strange one. The solemn service, with troops fully armed, drawn up in front of the ministers; the large gathering of people, some sad, some curious; the eagerness of the brave boys to go to the front, to join the gathering of the army; the songs and the hurrahs of the soldiers, as they passed down the main street, the tears and prayers of wife and mother, as with bended head they mingled their tears with their prayers in the silence of the lonely home.

The church diary for the date named above says that in Company A, Forsyth Rifles, were the following, who are connected with the families of the church: William J. Pfohl, Samuel C. James, Henry W. Barrow, J. F. Shaffner, Gustavus E. Sussdorff, Benjamin Atwood, Alfred H. Belo, Edward A. Brietz, James A. Reich, Alexander Rights, P. T. Shultz. In Company B, Forsyth Grays, are the following who are connected with the families of the congregation: Captain Wharton, Francis Carmichael, Thomas Byron Douthit, Lewis B. Eberhard, Samuel G. Hall, Joseph H. Reich, James E. Shultz, Cornelius A. Shultz, Julius R. Vogler, David Murchison, Augustus B. Butner, Reuben L. Chitty, Augustus A. Clewell, Francis E.

GEORGE FREDERICK BAHNSON

THE TIME OF THE CIVIL WAR 239

Keehln, Henry Shore. In addition to these there were a number of men who were stated hearers in the services.

Eight days after this the Third Company of Volunteers from Forsyth, Captain Miller commanding, started to the front. Bishop Bahnson conducted a religious service in the camp before the departure of the troops. The members of this company were largely from the country around Salem, some of whom were connected with the congregations of Bethabara and Bethania. No names are given in the diary.

On Sunday, July 21, it was suggested by some of the members that a daily service of prayer be held, to intercede at the throne of grace for friends and relatives. The proposition met with a hearty response, and at eight o'clock each day the members gathered. On the second morning, that is, on Tuesday, immediately after the prayer service, news was received that a desperate battle had been fought at Manassas Junction, Virginia, and that the Confederate troops had gained the victory. It was almost certain that the Salem soldiers were in the battle, hence the suspense and anxiety were great.

The next day the anxiety had increased to such an extent that David Clewell was sent to Richmond with the hope that he would be permitted to pass through the lines and go to the front, in order that he could render assistance to our troops.

From later information it was learned that our young men had not suffered. They had been exposed to severe cannonading, but having been intrenched they were mercifully spared from shot and shell.

This same anxiety appeared from time to time during the war, after the great battles, especial mention being made in May, 1863, after the battle of Fredericksburg.

As the months and the years passed, the cloud of sorrow fell upon one and another household. We find notes in the diary, which, though brief, tell a story of suffering for many hearts, and formed a portion of the great stream of distress which covered the land like a flood.

"At eleven o'clock this morning the young man, Augustine Hauser, departed this life. About six weeks ago he returned from the army, having by exposure in camp contracted the disease that carried him off. How many men in the prime of life have fallen victims to disease in this dreadful war." November 23, 1862.

"To-day at one o'clock was the funeral of our brother Armenius Lash, whose death took place at Petersburg, and his remains were brought here by his brother." December 6, 1862.

"The funeral of Lieutenant Jacob Sheppard took place. He was killed in the battle of Fredericksburg. Bishop Bahnson preached the funeral sermon." December 22, 1862.

"Henry C. Banner died at Petersburg, December 21, from a wound received at Fredericksburg, and was buried here to-day." December 24, 1862.

"To-day we received the news of the death of Charles J. Clauder, who had fallen on the battle-field near Fredericksburg. He was found dead, by the litter bearers, with his Bible open on his breast." May 13, 1863.

"About twelve o'clock to-day Frank Reich died, from sickness brought on by exposure in the army. His naturally strong constitution could not resist the strain. He leaves a wife and child." September 3, 1863.

"Noah Lewis, a soldier, died in the hospital here, and was buried at four o'clock to-day." Sunday, September 27, 1863.

THE TIME OF THE CIVIL WAR

This same sad record could be increased, for many a mournful procession passed beneath the rows of cedars, bearing the remains of loved ones, brave boys like Henry Belo and William Pfohl, who died in the struggle and the conflict. Or we could tell of those who fell, and whose friends did not even have the comfort of placing their remains in the home graveyard, as was the case of Wiley Gray, and many another.

The development of the war changed toward the end of 1863 and in 1864. September 10, the Twenty-First North Carolina Regiment passed through Salem, as it had been ordered to some of the western counties to suppress certain hostile demonstrations. There were between three and four hundred men. As they passed through Salem they were supplied with a dinner in the public square. Many of these men were from Forsyth County, and their relatives and friends were present to greet them. It was a joyous meeting, only to be followed by a sad parting, as the troops passed on to their destination. The band connected with this regiment came to Salem on November 2, and among the members were several men from our town.

Coupled with the movements of the troops we notice the feeling of desperation which was filling the minds of the people of the South as they felt the lines of the opposing military power drawn closer and closer around them. From the North, from the South, from the West, on the ocean, with steady progress these forces were closing in. The food supply became less and less, there were no medicines, clothing could be secured in very limited quantities, ammunition was running short. All this will explain why, in 1864, we see items in the diary which point to a desperate attempt to rally all the forces possible for the final decisive struggle.

The record says that the examining board met in Winston, in March, 1864, and that the treatment of many who had been previously exempt was severe and harsh. They were placed under guard, as if they had committed some offence, were sent under escort through the town, and were confined in the guard-house like prisoners. Thus efforts were made to increase the army by pressing into it those who had hitherto been exempt.

The same thing is seen in the strong and determined effort made to fill the ranks by the capture of deserters. The desertions increased as the sufferings and privations increased, and August 20, 1864, the Home Guard of Salem was called out to hunt deserters. At a later date the record condemns the severity of the measures used against these poor fellows. Thirty of these captured deserters passed through Salem, October 26, 1864, from Guilford County. They had attempted to escape and pass the lines, but had been apprehended, and were heavily guarded as they continued their unwilling march back to the army.

As a result of this special effort to increase the list of fighting men, a number of the older and also of the younger men from Salem went to the army at this time. The diary says that many were heads of families, and earnest prayers for their safety followed them.

Toward the close of 1864, the rumours and the news began again to change. They heard of the fall of Atlanta, and the nearer approach of the invading army. In 1865 the first rumours of possible peace reached them. Then came the report that Petersburg and Richmond had been evacuated, and finally they heard of the surrender of the southern army at Appomattox.

After the surrender the army was disbanded and the

THE TIME OF THE CIVIL WAR

soldiers returned to their homes. This home-coming was both happy and sad. It was happy because of the reunion of loved ones and the return of peace. But it was sad because of the struggle for existence which awaited them. The difficulty of this struggle can scarcely be realized in our day. Many returned suffering from wounds, from exposure, from hardships, from prison life. The war had impoverished the land, destroyed business, and left no opportunities for earning a support for themselves and their families. It is said that many men who bravely faced the foe in the field of battle shrank discouraged from the difficulties which confronted them after the surrender in 1865.

This home-coming, as well as the horrors of the war itself, is graphically pictured in a lecture delivered in the Academy chapel by one who was in the thickest of the struggle, who tasted to the full the hardships of prison life, and who remembers those days by the results of the wounds he received. He says:—

"We were paroled at Farmville, and begged food by the way, sometimes welcomed, often repulsed, and walked by slow stages on account of our weakness to Clover station, where we found a train that carried us to Danville. Here we appropriated a construction train, and standing on a flat car, rode to a burned bridge ten miles from Greensboro. Walking on, I reached home the second morning thereafter. I had been mourned for as dead. Some of my companions had taken the description given by a burying detail, of a young fellow resembling me, and marked his grave with a board on which they carved my name. My welcome home may be imagined.

"I had lost thirty-eight pounds in the three weeks since we left Petersburg, and was so emaciated and filthy that my father did not at first recognize me. As I emerged from the nasty underclothing I had worn night and day for seven consecutive weeks, and enjoyed the luxury of a warm bath, and donned clean garments, and again sat in a chair, and ate with a fork, and drank water from a glass, and joined in the family prayers, and slept in a bed, all the glamour and illusions of the pomp and pride and circumstance of glorious war were forever dispelled. I certainly was not built for a soldier. I don't want to impugn the veracity, nor would I curtail the pleasure, of those old soldiers who speak and write so enthusiastically of the duty of patriotism and the glory of war. But I must express my selfish regret that they so successfully concealed their real feelings at the time. If any single one among the thousands I saw felt at all happy or contented, he failed utterly to show it. I know if I had been half as badly scared as everybody around me looked, I never would have stayed to go into a single battle. Speaking for myself, I have few pleasant recollections of the war. To my mind come only sad and grim and gloomy memories: the forms of my comrades and friends hurried to an untimely death by disease and wounds; left a prey to the birds of the air, and the beasts of the field, at best hastily and unceremoniously shovelled into a shallow trench; if haply surviving, maimed and crippled, and marred in health and usefulness; the privations and sufferings from fatigue and hunger, and heat and cold, and filth and nakedness, in comfortless camp, on toilsome march, in ruthless conflict, in loathsome hospital, in pitiless prison; fields deserted, homesteads and towns pillaged and burned, graves violated,

THE TIME OF THE CIVIL WAR

sanctuaries defiled, Sabbaths desecrated; the havoc and ruin, the wanton waste and destruction, the merciless carnage; the unutterable agony of heartrending grief that hung like the smoke of torment over tens of thousands of blasted homes; the abomination of desolation!

"May justice and righteousness dwell in this land; may mutual toleration and forbearance take the place of sectional jealousy and bitterness; may the God of love so completely fill the hearts and minds of this people that the god of battles can nevermore find room in their thoughts; may the reign of the Prince of Peace speedily begin and his blessed dominion extend over all God's beautiful earth."[1]

The following is a list of some of the soldiers from Salem, Winston, and from some of the neighbouring Moravian congregations. There are also some names of men who did not enlist with the Forsyth companies, but have since become citizens of our towns. It is only a partial list, since there were many soldiers who served in other sections of the country, and whose names do not appear on any register accessible to the gentlemen who prepared this list. By request, an examination of the rolls of the companies from our county was made by Dr. J. F. Shaffner, T. B. Douthit, C. B. Brooks, W. H. White, C. B. Pfohl, and Captain J. C. Bessent, and the following names were found. It is quite certain that all names could not be discovered, but it is probably the most complete list of Winston-Salem men thus far prepared. Space has been left between the letters of the alphabet, and in these spaces additional names may be written. The writer will be glad

---

[1] Lecture delivered by Dr. H. T. Bahnson in chapel of Salem Female Academy.

HISTORY OF WACHOVIA

to receive the names of men who enlisted from Salem, Winston, or from any of the Moravian congregations.

Atwood, Benjamin, killed. Atwood, Jesse, died. Atwood, J. S., wounded. Anderson, Elisha G.

Brooks, C. B. Brietz, E. A. Brietz, Samuel. Barnacastle, H. F. Barnacastle, John. Barnacastle, Yerby. Barnacastle, E. Bahnson, C. F. Bahnson, H. T., wounded. Butner, James. Butner, E. J. Butner, A. B. Butner, W. N. Butner, John. Butner, L. E. Butner, F. A. Butner, Augustus L., killed. Butner, Augustus. Butner, Henry L., died. Barrow, David. Barrow, Henry W. Barrow, William. Boner, Edward J., wounded. Bowles, J. C., died. Bowles, William, died. Bowles, J. S. Bowles, J. P. Billiter, P. L. Billiter, Amos. Bevil, A. W. Beckel, Samuel W. Brewer, W. H. Brewer, Wesley. Banner, Henry C., killed. Brown, W. R. Brown, Haywood. Brown, David. Brown, Nathaniel, wounded. Brown, H. A. Brown, T. J. Byerly, J. E. Burk, J. J. Burk, H. F. Burk, W. J. Burk, Andrew. Burk, George. Brendle, Gottlob. Brendle, R. A. Brendle, J. P. Best, T. T. Belo, A. H., wounded. Belo, R. W., wounded. Belo, Henry, killed. Belo, C. E. Bitting, J. Walter. Blum, James. Beard, William.

Carmichael, L. F. Carmichael, W. F. Chitty, Henry N. Chitty, Henry. Chitty, Lafayette. Chitty, Reuben. Crowder, N. Cooper, J. A. Cooper, W. J. Clewell, Augustus A. Clewell, Francis C. Crouse, Harrison. Crouse, Samuel. Crouse, Daniel. Coley, J. H. Creekman, G. N. Crater, L. J. Crater, R. J. Crater, Allen. Craver, Allen. Calhoun, J. Y., died. Conrad, Alpheus S. Conrad, John C. Conrad, Wiley. Conrad, J. H. Conrad, B. C. Conrad, J. Carlos. Conrad, G. H. Conrad, R. J. Crouch, Augustus, killed. Crouch, John. Clodfelter, W. C. Campbell, R. Chaffin, N. S. Crist, T. F. Church, Robert, died.

Douthit, T. B. Dull, Edward C.

Everhard, L. D. Essic, Theophilus. Essic, Valentine. Ernest, Henry. Ebert, Alfred. Ebert, Murchison.

THE TIME OF THE CIVIL WAR 247

Fogle, C. H. Fogle, Samuel. Fuller, Dave. Fansler, William, wounded. Faircloth, W. H. Fletcher, A. Fry, David.

Gillam, A. H. Griffin, J. A. Goslen, L. H. Goslen, J. W. Glasscock, William H. Glasscock, M. V. Garboden, Lewis. Gray, S. Wiley, killed. Gray, James A. Gorrell, A. B. Gorrell, R. D. Gorrell, Ralph, killed. Gilmer, J. E. George, Peter.

Hunter, Thomas. Hendricks, Nicholas, died. Hendricks, Nathaniel, killed. Hendricks, John, killed. Hendricks, Lee. Hendricks, Mat. Hensdale, David, killed. Hinshaw, William. Hauser, C. H. Hauser, Nerva. Hauser, Augustine, died. Hauser, Francis. Hauser, C. E. Hauser, R. A. Hauser, William. Headley, P. D. Hughes, Henry. Harald, William. Holder, W. C. Holder, E. Jack. Holder, Henry A. Holland, L. E. Holland, E. E. Holland, Junius R., killed. Herville, William. Hine, W. C. Hine, L. F. Hine, E. A. Hine, J. H. Hine, Theodore. Hine, Lewis. Hine, L. I. Hege, Daniel. Hege, Edward. Hege, Z. G. Hunter, J. W. Hall, S. G. Hall, W. H. Hall, J. O.

Ingram, Clint. Ingram, John.

James, Samuel C., killed. Jenkins, Robert M. Jenkins, R. A. Joyner, Elias. Jarvis, John, killed.

Keehln, T. F. Keehln, F. E. Kessler, Samuel. Kennedy, Joel. Kiger, Alexander W. Kreeger, James. Knott, William R. Kimel, Lewis, wounded. Kapp, William. Kapp, Alexander. Knott, George. Knott, R. W. Koonce, M. Kennedy, T. Van.

Lineback, Phil, killed. Lineback, J. A. Lineback, J. H., wounded. Lineback, J. W. Lineback, R. C., killed. Lineback, Edgar. Lineback, L. W. Lineback, P. T., killed. Lineback, Emmanuel. Lineback, J. B. Lineback, Allen, died. Lineback, Timothy. Lineback, W. H. Lewis, Isaac. Lewis, Noah, died. Lehman, O. J. Lehman, P. T. Loderick, John. Livengood, Henry. Lash, Armenius, killed. Lash, Augustus. Lash, Henry. Lemly, W. A. Lemly, I. T. Lumly, David. Landquist, John. Lowman, William.

Mickey, F. W. Mickey, S. T. Murchison, D. B. Miller, D. B.
Miller, Alex., killed. Miller, John, killed. Miller, Samuel E. Miller,
Carlos W. Miller, E. Miller, F. P., killed. Miller, G. L. Miller,
V. B. Miller, F. W. Merritt, John. Moss, S., wounded. Mock,
Christian S. Mock, Nathaniel. Mendenhall, Frank. Meinung, Edwin. Meinung, Alexander. Mann, J. E. Mastin, J. H. Mast, D. P.,
wounded.

Nissen, G. E. Newsom, Green. Newsom, John. Nelson, W. F.
Nading, John. Nading, N. W. Nading, F. A. Norfleet, M. W.

Owens, Larkin, killed. Ogburn, M. L. Ogburn, William. Ogburn,
C. J., wounded. Ogburn, J. W. Ogburn, S. A.

Porter, John H. Porter, F. M. Porter, G. W. Phillips, C. T.
Pack, David. Pack, Calvin, died. Pfohl, W. J., killed. Pfohl, W.
Thomas. Pfohl, E. A. Pfohl, A. F. Pfohl, C. B. Parsons, William.
Pratt, J. L. Painter, William, wounded. Padget, Charles A. Pitts,
Harrison. Pfaff, Philip. Peterson, William. Peterson, Edward.
Pratt, T. J. Pratt, Francis. Pratt, Wm., Jr. Petree, W. W.

Reich, J. E., died. Reich, W. A. Reich, Lewis (Salem), died.
Reich, Lewis (Old Town), died. Reich, John. Reich, G. A. Reich,
J. H. Reich, James. Reich, Parmenio, died. Reich, Constantine,
killed. Reich, B. F., died. Reich, William. Reich, John L. Reich,
L., killed. Reich, H., killed. Rothrock, J. M. Rothrock, Charles,
wounded. Rothrock, John. Reed, James L. Reed, D. S. Reed,
John. Reitzel, Christian, died. Rights, J. A. Rempson, John.
Rominger, W. J. Rominger, J. A., died. Rank, Eugene, killed.
Robertson, David. Riggs, Jesse.

Shultz, James. Shultz, C. A. Shultz, P. T. Shultz, J. P., killed.
Shultz, J. A. Spear, Solomon. Shepperd, W. H., wounded. Shepperd, Frank. Shepperd, Hambleton. Shepperd, Jacob, killed. Shouse,
C. A. Shouse, Wiley, wounded. Shouse, Edwin. Shouse, Christian.
Shore, H. L. Shore, Augustus. Shore, N. T. Shore, Sanders. Shore,
John H. Shore, J. H., killed. Shore, W., killed. Shore, Isaac, killed.

THE TIME OF THE CIVIL WAR

Swaim, Eli, killed. Swaim, W. F. Spaugh, W. E. Spaugh, Frank. Spaugh, Obadiah. Spaugh, J. E. Spaugh, Simon, wounded. Spaugh, E. J. Spaugh, Jonas, wounded. Spaugh, B. A. Spaugh, William. Spaugh, W. J. Spaugh, D. A. Siewers, N. S. Siewers, J. B. Sussdorff, G. E. Samuels, James A. Sites, George W., wounded. Stephens, Alfred. Styers, Jesse J., killed. Styers, Edward J. Styers, N. R., killed. Starr, A. Shaffner, J. F. Snyder, Sanford. Snider, William P. Strupe, L. J. Strupe, Eugene. Strupe, Ephraim. Stauber, J. C., died. Stafford, J. C., killed. Shober, Charles E. Sides, Sandford. Shutt, Lewis. Swink, George. Siddall, H. A.

Thomas, W. H. H., wounded. Thomas, Columbus, died. Transou, Julius. Transou, Reuben, died. Transou, A. E. Transou, Lewis. Transou, O. C., died. Tise, Jacob.

Vogler, J. R. Vawter, A. L., died.

Winkler, J. C. Wharton, R. W. Webb, A. H. Webb, J. C., wounded. White, W. H. White, Tandy. Wright, L. D., killed. Wright, Silas. Waugh, Samuel, wounded. Woolsey, William, wounded. Woolsey, Franklin. Wren, Calvin T. Wren, Jerry. Wimmer, John, wounded. Whitfield, Nicholas. Wheeler, W. H. Wheeler, Henry, wounded. Watson, C. B. Watkins, C. J. Warner, J. A. Winchester, Luther. Welfare, Edward, wounded. Welch, J. J. Welch, Henry, killed.

Young, J. G.

Zimmerman, Martin.

We turn now to another phase of the war. The Indian foe invaded Wachovia in 1759, the British during the Revolution, and in the Civil War the Federal troops passed through Wachovia, and even encamped for a season in Salem.

April 2, 1865, an alarm was sounded, and preparations

were made for the dreaded invasion. News of the severity of the Union army in Tennessee, in Georgia, and in Virginia had reached them, and they feared the worst. The clerk of the court distributed his books and papers in private houses, so that, if one house was burned or looted, another would probably be spared. Cotton and cloth were also stored in private houses with the same object in view. Horses were taken to unfrequented spots, and there tethered till the army had passed. In the vaulted cellar of the principal's house is a sunken place in the floor, where an excavation had been made; in this the money and jewellery of the pupils and the valuable property of the school had been placed. In the large space under the Main Hall of the Academy Mr. Fogle put the two fine black horses of the school, and thus saved them. In every possible way preparations were made for the approaching foe.

The first report was false, but April 10 they did arrive. During one of the Easter services in Bethania, while the congregation was assembled in the church, the Federal troops, under General Stoneman, suddenly entered and took possession of the town. It was an astonished congregation that left the church that night. Houses that had been locked were broken open and drawers and closets were ransacked. No resistance was offered, hence no overt act, such as burning buildings, occurred. But there was so much plundering and thieving that the inhabitants of modern Bethania felt, after Stoneman's troops had gone, as did the inhabitants of Bethania of old when Cornwallis and his army took their departure.

Before the troops entered Salem, April 10, 1865, there was some excitement, attended with pursuit and capture of the scouts, but, in the end, the mayor of the town, Joshua Boner, the principal of the academy, Robert de

Robert William de Schweinitz

THE TIME OF THE CIVIL WAR 251

Schweinitz, and some others, met General Palmer, surrendered the town, and requested protection for the school and the citizens. This protection was accorded in a thorough and satisfactory manner. The government building on Marshall Street contained a large store of supplies, and these satisfied the wants of the troops, hence little damage was done to the town, though there was some breaking down of barriers in one direction and another.

General Palmer had his headquarters in Joshua Boner's house, and the soldiers encamped below the creek. With the exception of the clatter of the hoofs of the horses as they filed down Main Street, no one would have been able to realize that a body of three thousand troops were passing through. During this occupation of the town by the raiders, one body of troops by some error entered Cedar Avenue and the graveyard, but many dismounted and walked through the enclosure, and in some instances hats were removed as a mark of respect for the dead.

The next month a body of cavalry arrived, and remained in camp several weeks. They were in the town from May 10 until July 13. They belonged to the Tenth Ohio Volunteer Cavalry. By this time Lee had surrendered (April 9, 1865), hence hostilities had ceased, and the soldiers were no longer hostile, as in time of war. They were awaiting the orders to be mustered out. Hence they fraternized with the people, and were hospitably received into many of the homes.

The camp was on the plot of ground now occupied by the steel tank of the Salem Water Supply Company, and the officers had their headquarters in the house now occupied by Dr. J. W. Hunter.

The chaplain at one time addressed the Salem Home Sunday-school, and at another time he visited and preached in the coloured church, exhorting the negroes to settle down and become honest and industrious citizens. The Fourth of July was signalized by a celebration in the square, and many people came expecting to witness remarkable things, but they returned to their homes disappointed. On pay days there was much drunkenness and rowdyism, and in one or two instances men were killed. The soldiers treated the negroes very harshly, as they were strung up by the thumbs, and maltreated in other ways. The diary closes the account of this two months' stay with the following emphatic words, "Everybody, or at least the vast majority, rejoiced that they left this morning."

In April an unusual scene was witnessed in the town. The church bell was rung, but it was not a fire alarm. All the citizens and the soldiers who had returned from the army responded, and gathered in groups at the hotel or in the square. This unusual sight was necessitated by the presence of a number of Confederate troops, who evidently were on a foraging expedition, and under plea of searching for government cloth, which they claimed was secreted in the homes of the citizens, they proposed to forcibly enter and search the houses. Knowing that robbery was the real object, the citizens determined to resist; and when the strangers saw the arms and the determination, they withdrew, though with many a dreadful threat of what they would do when they returned with a larger force of men.

The confusion which followed the surrender of Lee was widespread. The governor of the state declared that he had no further authority; the town officials took the same position; the country was filled with a reckless class of men, many of whom were bad, bent on plunder, as is

THE TIME OF THE CIVIL WAR

shown in the preceding paragraph. This state of affairs lasted nearly a month, till the arrival of the Union troops in May. During these weeks, when Salem was without a government, the citizens organized a vigilance committee, composed of the citizens and the soldiers who were now returning from the war, and patrolled the streets day and night, holding in custody all who could not give a satisfactory account of themselves. The work of this vigilance committee was no light task, but order was maintained and property and lives protected till the organization of the new government was effected.

It is not necessary to add much to what we have already given of the daily life of the people, but it will be in place before closing the subject to allude to the great privations which the community suffered. Many articles, common in our day, were unknown to the people in those years. Principal de Schweinitz rejoiced when on one occasion Governor Vance sent two barrels of sugar for his school family. Prices made the articles prohibitory, even if they could have been obtained. Salt sold for $20 per sack, corn was $10 per bushel, bacon $2 to $3 per pound. In estimating the cost of a love-feast it was stated that with the smallest size cake, and without coffee, the expense of the service would be $125. Later the terrible depreciation in money added to the confusion. A certain collection in the church amounted to $500. On the collection plate was placed a silver dollar, and the diary says that the silver dollar was worth as much as $40 in the depreciated currency.

A pleasing feature of these years of hardship appears in the earnest and self-sacrificing manner in which the church and community laboured to ameliorate the sufferings of the soldiers, especially in the latter portion of the struggle. The residents of Salem, in 1863 and 1864, will recall the long lines of cloth tacked to the fences, in the avenue, or around the private lots in the town. These long strips were being painted and made into "oilcloth," to protect the soldiers from the weather, and to serve them in other ways. The Fries mills were running day and night to weave the famous gray cloth used in the army. The clatter of the wooden shoes was heard, as the boys and girls came and went from school; and while the children rather liked them, because they did make so much noise, the real object of this use of wood instead of leather was to send so much more leather to the soldiers. Even the little folks picked quantities of lint for the wounded, while their elders wound numberless rolls of bandages for the surgeons' use.

One of the heroic acts of the war was the journey of a number of our ladies to the hospitals, to act as "red cross" nurses, even at that early day. Among those who went to Blantyre Hospital were Mrs. Eliza Kremer, and Misses Lizetta Stewart, L. Shaub, Laura Vogler, and Margaret Clewell.

The experiences within the Academy were interesting, and leave a bright spot in this dark history. The school was a place of refuge in this time of storm. Parents sent their daughters from various motives. Some came for the sake of the education only; others came from sections which were not safe because of hostilities in those portions of the country; still others came because they were refugees, driven out of home by fire and sword. All during these years the school sheltered two hundred or more of these young people, and no harm came to this precious charge.

THE TIME OF THE CIVIL WAR 255

The details of how provisions were supplied are interesting, as told by those who lived through the years 1861–1865. It was not an uncommon thing to see the principal ride up to his office after a long journey, mud-bespattered and weary; and when the object of his journey was ascertained, it was found that he had heard of the possible purchase of a few bushels of corn, or a little bacon, ten or fifteen miles away, and had ridden thither to secure it. Or his assistant in this difficult task, Augustus Fogle, would arrive at midnight, after a most difficult ride to secure a beef, and was informed that a score of miles away two pigs might be bought; having taken an hour or two of rest, he would be off again at three o'clock in the morning. It was no light task to feed and shelter a family like this during the days of the Civil War.

One bright and happy event occurred at the close of this period. It was the celebration of the centennial of the founding of Salem. This was in 1866. The relief which came with the return of peace had enabled the congregation to rally and to begin to lay plans for the future, and it was determined to celebrate the occasion in a worthy manner. The church was beautifully and elaborately decorated. At that time the pulpit was on the north side, with galleries on the three remaining sides. The exercises were carefully arranged, the music was fine, and in this celebration the congregation seemed to gain strength and encouragement for the future, and to realize that the Lord who had guided them thus far would continue to hold his protecting hand over them.

CHAPTER XXVI

THE DECADE FOLLOWING THE CIVIL WAR

1865–1875

WACHOVIA'S trial, after the War of the Revolution, was the prevalence of smallpox. Wachovia's burden after the Civil War was the time of reconstruction. This is the name applied to the series of errors made by the Federal authorities after the assassination of Lincoln. It is believed by many that when Lincoln was shot the South lost the friend who could have done the stricken land the greatest amount of good. As it was, the President was shot, and the men who assumed the reins of government were not fair, nor were they just, toward the southern people. It may not have been intentional ruin of the country, but such it was. Millions of slaves were freed and given the ballot; millions of white men who were able, and were again loyal citizens of the land, were disfranchised. The whites were able to govern, but they could not vote. The blacks were unable to govern, and they assumed the power. At this juncture a company of adventurers came in, made their way into the highest offices, bought or controlled the entire negro vote, robbed and plundered, and what the war left these men finished. State after state was brought face to face with utter ruin. Then the whites took the next step; they determined to drive these men out by force. These things brought about the reconstruction days, with the unrest and violence attending them.

DECADE FOLLOWING THE CIVIL WAR

Wachovia did not feel these evils as much as many other sections. The church work seemed to stagnate. There were fewer accessions than usual. The ministers were discouraged. The little money reserve which the Province had, after the settlement with the Unity's conference, was steadily diminishing. The church services were not attended as they should have been, and everything seemed to be at a standstill.

In the Academy the patronage was growing less and less. The old, tried, and true friends were not able to send their children to school. Their slaves liberated, their plantations devasted, their homes burned, these things left the friends of the school in abject poverty, in very many cases.

This picture shows us the decade following the war, — business dull, opportunities few, services poorly attended, school interests depreciated, everything moving feebly.

Then there came a time when the crisis was passed. As the new fresh blood sends the life and strength through the body, after a severe illness, so the pulsation of public affairs began to show renewed life and health. The disfranchised men were given the right to vote. The obnoxious leaders had been driven out of the land, or had come into sympathy with the interests of the state, and North Carolina awoke to a day of better things.

It became apparent that there must be a revolution in methods in Wachovia, both in school and church. The plans worked slowly at first, but there was a steady advancement of all interests. The marked changes appeared later.

The renovation of the Salem church was one of these indications. The congregation, with an effort, raised a sum of money, to make material internal improvements.

The pulpit was placed at the east end, and a gallery was added on the north side; pews replaced the old-time benches.

In the town one of the steps of far-reaching importance was the prohibiting of the sale of intoxicating drinks, by an almost unanimous vote, and since then the sale of liquor has not been allowed.

The Academy added the two upper stories to South Hall.

These and other things indicated that the period of prosperity was steadily advancing.

CHAPTER XXVII

A NEW ERA

1875–1902

ABOUT the year 1875 a new era began to dawn. Winston received a business impetus which sent it forward on the road to prosperity. The railroad between Greensboro and Winston-Salem was finished. The old houses were replaced by new and better buildings; the blocks of stores around the court-house were remodelled, or new ones erected. The tobacco interests, which have since become such an important feature, attracted the attention of a new class of people. The population rapidly increased, and the value of real estate was greatly enhanced.

In Salem the growth was less rapid, but none the less real and permanent. The young men took hold of the new state of affairs and entered upon the task of building up the town. In former years almost every line of business was represented on a small scale. There was one man with a comfortable salesroom and a small workshop manufacturing hats; another conducted a cooper shop, and to this day his genial face can be remembered as he stood in the doorway and had a pleasant word for each passer; still another had a bookbindery, in which he did work for customers all over this section of the state; then there was the locksmith, the confectioner, the saddler, the silversmith, the carpenter, and the carriage maker, in fact almost every line of manufacture was represented on a small scale. With the dawn of the new era it became apparent that the business enterprises must be planned on a larger scale, and hence we see the modest carpenter shop exchanged for the more pretentious planing-mill, with improved machinery, ready to build the new young city; the blacksmith shop is replaced by the large iron works, destined to send their manufactures all over the world; the most pretentious business enterprise of the town, the cotton and woollen mills, were increased by the erection of a large modern mill. Thus at the beginning of this last period, which we have termed a new era, the business pulse of the two chief towns of Wachovia was beating in harmony with the beginning of that wave of enterprise which, at the end of twenty-five years, has covered the entire South and is marvellous in its extent and importance.

Within the church equally marked changes were taking place, or we may better say, were being prepared.

In 1880 negotiations were begun with a view to the organic union of the Northern and Southern Provinces, with the government in the hands of one board. Commissions were appointed and for three years the details were studied and plans considered. The effort was finally abandoned, in 1883, and this action of the commissions was approved by the synods of both provinces. The two sections of the Moravian Church in America have the most friendly feelings for each other, and at the present time calls can be extended to ministers, directly, from one province to the other. In all respects, except in actual administrative functions, the two provinces are really one.

The men who had faithfully carried the church through the time of war, and through the reconstruction period, were beginning to feel the weight of years; De Schweinitz, Grunert, Leinbach, and Rights had given the service of a

Emil Adolphus de Schweinitz

A NEW ERA

lifetime to the upholding of the church and Province, and will always be held in loving remembrance. They lived to see the beginning of brighter days.

It was at this time that Rondthaler was called to the pastorate of the Moravian Church in Salem, and began a service which has now reached a quarter of a century, and during this time has been a wise and successful leader, retaining all that is good in the old, and reaching out to adopt all that is wise and desirable in the new. During this quarter of a century the church and Sunday-school work has expanded, the congregation has enlarged, and the provincial interests have reached out into many new fields of usefulness.

CHAPTER XXVIII

HISTORY OF THE WATER SUPPLY AND FIRE PROTECTION

1766–1902

A RECENT writer is responsible for the statement that in locating a home a German first asks for a spring of water, and then locates the home near the spring. An Englishman will first select an elevated point, locate his home, and then consider the question of bringing the water to the home. Be this as it may, the builders of Salem first searched for springs, discovered them in the grove (south of the present site of Calvary Church), and having run the level, then located the principal buildings of the town at a place where the water could be brought from the springs into the houses, by gravity. The distance from the springs to the Salem square is a mile and more, hence the task of piping the water from that point was a difficult undertaking.

In 1774 the first steps were taken to provide the town with a water supply. In that year the plot of ground was fenced and a cover was placed over the spring. Then the matter was left until the way should be opened for further work.

Early in 1778 active operations were begun. The best heart-pine timber was brought from the surrounding country, and these logs were bored their full length, thus being made into pipes. The ends were trimmed and fitted into each other. The water was brought to the main street of the town by gravity, and thence distributed to five stations.

WATER SUPPLY AND FIRE PROTECTION

February 26, 1778, the laying of the pipes from the spring to the upper cistern was finished.

March 18, the pipes were laid to the ironing room of the Sisters' House.

March 21, pipes laid to the hotel.

March 25, the work was finished when the pipes had been laid to the Brethren's House.

Thus the first water supply was completed March 25, 1778.

This system furnished the needed water for the town during a period of fifty years.

In 1827 work upon a new system was inaugurated, and in 1828 it was completed. The method employed to supply the town in this second system was both ingenious and efficient. In the ravine, east of the terminus of Bank Street, is a spring of clear, cold water. Here it was determined to erect a house, install a triple pump, and use a large overshot wheel as the power to run the pump. The water was forced up the hill, perhaps one hundred feet, to a supply cistern at the south end of Cedar Avenue. Thence by gravity it was distributed to a dozen or more cisterns. The pipes used in this system were glazed terra-cotta pipes. This was before the day of steam pumping, and the power was procured in the following manner: —

Starting at "bath branch," above the present railroad culvert, the water to turn the wheel was conducted along the hillside in a wooden trough, a distance of two miles. In crossing the ravine east of Park Avenue, it was necessary to support the trough on a high trestle. Thence the water passed through the Academy Park, and when it reached the wheel-house, it had sufficient elevation to fall upon the great fifteen-foot wheel, which revolved ceaselessly day and night. This second water-supply system served the town a full half century, from 1828 to 1878.

The third system, which is now in use, though supplemented by later additions, was begun by the Salem Water Supply Company. This company was organized in 1878, with J. F. Shaffner, Sr., as president. It secured all the rights and privileges of the old company, and at once proceeded to the preparation of a reservoir on the Fogle lot, on Belews Creek Street. This reservoir had a capacity of sixty-five thousand gallons. A well was dug near "bath branch," not far from the point at which it empties into Salem Creek. The pump was operated by an overshot wheel, with water brought from the same stream which turned the wheel in 1828, though the supply trough, or race, in this case is only a few hundred feet in length. Reuben Chitty was a familiar figure in his attention to this wheel, as well as to the property of the earlier system.

Seven years later a second well was dug, the pump being worked by an overshot wheel, with water from "bath branch." This is a few hundred yards north of the first well. The pipes from these two wells join, and feed the common reservoir.

A large steel reservoir, with a capacity of half a million gallons, was constructed in 1887, near the site of the first reservoir, and this is still in service in 1902. Arrangements were made about this time to connect the Winston and Salem systems, so that in case of a widespread conflagration, the firemen could draw from the supply of both towns.

In 1890 the Salem Water Supply Company bought what is known as the Reynolds Spring, about a mile southeast of Salem, and erected a steam pump, connection having been made with the general system of mains.

WATER SUPPLY AND FIRE PROTECTION 265

Previous to 1890, the enterprise was strictly a private concern, supplying the town with fire protection, but without compensation. In the above year a contract was entered into between the town and the water company by which the company received $25 per year hydrant rent, on about fifty hydrants, located on the eight miles of mains.

A year or two later work was begun on the new reservoir, near the Reynolds Spring, and this is now completed with a capacity of a million and a half gallons, giving the town of Salem a reservoir capacity of two million gallons.

A very important development in the history of the Salem Water Supply Company occurred in 1901. The company, Colonel F. H. Fries, president, purchased in fee simple, or secured the water rights, to about two hundred acres of land, in what is known as the Butner or Fogle bottom, and thence eastward. This is the basin of a large watershed, with a water-bearing gravel substratum. This gravel stratum will supply a million gallons per day, of the purest water. This can be increased to five million gallons per day by the use of the creek water, the purest stream in this section, and the supply will then be sufficient for a city of fifty thousand inhabitants. A pumping station has been erected at this point and connection made with the reservoir. The value of the plant at the present time is $60,000.

The men who have been most energetic in this work, since 1878, are Dr. J. F. Shaffner, Colonel F. H. Fries, Charles Fogle, C. H. Fogle, and Henry F. Shaffner. The first-named gentleman furnished the above facts concerning the Salem Water Supply Company.

The Winston Water Company was organized in 1880, G. W. Hinshaw, superintendent, and Thomas J. Wilson, president. The supply well is near "Belo's Pond," and the reservoir, with a capacity of one million gallons, is located at the upper end of Trade Street. The well which supplies the water has a diameter of thirty feet, to a depth of thirty-two feet, and a twelve-foot diameter for a distance of twenty feet more. Its supply is from seventy-five to one hundred gallons per minute.

The company was a private corporation from 1880 to 1894, when it was sold to the city of Winston.

At present, nearly ten miles of mains have been laid, and the value of the plant is $110,000. The present supply pumped into the reservoir is between four and five hundred thousand gallons per day. The pumps have a capacity of two million gallons per day. An automatic filter purifies the creek water that is used, and there is at the pumping station a storage reservoir, with a capacity equal to the one on the hill. The pumping station is so arranged that the pressure can be thrown directly on the pipes, thus gaining any amount of pressure for throwing water from the hydrants.

The above information was kindly furnished by G. W. Hinshaw, former superintendent, and J. O. McGruder, present engineer.

Thus we see that the Twin City has a combined reservoir capacity, including the Winston storage reservoir, of four million gallons.

We note the marked contrast between the little rivulet of spring water trickling through the wooden pipes in 1778, and the steam and electric pumps, ready to force two million gallons daily into the reservoirs.

Logically connected with the water supply is that of the history of the protection against destruction of property by fire. A detailed history of the Salem Fire Department is given in a pamphlet entitled "Fiftieth Anniversary of

WATER SUPPLY AND FIRE PROTECTION

Salem Fire Department," by W. S. Pfohl. Fire inspectors were appointed whose business it was to examine the condition of affairs in the buildings, and to have corrected that which in any way threatened the safety of the property. This inspection of the buildings has been continued all through the one hundred and thirty years, and no doubt this is one of the reasons why fires have been so rare. The regulations are quaint but effective. If perchance the reader is tempted to smile at this old document which we reproduce, let him remind himself that it was these regulations which gave to the towns practical freedom from fires, there having been only one fire each twenty-five years during the first century of the town's history; and as two of these were insignificant, it is right and proper to state that Salem had one building destroyed during the first fifty years of its history, and a second dwelling was burned during the second half century. Hence the following regulations call for our respect and interest: —

"At a meeting of the Fire Inspectors, held January 25, 1773, the following observations were made: —

" 1st. It would seem necessary that in the larger kitchens, as the hotel, the Sisters' house and the Brethren's house, the chimneys should be swept out five times during the year, whereas in family houses, twice or three times might be sufficient. But, as in the burning of dry wood, in stoves as well as in fireplaces, less soot is formed than where green wood is used, the fire master should consider the necessities of each case, rather than confine himself to stated periods.

" 2d. It is desirable that a young man be selected, who should be instructed in the business of chimney sweeping, who could relieve the regular sweeper from time to time.

Chimneys that measure 16 × 18 inches, also 14 × 18 inches, are most convenient to be swept. The latter, however, if not straight, will present some difficulties.

"3d. In reference to log houses it was resolved and ordered that all pipe openings in the chimney must certainly be examined once a year, and even if no special flaw be found, the plastering must be renewed. In this connection an instance was recalled, when a fire would no doubt have occurred, if this precaution had not been taken.

"4th. It was agreed that the compensation of the sweeper be the same as that paid for the same service in the congregations in Pennsylvania.

"5th. The question of the number of times of sweeping the chimneys was referred to again, and it was unanimously decided that in family dwellings chimneys should be swept once during the summer and twice during the winter. The sweeper was cautioned, when ascending the chimney, not to rest on top of it when his work is done, lest he fall with the chimney to the ground, as the brick are not laid in lime mortar.

"6th. In conclusion it was suggested that it be made a rule that all chimneys be swept in the future, and that 'burning out' chimneys be entirely discontinued."

Twelve years later, when the two engines arrived, the following regulations were made, and read at stated intervals to the citizens of the town: —

"1st. Precautions which may be taken to avoid danger of fire.

"(a) That no method of building be adopted whereby the community is endangered. This may happen if the foundation of the chimney is not carefully laid; if the chimney is not sufficiently large to admit of its

WATER SUPPLY AND FIRE PROTECTION

being swept; if it is not strong enough, nor plastered; if it is not provided with at least one damper, or does not extend high enough above the shingle roof.

"(b) That no chimneys be 'burned out.'

"(c) That in front of each fireplace a sufficiently broad and plastered hearth be laid, so that the flooring is not placed too near the fire.

"(d) That tile stoves be not placed too near to joists or wooden partitions, and that provision be made against the possibility of coals falling out of the stoves.

"(e) That no dangerous practices be allowed, such as drying wood on the stove, or piling it up between the stove and the wall; wood which is too long for the stove is a menace, because when it burns in two pieces, one may fall out of the stove door, which of course cannot be closed; rags should not be hung upon the stove to dry, nor should any other combustible material be placed on the stove.

"(f) That bake ovens should be carefully located, and the coals which come from the oven should be carefully provided for.

"(g) That no smoke chambers be constructed at chimneys in dwelling houses, unless they are entirely fireproof.

"(h) That lighted candles and coal pans be not allowed to stand where they will imperil property; that no open light be taken into stables, lofts, or any place where hay, straw, tow, or other combustibles are kept, but that lanterns be used. Neither shall any one enter such places with lighted tobacco pipes. It is even doubtful if smoking in the yards and streets is wise.

"(i) That spittoons be not filled with sawdust.

"(2d.) The fire inspectors are to meet four times a year and shall carefully consider the following matters. They shall look after the Institutions, which in times of danger are to be carefully guarded. In their meetings they shall see if any one intrusted with special duties has been unfaithful, and how soon they can be replaced. They are to decide how often inspections are to be made. They are to examine the engines, the hooks, and the ladders, and see that the buckets are in place and in sufficient quantities. They are to provide the necessary supplies to the responsible parties, such as keys for the houses, buckets when needed, and they are to recommend localities where cisterns may be located, and report to the wardens' college, calling attention to the special needs.

"3d. How to act in case of fire, and what arrangements to make therefor: —

"(*a*) Any one discovering fire, whether by day or by night, shall first notify the inmates of the house; then they shall notify the men in the single brethren's house and then the fire overseers. Whenever the night watchman suspects the presence of fire he must immediately examine into the matter, and communicate with the watchman in the single brethren's house, in order that he may be ready to aid him. In case of actual fire, the alarm bell shall be rung, and the watchman shall go from house to house to alarm the citizens.

"(*b*) The fire overseers shall hasten to the fire, and shall have the entire control, no one having any right to countermand.

"(*c*) The engine masters and their allotted helpers shall take the engines to the scene of the fire, twelve persons for the large, and four for the small engine. They shall remain with the engines till the danger is at an end, and shall not intrust them to the care of any one else.

"(*d*) In like manner the four who attend to the ladders, the three with the hooks, and the three who

WATER SUPPLY AND FIRE PROTECTION 271

have the axes, shall all be under the direction of the chief overseer."

The paper from which the above rules have been taken gives a number of more explicit directions, so that all the inhabitants in the village had a place assigned to them.

The first of the two disastrous fires occurred in 1781. It was then that the hotel burned, and the lives of the inmates were in great peril. This loss, as well as the danger to life, no doubt had its influence in causing the authorities to take steps to purchase the fire engines. Two were ordered from Germany and were received in 1785. The one was a large engine on wheels, while the smaller one was carried by handles. It was to be used either inside the house, or outside, as occasion required. This smaller engine has been preserved, and is now in the rooms of the Wachovia Historical Society. These two engines were tested May 25, 1785, and it was found that both the large and the small one threw water over the highest buildings in the village, though the diary says "one objection is that the stream of water scatters too soon."

The list of engines used in Salem are the following: —

1785, the larger engine on wheels.

1785, the smaller hand engine, now in the Wachovia Historical Society rooms. These two were housed in the building on the west side of the square.

1832, the Vigilant, bought in Philadelphia, at a total cost of about six hundred dollars. Housed west of Tar Branch, on Academy Street. This engine is now in Bethania.

1855, the hose carriage, now in Bethania.

1858, the Rough and Ready, or Fries engine, housed near the wool mill. Used until 1884.

1884, a Button hand engine, housed north of Meinung's shop, Main Street. Later exchanged for a steamer.

1886, a Button steamer, in use at the present time, and housed on the first floor of Commissioners' Hall, Liberty Street.

In 1843 a fire company was organized in lieu of a military company, and was named the "Salem Vigilant Fire Company." This did duty till 1861, a period of eighteen years.

May 13, 1868, the "Rough and Ready Fire Company" was organized and chartered, and is still in control of the engine and hose.

A new hose wagon was added in recent years, and a hose carriage which is controlled by the Eagle Hose Company, in West Salem.

The number of fires in Salem have been very few:—

The hotel burned in 1781.

Siewers' shop in 1845.

Foltz's kitchen, in 1853.

Shaffner's dwelling house in 1864.

The total number of fires and false alarms during the first hundred years in Salem were ten.

The Winston Fire Department purchased their first steamer in 1882, a La France, which is in charge of Volunteer Company No. 1. Some years later the large steamer was purchased and also a hook and ladder wagon. A second hook and ladder company is made up of coloured people. Eight horses are kept by the town, and the entire eighty men receive some compensation, though only six are paid full salaries.

The two towns are supplied with the Gamewell fire alarm telegraph system, with twelve boxes in Winston, and five in Salem.

The water supply and three steam fire engines, with the auxiliary companies, afford fine protection. Since this excellent system has been in existence, there have been few disastrous conflagrations.

As great as was the contrast between the wood pipes of the early days, and the steam pumps with a two-million-gallon capacity, so great is the contrast between the little hand engine of 1785, shown in the illustration, and the powerful steamers as they pass swiftly over our streets, leaving behind a train of steam and smoke, on their errand of protection.

CHAPTER XXIX

GROWTH OF THE TWIN CITY

THE population of Winston-Salem at this date is uncertain, as is the case with any growing town at any fixed date. The census is not always reliable, since there are suburbs, with street car and telephone connections, and with people who find employment in the town, but who would not be included in the list of the census taker, as they live outside the corporate limits. A conservative estimate would probably place the number of inhabitants at fifteen thousand, while many claim that, with the suburbs added, and also with the many workmen who spend much of their time here, but register elsewhere, the sum will approximate twenty thousand.

There are at the present time railroads from four points entering Winston-Salem, — from Charlotte, from Wilkesboro, from Roanoke, and from Greensboro, that is, from the south, the west, the north, and the east. Three of these are under the control of the Southern Railway, and the Norfolk and Western Railroad has control of the other. The first railroad was built about thirty years ago, between Greensboro and Winston-Salem, Edward Belo, president. It was then known as the Northwestern North Carolina Railroad.

A number of years later the citizens of the Twin City decided that the interests of the town demanded certain railroad connections north to gain needed business prerogatives. Colonel Fries was chosen president, and the capital was supplied in part by home men, and the 120 miles of road were built. Later it was sold to the Norfolk and Western, and the name which it had borne previous to this time, the Roanoke and Southern, was exchanged for that of the new owner. Then the Wilkesboro road was constructed by the Southern Railway. A road to Mooresville completed the connection with Charlotte. Winston-Salem has become a centre as a freight-distributing point.

At this time an impetus was given to the tobacco interests of Winston. There were certain advantages which commanded the attention of experts, and the town grew into one of the larger markets of the world for the sale and manufacture of tobacco. The extent to which this interest has grown will be shown by the fact that last year the sales of leaf tobacco in the warehouses approximated twenty million pounds, with a value of $2,000,000. The factories shipped about the same quantity of manufactured tobacco, which was sold for $8,000,000. The number of persons employed in this business is five thousand. The tax paid to the United States government through the Winston office, largely on tobacco, is almost $3,000,000 a year.

The earliest mention of an attempt to engage in manufacturing on a large scale in Salem was in 1837. This was a cotton factory organized and operated by a company. It was conducted on a scale of some magnitude, but did not pay, and was finally sold.

In 1840 the Fries wool mill was begun. To this was later added a cotton factory, and at a still later date the large Arista cotton mill. In more recent years the South Side cotton mill began work, with H. E. Fries, president. The large mills at Mayodan, and Avalon, and at Fries,

Virginia, are all under the direction of Colonel F. H. Fries as president.

The wood and iron works of Fogle Brothers, Vance and Hege, in Salem, and the South Side chair and iron bedstead factories, under the direction of Charles S. Siewers, and the Spach and Nissen wagon works, add to the importance which Salem is assuming as a manufacturing centre.

In Winston, in addition to the tobacco business, are the chemical works, the knitting mills, the furniture factories, and others that might be mentioned.

One of the interesting and marked improvements of recent years was the erection of the Fries power plant at the Yadkin River, by means of which electricity is generated and sent over the wires thirteen miles, to furnish the motive power for nearly all the factories, to run the street cars, and to light the streets and houses.

The street car line has nine miles of track, with good service, both for the pleasure and the use of the people of the city.

There are two telephone companies in Winston-Salem, with long distance connection, and with about seven hundred phones in use in the two communities.

Both the Western Union and the Postal Telegraph Companies have offices in the Twin City.

There are perhaps a score of churches in Winston-Salem, representing almost all the denominations, and some of these congregations have handsome places of worship. The schools have also kept pace with the times, and as we have shown elsewhere, there are at this time thirty-seven hundred children under instruction in Winston-Salem.

A brief chapter can only imperfectly outline the material growth. Perhaps the best way to impress the contrast between the past and the present is to state the purchase price then and the present value. Wachovia, which was about half the size of Forsyth County, was purchased for a little more than $32,000, interest, quit rents, and principal. The tax valuation of Forsyth County is nearly $10,000,000. Winston site, original size, was purchased of the Moravian Church for $255. The present tax list valuation is nearly $5,000,000.

CHAPTER XXX

SUNDAY-SCHOOL ACTIVITY

1817-1902

IN 1817, we are told by the writer of the memorabilia that a Sunday-school was organized for the young people of the neighbourhood, which was in charge of some of the ladies from the Sisters' House. The character of the work was to give intellectual training, in reading and writing, but of course the religious training had its important place in the hour. This is not the beginning of the Sunday-school work in the Province, since in the same paragraph which mentions the beginning of the work in Salem, it is said that the already existing Sunday-school work some four miles from Salem is regularly conducted by the teachers of Salem Female Academy.

Several notices of the Sunday-school work are given during the following years, indicating that it had become one of the accepted means of grace in the Province.

A decade later, that is, in 1828, we find a notice of the influence of the American Sunday-school Union. We are told of Sunday-schools all through Stokes County, and the names of some around Salem are given, for example, Brushy Fork, Pleasant Fork, and Liberty or Calahan. The following year, 1829, a great celebration in the Salem church and the Salem square is described. Six hundred children were present, besides the strangers and the members of the Salem congregation. The Salem church was not large enough to hold the company, so the service was

SUNDAY-SCHOOL ACTIVITY 279

conducted in the Salem square. Shober was the president of this interesting work, and made an earnest address. Reichel preached the sermon, and love-feast was served in the afternoon. The weather was fine, and the day was a blessed one. On this occasion the Salem Sunday-school (probably the mission school) joined the American Sunday-school Union. At a later celebration there were present twelve hundred children, and a total attendance of parents and children of two thousand.

A few years later the work of this Union declined, and the individual churches assumed the responsibilities.

The first mention of organized effort at what is termed Sunday-school work in the Salem congregation is found in the diary and memorabilia of 1828 :—

"Sunday, November 23, Sister Fredericka Boehler organized a school among the older girls, as she felt herself called upon to do some special work for those committed to her care. She decided to hold the sessions of the school each Sunday afternoon from two to four o'clock, and her object was to assist them to retain and remember the instructions of the week. Her plans were endorsed by her parents, and sanctioned by the Provincial Elders' Conference. Brother Schaff was present on this first occasion, and formally began the work, by a service of song and prayer, especially commending this labour of love to the blessing of the Lord."

This Sunday-school seems to have been continued without interruption during the following years, until all the several lines of work were gathered together and moved into the church in 1849. We find that at the beginning this school gave attention to reading and writing, though we have no reason to suppose that the religious instruction was in any respect overlooked. There are notices of the addition of a library, of the distribution of Sunday-school papers, of anniversary days when the mission box was opened, and donations made to the Cherokee schools; thus the Sunday-school among the girls appears to have been successful and continuous from 1828.

The work among the boys was less regular, though the effort was never finally abandoned, either among the young men or the boys. In 1828 the remark is made that, as the Sunday-school work was so successful among the girls, it was the desire of the congregation to have similar advantages for the boys, and that during the year this wish was realized. Mention is frequently made of the Sunday-school work among the boys, and the Sunday Bible classes among the young men, but the remarks from time to time bearing upon the "reorganization" of the work seem to indicate that the success was not as great as in the case of the girls. From this, however, it must not be inferred that the spiritual work among the boys and young men was neglected. On the contrary, there was regular instruction in the day school, there were special week-night hours for reading, and lectures on church history for them, and the missionary and other societies flourished.

Twenty-one years later, almost to the day (November 25, 1849), the children were all gathered in the chapel of the church, and the work was thoroughly organized, and thenceforward the sessions were held in the church. The diary for that date says:—

"Bishop Bahnson began, in the chapel, a Sunday-school, especially for our own young people, whom we hope to incite to a better observance of the Lord's day. There were present thirty-six boys and twenty-one girls, which was a happy beginning."

SUNDAY-SCHOOL ACTIVITY

The Sunday-school was later transferred from the chapel to the church. Under the superintendency of James T. Lineback it grew in numbers and efficiency. As the number of Moravian schools in Salem increased, it was necessary to give this one a special name, so that in later years it has been called the " Salem Home Sunday-school." It is now and has been for many years in charge of Colonel F. H. Fries. In addition to the members of the age included in the list named in 1849, there have been added other departments, — the infant class department, the men's Bible class, the woman's Bible class, and the home department, — and the entire school now numbers 364.

The Sunday-school work among the Moravian churches in Winston-Salem has continued to increase as the towns have grown, and the following schools are within the Twin City limits or its immediate suburbs: Home Sunday-school, Elm Street, East Salem, South Side, Calvary, Christ church, Fairview, Academy, Cotton Mill; and if to these we add the number on the roll of the coloured Sunday-school, we have a list of almost two thousand in attendance at the beginning of the year 1902.

During the earlier years of the Sunday-school activity in Salem and in Stokes County, we find that great zeal was displayed in the cause by Friedberg and Friedland in the neighbouring country. In the former congregation, Henry Shultz was particularly active, and the work at Cool Spring met with marked results. One of the first small buildings used for Sunday-school by Shultz was on the identical lot later purchased for Advent congregation, and on which this church now stands. At Friedland, Pfohl and Vogler laboured with success, aided by other members from Salem.

After 1850 the influence of the county Sunday-school

organization departed, and the schools became thoroughly identified with the individual congregations, and came under their control. Previous to this time they were supported by the members from Salem, Friedberg, Friedland, and other congregations, but they owed allegiance to the Stokes County Sunday-school Union, and this in turn to the American Sunday-school Union. This uncertain and indefinite relation was changed to a certain and definite and organic connection with the several congregations of Wachovia.

During the last quarter of a century the Sunday-school work has assumed still another phase. Under the general direction of the veteran Sunday-school worker, James T. Lineback, it again became the plan of the church to organize new Sunday-schools, but this time as direct feeders to the church. The Sunday-school was begun with the intention of soon establishing a congregation. This was the case at Oak Grove, Providence, Fulp, Wachovia Arbour, Bluff, and other places that could be mentioned.

Every one recognizes the encouraging growth of the church in this period, and it is quite plain that the Spirit of God has used the Sunday-school as one of the chief means to bring about this happy result. The present aggressive period in our history could appropriately be called the Sunday-school period.

CHAPTER XXXI

ENLARGED CHURCH WORK

THE beginning of the twentieth century shows to even a casual observer that the church in Wachovia has witnessed a growth and expansion, and in this chapter we will study a few features as we see them in the several congregations.

The old mother congregation at Bethabara still claims the sympathetic interest of the Province and of visiting strangers. The church building has been renovated in recent years, and is picturesquely situated, as the view given in this book will show. The graveyard, on its beautiful hilltop, is faithfully cared for by the congregation, and it can be truly said that " Old Town " is a favourite spot. A number of celebrations have taken place, at which the members from all the congregations have been present, notably that of 1853, the centennial of the founding of the Province. C. D. Crouch has the pastoral charge, and the work is doing well, though the membership, by force of circumstances, is small.

Bethania continues its good work, and will soon think of celebrating its sesquicentennial. The town has not lost in size and numbers, though business has been diverted to the line of the railroad, some two miles away. The church has been very active in recent years, and has surrounded itself with a circle of affiliated chapels, Alpha, Mizpah, and Olivet. All these have done much to keep alive the spiritual work, and the Bethania pastor, F. W. Grabs, has five hundred names on the church register.

Of Salem much has already been said. The Old Home church followed the plan of locating the chapels where the people live, hence we find in addition to the Elm Street chapel, and the church for coloured people, the East Salem church, about a mile eastward, and the South Side church, a mile or more south, and near this the Cotton Mill school. To these have been added Calvary church in Winston, and Christ church in Salem, westward half a mile. Edward Crosland lives in the comfortable parsonage which adjoins Calvary, and Howard E. Rondthaler occupies the equally attractive parsonage at Christ church. Fairview, a comfortable brick church three miles north, has recently been built. Bishop Rondthaler, with his assistants, Howard Rondthaler and Edward Crosland, minister to a membership of about eighteen hundred. The coloured church is under the care of W. E. Spaugh, and the South Side work of C. D. Crouch. Eden and Wachovia Arbour, two smaller congregations, each about three miles from Salem, are usually served from the latter congregation.

Friedberg has followed the plan adopted by the others, and her membership has actively taken hold of the work in the neighbourhood, and on one side has erected a chapel to which has been given the name Enterprise, and on the other side has built a place of worship which they have called Advent. This congregation, with its six hundred and more members, has J. F. McCuiston as its pastor. The church and newly finished parsonage stand in a beautiful grove in the country. It is a conservative congregation, earnest and devoted, and clings closely to the traditions of the Unity.

EDWARD RONDTHALER

ENLARGED CHURCH WORK

Friedland still occupies its quiet location, with church improved, and graveyard recently neatly fenced. Union Cross is affiliated with it, and the membership is about 250. The work is in charge of C. D. Crouch.

In this same general section is Kernersville, with its neatly decorated brick church, and with the graveyard recently improved. Kernersville congregation is in a town of some twelve or fifteen hundred inhabitants, and the members have established a flourishing branch church a mile or two away — Carmel by name. E. S. Crosland is in charge, and the lists show 134 members.

Not far from Oak Ridge, in Guilford County, is a newly organized church, Moravia, which is served by Howard E. Rondthaler.

New Philadelphia has one affiliated church, Bethesda, and its membership is 333, with F. W. Grabs in charge. This congregation recently celebrated the fiftieth anniversary of the consecration of the church, which occasion was largely attended, and was greatly blessed.

Mt. Bethel in Virginia has received new life and energy, within the last few years, and though it is considered a home mission field, it is an active congregation, and on the side of the Blue Ridge has established another congregation, Willow Hill, C. D. Crouch, pastor.

Along the line of the Norfolk and Western Railway have been established a series of congregations; the nearest are Oak Grove and Providence, some eight miles from Salem. Then we find Fulp, about fifteen miles, and Mayodan and Avalon, thirty-five miles. The last two are in the villages which have grown up around the cotton mills, and the resident pastor is W. E. Spaugh.

Hope and Macedonia are near to the new Clemmonsville work, and are under the care of James E. Hall.

Hope has erected a new and attractive place of worship, and registers its membership with Clemmonsville. Macedonia is the only church beyond the Yadkin River, and has a list of 274.

The Clemmonsville work is one of the more recent enterprises of the church and calls for special mention. The following sketch has been prepared by the pastor, James E. Hall.

Edwin Thomas Clemmons died December 20, 1896, seventy years of age. He was born in Clemmonsville, eleven miles southwest from Salem. By his will a generous sum of money was left for the founding of a Moravian church and school at his native place. The actual beginning of the work was in 1899. The first service was held in the second story of Strupe and Son's store building, in the village of Clemmonsville, October 27, 1899. In November James E. Hall was called to take charge of the work, and regular services were continued as they had been in the past, before the official call had been given.

In the spring of 1900 land for the new enterprise was purchased, and the location for the buildings was decided upon. It was the Kinney-Bradshaw plot. On the 29th of March the centre of the plot of ground was marked, and an iron rod was driven deep in the ground. In the latter part of the year 1900 the neat and attractive parsonage was erected. August 13, 1900, the congregation was formally organized. The sermon was preached by Bishop Rondthaler, and in the two services which were held, the pastor, James E. Hall, was assisted by McCuiston, Pfohl, and Sheets. Before the second service, those who were to form the group of charter members assembled in the Strupe home, the same building in which Clem-

ENLARGED CHURCH WORK

mons had lived years ago, and after a brief religious service, the procession proceeded to the Methodist church, and after the reception of forty-four members, by the right hand of fellowship, the Holy Communion was celebrated.

During the summer of 1900 preliminary steps were taken to begin the school work also. J. Kenneth Pfohl was called to this work, and he spent a number of weeks in visiting the homes of the people and attending to other necessary preparations. He was joined by the pastor of the church in these efforts. The school was opened October 9, 1900, in what is known as the Douthit store building, the property of H. W. Fries. The house had been carefully prepared for school use during the year, and with its fresh coat of paint, and with the new furniture, was very inviting and attractive. The principal was assisted by Misses Bessent and Whittington. The scholars, seventy or more in number, assembled at the school building in the morning, and went to the Methodist church in a procession. Here the formal exercises took place. These were participated in by Bishop Rondthaler, and the ministers, Hall, Clewell, and Wood. The opening was very encouraging, both in numbers and interest.

The parsonage at Clemmonsville was so far completed that it could be occupied February 22, 1901. In April the first love-feast was celebrated, with an attendance of one hundred. May 15, 1901, the first brick for the new school building was laid, by James E. Hall, and on the next day the corner-stone was laid by Bishop Rondthaler, in the presence of a large congregation, with appropriate ceremonies. Among the visitors was Mrs. Clemmons, widow of E. T. Clemmons, and also G. F. Bahnson, pastor of the congregation of Schoeneck, Pennsylvania. The Salem church band was present on this occasion.

The school took possession of the new building October 8, 1901, with appropriate exercises. It is a large, modern building, with a capacity of 200 or more scholars, and with an assembly room seating 250.

A church building, similar in size to the schoolhouse, will be erected in the future, but for the present the auditorium of the school will be used for preaching and Sunday-school purposes. The first sermon was preached October 13, 1901, and the Sunday-school was organized a week later.

The graveyard is on Clemmons Hill, a short distance from the church, and roads have been laid out and the entire plot of ground around the church prepared so as to gain the best results in the future.

The founding of the church and school at Clemmonsville is an important event in the history of Wachovia. The plans, as they have been made, contemplate the organization of a " Place Congregation " (*Orts Gemein*). All the work thus far points to this: the selection of a plot of ground to be sold to members at a low rate; the establishment of a good school and a substantial church building; the erection of adjoining homes for those who will have the work in charge.

The conduct of affairs has been in charge of the following officials: Bishop Rondthaler, James E. Hall, J. W. Fries, C. T. Pfohl, W. T. Vogler, E. F. Strickland, and J. K. Pfohl. Their zeal is equal to that of the Moravians in the early days of Wachovia. They have done their work well. The money left by Clemmons has been used as he wished it to be. The sum left is generous, but it requires careful management to carry out his will. Every dollar in the hands of this committee seems to have gained three times the result it would have gained in the hands of many another committee. The site is ideal; the buildings erected thus far are both attractive and satisfactory; the church enrolment already shows 140 names; the young but excellent school has long since passed the one hundred mark; and the entire work forms one of the most encouraging features of this period, which is altogether so bright and promising.

CHAPTER XXXII

TWO CENTENNIALS

IN 1900 the Salem church building attained an age of one hundred years. It was decided to celebrate this event in a fitting manner, and during the weeks preceding the dates, committees were busy making preparations.

Friday morning, November 9, between eight and nine o'clock, the congregation gathered in the church. As the clock struck nine the assembly was notified that the old century had closed and a new century had begun, and voices and instruments blended in a happy thanksgiving hymn. The special feature was a strict adherence to the programme of the dedicatory exercises of a hundred years ago. The same form of service was followed, the same Scripture passages were read, the same hymns were sung, the same tunes used. The record of the consecration service of 1800 was communicated to the audience. The weather was cold, the time early, yet the church was filled and the hour was very impressive.

Friday night was given to the reading of papers on the subject of "Woman's Work during the Century," and these papers have been published in the *Wachovia Moravian* and the *Academy*.

Saturday, November 10, the service in the evening was given to the young people's work in the congregation. It was found that there are more than a score of active societies. The "one minute reports" were listened to with marked attention as they set forth the various lines of work.

Centennial Sunday presented a full programme. The weather was not promising in the morning, but the sun made all things bright before the day was done. The pastor, Bishop Rondthaler, preached the centennial sermon, the text being, "O Lord, thou hast been our dwelling-place in all generations." The sermon has been printed in full in the *Wachovia Moravian*.

The love-feast brought together a large congregation. The auditorium was filled, the galleries, the rooms front and back; all together more than a thousand people were served.

In this meeting were read greetings from the various boards in this and other lands; also a paper giving an account of the love-feast and Communion of one hundred years ago.

The Holy Communion followed the love-feast, and the pastor, Bishop Rondthaler, was assisted by the ministers, Hall, Clewell, Thaeler, and H. Rondthaler. There were present many communicant members of other churches.

In the evening the closing service partook of the nature of a Sunday-school rally. The attendance surpassed that of all the other meetings. More than twelve hundred people were within the walls of the church. The names of the various Sunday-schools of the Province were called, and the members of the schools responded by rising in the audience. It was found that all the Sunday-schools were represented.

The plans for the celebration had in view more permanent blessings than those which were connected with the exercises of the three days. It was proposed to establish memorials to signalize the happy event. Hence committees were appointed to devise preliminary measures for improving the surroundings of the graveyard, for adding wider facilities to the Salem Boys' School, and for providing permanent endowment for Salem Academy and College. These plans were discussed and enlarged during the following weeks, and finally resulted in the selection of a committee of eight members, representing a Centennial Society, the latter made up of all those who contributed any sum to any of the funds.

The committee has done a very important work during the nearly two years since the centennial celebration. A stone wall has been built of huge granite blocks, on the west and north sides of the graveyard and avenue, at a cost (when completed) of $3000. A thousand dollars has been secured to strengthen and improve the Salem Boys' School. An equal sum has been raised for the Academy, and with it improvements have been added, the committee working with the school authorities to assist particularly in those things which were needed, but which would probably not have been undertaken by the trustees without this special outside interest. Of as much, or even more, importance is the influence the committee has had in enlisting the special support of the community in the work of the Academy.

Before leaving the subject of the celebration of the centennial of the Salem church we will allude to the decorations. The *Wachovia Moravian* of December, 1900, gives the following description of the tasty and elaborate work done inside and outside the venerable building : —

"Clustered about the pulpit and lower platform were eight tall and graceful Gothic arches, rising well toward the ceiling, and covered with cedar and laurel. Cedar festoons draped the gallery front and pillars, while from the central chandelier broad folds of the Moravian colours (red and white) were swung to various portions of the church. Studding the arches, like diamond points, were lines of tiny electric lights, half hidden in the foliage. Suspended in the arches, in letters of red and white, were festal texts of special appropriateness to the occasion.

"For the first time the exterior of the church was electrically decorated; lines of coloured lights depending from the belfry made brilliant the scene, and the old belfry itself shone out with the two sets of figures, indicating the beginning of the first and of the second century. The electrical decorations were a beautiful feature of the celebration."

The second centennial to which allusion is made by the heading of the chapter is still a future event. It is that of the Salem Female Academy, or, as it is sometimes called since the introduction of the collegiate department, Salem Academy and College. October 31 of this year, 1902, the full century since the calling of the first principal will be rounded out. The friends in Winston-Salem and the pupils all over the country have decided to signalize the event in a proper manner, by a week of festivities, and in other ways. This event will be celebrated about a month after the publication of this "History of Wachovia," hence what is said will be based upon the plans which are under discussion, and will not be a history of the event itself.

Preliminary work leading up to this celebration has been done during the past years. It appears directly or indirectly, in many ways. The work of the Alumnæ Association has always had this in view. So too the gifts of the class memorials showed the same spirit of permanent interest in the school home. These memorials have been erected or are being prepared, and we note the Vance window, the organ, the granite entrance to the park, the iron grillwork entrance north of Main Hall, the proposed electric chandelier, the bust of Comenius, the chairs, the painting, the Emma Moore memorial.

The plans of the committees as they have been developed in March, 1902, for the celebration are as follows: —

The evenings of May 22 to 24 will treat of historical subjects, school and general. Essays will be read by the graduating class, bearing upon these topics, and addresses will be made by distinguished men. The music is being prepared with the greatest care, and a number of the successful musicians, pupils and teachers, of former days will unite with the present musical portion of the school, and to this will be added the local talent. All together the music promises to be a special feature of the centennial celebration.

Sunday will be the day for the centennial sermon.

Monday will be Senior Class day, with the grand concert in the evening.

Tuesday will be a day for receptions, class reunions, art exhibits, and at night a series of historical tableaux in front of Main Hall.

Wednesday will be given over to the alumnæ. It is proposed to give a banquet, and at night to have a special programme to commemorate the great work done by the school in sheltering and protecting so many young people during the Civil War.

Thursday morning, May 29, the diplomas will be presented to the graduates, and the corner-stone of the Cen-

SALEM ACADEMY AND COLLEGE

tennial Memorial building will be laid, and there will be addresses by a number of the distinguished visitors.

The lot selected for the Alumnæ Centennial Memorial building is the one in front of the Salem church, now occupied by the principal's house. If the present general plans are carried out, the building will provide for the accommodation of two thousand people.

Whether the plans develop as expected, or whether modifications will be introduced, will be known soon after the publication of this book; in fact the publication has been hastened in order that it could be used in connection with this occasion, so that, in one sense, " History of Wachovia in North Carolina " may be considered as associated with the centennial celebration of Salem Female Academy.

CHAPTER XXXIII

THE MORAVIAN CHURCH IN WACHOVIA AS IT IS TO-DAY

1902

As we conclude our historical review of a century and a half we naturally ask, " What is the condition of the Moravian Church after the lapse of these many years; what relation does it bear to the world about it; what is its special call at this time; and what are its prospects for the future?"

We believe the best reply to this question will be to institute a comparison between the two periods, then and now, and when this has been done the deductions will not be difficult.

The honest comparison shows well for the church of to-day.

The church is true to the cause of the Master in all the details of life.

The spirit of its members is the spirit which shines in the life of the Prince of Peace.

As faithful stewards of the talents intrusted to them the members believe that to the talents given, other talents should be added: they believe this is true in the professional life, in the business life, in the humblest calling; and by following this pathway the scope of the responsibilities are being widened and increased in our day.

"Feed my lambs" was the command of the Master to his disciples, and the church in Wachovia to-day finds that

THE MORAVIAN CHURCH TO-DAY

it has more young people under its care than was the case a generation ago.

" Preach the Gospel " is another great command, and this is being done with zeal and success and to the salvation of many souls.

The past is sometimes emphasized at the expense of the present. This is an error. The true student will find that the day of enlarged work for the Master is now dawning for the Moravian Church of Wachovia. Its pure doctrine, its beautiful customs, its inspiring history, its successes in the past and in the present, its consecrated ministry, its devoted membership; all these things point forward to a bright and successful future which will not only bring bright jewels of success to the church here on earth, but will gain for it the smile of approval of the King of kings and the Lord of lords.

PART II

THE DOCTRINAL POSITION OF THE MORAVIAN CHURCH

HISTORICAL SKETCH OF THE MORAVIAN CHURCH

BIOGRAPHICAL SKETCH OF THE PRINCIPALS OF THE SALEM FEMALE ACADEMY

LISTS AND STATISTICS

THE DOCTRINAL POSITION OF THE MORAVIAN CHURCH

BY RT. REV. EDWARD RONDTHALER, D.D.

THE Church of the Unitas Fratrum, or the Moravian Church, as it is usually called, separated itself at a very early date from the Romish Communion. It was in the ten years between 1457 and 1467 that this separation was consummated. The reasons for the establishment of the Unitas Fratrum so long before the Lutheran, Reformed, and Anglican churches came into being, were not, in the main, doctrinal ones. Our fathers were, by no means, so widely separated at first from the Romish creed as was afterward the case with them and the other Protestant churches. The question of pure, earnest, and united Christian living was what pressed heavily on the consciences of these Moravians. We see this very distinctly in the first document of the Moravian Church, still extant, "The Statutes agreed upon by the Brethren in the Mountains of Reichenau, 1464." In this venerable paper the stress is laid on Scriptural obedience, kindness toward one another, mutual encouragement, good Christian example, charity toward the orphan, the widow, and the destitute, correctness of conduct between masters and servants, and honesty in business dealings.

But it turned out as the Saviour said (John 7 : 17), "If any man will do his will he shall know of the doctrine." Each of the published Confessions of the young

Unitas Fratrum became clearer, more Scriptural, and more evangelical. At the same time their freedom from any original doctrinal bias enabled them more readily to appropriate light from whatever quarter it might reach them. Because they were always seeking for a better Christian life and only using doctrine as a help toward this, their main end, they were not ashamed to acknowledge the greater clearness which had come to them on the subject of justification, through the teachings of Martin Luther, and their equal indebtedness to the Reformers at Strasburg and Geneva, with whom they stood in the most intimate and fraternal relations.

When after the wonderful and gracious renewal of the Moravian Church, in the early part of the eighteenth century, the brethren were brought into Providential connection with Zinzendorf and his friends, the same spirit manifested itself among them as had been shown by their spiritual fathers in old Moravia and Bohemia. Christian life was their first consideration, and its doctrinal expression took the second place. In the former respect, they did not allow Zinzendorf to divert them from their standpoint, and make Lutherans out of them. On the contrary they stoutly declared, even to him, their self-denying patron, that they already were exiles on account of their faith, and would wander still farther on into the wide world, if he could not reconcile himself to the Moravian Church and its apostolic practices. But when Zinzendorf yielded generously to their Moravian principles of Christian life they very heartily allowed themselves to be influenced by his doctrinal views. Sometimes, indeed, as a poet-theologian, he led them into vagaries for which both they and he were afterward sorry. But these divergencies were unessential and temporary. The main drift of his teaching was sound and salutary. It is contained in his famous dictum, "I have but one passion and that is Christ." It is set forth in his stanza which is sung both in our baptismal and in our burial service:—

> "The Saviour's blood and righteousness,
> My beauty is, my glorious dress,
> Thus well arrayed I need not fear
> When in his presence I appear."

The love of a sin-forgiving Saviour, through Zinzendorf's influence, became the centre of Moravian practice and the light in which its doctrines and regulations were understood and interpreted. From this point of view they could cordially accept the Augsburg Confession, and, with equal cordiality, the confessions of the Reformed churches. The main thing with these Moravians was to cling to Christ and to enjoy the power of his atonement, and both these truths they found in what they called the Lutheran trope (or manner) and the Reformed trope, to either of which a Moravian may attach himself to this day.

The Zinzendorfian view of the Saviour's love has pervaded the school training for which the church is famous both in the Old and the New World. It centres around the question, "My child, do you love the Saviour?" and from this point of view are settled the various problems that arise in school ethics.

With the same message the Moravians have gone confidently to the most degraded heathen. Beside the Indian who a few minutes before had tried to drive his axe into Zeisberger's brain, the missionary sat calmly down and told him, "God loves you and has died to save you from your sins," and then and there won him for the Lord Jesus Christ.

The Moravians, therefore, were and still remain profoundly grateful to Count Zinzendorf for his spiritual guidance. It transfused their old and somewhat sombre Christian ethics with the genial light of a Saviour's love, so that the merest child or the most ungifted heathen could simply and happily respond to the teaching and blend his doctrine and his ethics in the one statement of our Lord, "If ye love me, keep my commandments."

With this central position firmly established, and made paramount, Moravians could gradually, if not at once, shake off any minor eccentricities into which Zinzendorf or others might have persuaded them. This was done most effectually in the treatise published by Zinzendorf's spiritual successor, the learned, devout, and intensely practical Bishop Spangenberg, the chief founder of the Moravian Church in America, and especially of its Wachovian district in North Carolina. His work was issued in 1778, and is called "Idea Fidei Fratrum" (Abstract of the Faith of the Brethren), and which, without special enactment of the church, is still regarded by Moravians as the best exposition of their doctrine.

The Moravian Church, throughout the world, is governed, in the last instance, by the General Synod, which convenes once in ten years. One of the chief duties of this representative body is to watch over the doctrine of the church. The last utterance which the General Synod made upon the doctrine was in 1879. This statement has been unanimously reasserted by the General Synods of 1889 and 1899. It is contained in Sections 5, 6, 7, 8, and 9 of Chapter 2, "Synodal Results."

We make the following quotations: —

"The Holy Scriptures of the Old and New Testaments

DOCTRINAL POSITION OF CHURCH

are and shall remain our only rule of faith and practice. We venerate them as God's Word, which he spake to all mankind of old time in the prophets, and at last in his Son and by his Apostles, to instruct us unto salvation, through faith in Christ Jesus. We are convinced that all truths that declare the will of God for our salvation are fully contained therein."

"The Standard of Doctrine," Chapter 2, Section 5, "Synodal Results of 1899":—

"We esteem every truth revealed by God as a precious treasure, and sincerely believe that such a treasure dare not be let go, even though we thereby save our body or our life (Luke 9:24). But most especially do we affirm this of that doctrine which the Renewed Church has from the beginning regarded as her chief doctrine, and over which she has hitherto, by God's grace, kept guard as a priceless jewel, 'That Jesus Christ is the propitiation for our sins; and not for ours only, but also for the whole world' (1 John 2:2). For 'Him who knew no sin God made to be sin on our behalf; that we might become the righteousness of God in Him' (2 Cor. 5:21), or, as we sing in one of our hymns:—

> "'Whosoever believeth in Christ's redemption,
> Will find free grace and a complete exemption
> From serving sin.'"

With this our leading doctrine, the following facts and truths, clearly attested by Holy Scripture, are linked in essential connection, and therefore constitute, with that leading doctrine, the main features in our view and proclamation of the way of salvation:—

(*a*) The doctrine of the total depravity of human nature,

that since the fall, there is no health in man, and that he has no strength to save himself (John 3 : 6; Rom. 3 : 23; 7 : 18; 1 : 18–32; 3 : 9–18; Eph. 2 : 8–13).

(*b*) The doctrine of the love of God the Father, who "has chosen us in Christ before the foundation of the world," "so loved the world that he gave his only begotten Son, that whosoever believeth on Him, should not perish but have everlasting life" (John 3 : 16; Eph. 1 : 3, 4; 1 John 4 : 9; Eph. 2 : 4).

(*c*) The doctrine of the real Godhead and the real humanity of Jesus Christ, that the only begotten Son of God, by whom all things in heaven and earth were created, forsook the glory which He had with His Father, before the world was, and took on Him our flesh and blood, that He might be made like unto His brethren in all things, yet without sin (John 1 : 1–3, 14; John 17 : 5; 1 John 5 : 20; Col. 1 : 17–19; Phil. 2 : 6, 7; Heb. 2 : 14, 17; 4 : 15).

(*d*) The doctrine of our Reconciliation unto God and our Justification before Him through the sacrifice of Jesus Christ, that "Christ was delivered for our offences, and was raised for justification," and that by faith in Him alone, we obtain through His blood forgiveness of sin, peace with God, and freedom from the bondage of sin (Rom. 3 : 24, 25; 5 : 1; 1 Cor. 1 : 30; Heb. 2 : 17; 9 : 12; 1 Peter 1 : 18, 19; 1 John 1 : 9; 2 Cor. 5 : 18, 19).

(*e*) The doctrine of the Holy Ghost and the operations of His Grace, that without Him we are unable to know the truth; that it is He that leads us to Christ by working in us the knowledge of sin and faith in Jesus, and "who beareth witness with our spirit that we are the children of God" (John 16 : 8–11, 13, 14; 1 Cor. 12 : 3; Rom. 8 : 16).

(*f*) The doctrine of Good Works as the fruit of the Spirit, inasmuch as faith manifests itself as a living and

DOCTRINAL POSITION OF CHURCH

active principle, by a willing obedience to the commandments of God, prompted by love and gratitude to Him who died for us (John 14 : 15; Rom. 6 : 11–14; 1 Cor. 6 : 20; Gal. 5 : 6, 22–24; 1 John 5 : 3–5; Eph. 2 : 8–10; James 2 : 17).

(*g*) The doctrine of the fellowship of believers one with another in Christ Jesus, that they are all one in Him who is the Head of the body, and all members one of another (John 17 : 21; Matt. 23 : 8; Eph. 4 : 4).

(*h*) The doctrine of the Second Coming of the Lord in glory, and of the Resurrection of the Dead unto life, or unto condemnation (Acts 1 : 11; John 6 : 40; 11 : 25, 26; 3 : 36; 5 : 25–29; 2 Thes. 4 : 14–17).

These truths and our adherence to them we do not hold as a rigidly formulated confession, but as our conception of the main contents of Christian doctrine, as it has found expression especially in that body of truth which our church has professed to hold for more than one hundred years, when annually praying the Easter Morning Litany ("The Chief Substance of our Doctrine," Chapter 2, Section 7, "Synodal Results of 1899").

THE MORAVIAN CHURCH

BY ADELAIDE L. FRIES

THE Moravian Church — Unitas Fratrum — is an ancient Episcopal church, antedating the German Reformation by more than half a century. During the years from 1402 to 1415, the kingdom of Bohemia was stirred from end to end by the earnest and eloquent preaching of John Hus, a native of the village of Husinec, Professor in the University of Prague, and pastor of the Bethlehem Chapel of that city. When he had sealed his faith with a martyr's death, the nationalists of Bohemia could be held in check no longer, and took up arms in a violent protest against the tyranny of Rome. But the revolutionists were not at one among themselves, the Taborites demanding a thorough reformation of the church and clergy, while the Calixtines sought little more than the recognition of a Bohemian National Church and the restoration of the Cup to the laity in the Lord's Supper. In the struggle that ensued the Taborites were completely crushed, while the Calixtines, in a large measure, attained their end. Many, however, felt that the conflict had come to be mainly a political one, and that the principles of Hus were as far as ever from general acceptance. In 1456, therefore, a company of these more spiritually minded men gathered on the estate of Lititz, about eighty miles from Prague, their object being to found a society, within the National Church, which should carry out the reformation begun by Hus, accepting the Bible as their standard of faith and

THE MORAVIAN CHURCH 309

practice, and maintaining a strict Scriptural discipline. This society assumed the name of Unitas Fratrum — the Unity of Brethren. It was carefully organized, and a body of principles, adopted by a general convocation in 1464, is still preserved in the Lissa Folios.

But the Unitas Fratrum could not long remain simply a society within a church from which it differed on many radical points, and after much consultation and prayer it was resolved to separate altogether from the National Church; and that there might be no question as to the validity of the ordination of their ministers, they resolved to secure the apostolic succession. At that time there was a colony of Waldensians living on the borders of Moravia, which had been on very friendly terms with the Calixtines during the Hussite War, and had renewed its ministry through them when it was in danger of dying out. In 1434 two Waldensian priests, ordained the preceding year by Bishop Nicholas, in Prague, had been sent to the Council of Basle, and were there consecrated bishops by bishops of the Roman Catholic Church. To these Waldensians the Unitas Fratrum turned, and finding two surviving bishops who were favorably disposed toward them, the deputation of three priests received the episcopate at their hands, with power to transmit it to their church.

The sources from which the Unitas Fratrum drew its membership were strangely varied. There were Calixtines and Taborites, priests ordained in the National Church, and others from the Church of Rome, noblemen, Masters of Arts, and "men of humble origin," and that this composite mass should have been welded into one harmonious whole argues much for the needs of the time, and the soundness of the Unity's doctrine.

Gathering strength by large accessions from every part

of Bohemia and Moravia, and spreading into Prussia and Poland under the influence of various sharp persecutions, the Unitas Fratrum came to be an important factor in the national as well as the religious life of these kingdoms. Schools were established in all their numerous parishes, with several higher institutions of learning and theological seminaries; their printing-presses were used with diligence for the dissemination of evangelical truth; a translation of the Bible into the Bohemian language was undertaken, and after fifteen years of labor the so-called "Kralitz" Bible — still the authorized version in Bohemia — was given to the public. A Catechism, Hymn Book, nine successive Confessions of Faith, and many other theological works were published. When Luther, Calvin, and the other Reformers of the sixteenth century became prominent, the Unitas Fratrum established pleasant and mutually beneficial intercourse with them. The Unity had more than four hundred churches in Bohemia and Moravia alone, where its ministers preached the Word to a membership of not less than one hundred and fifty thousand souls; and when, in 1609, the Emperor Rudolf II was forced to confirm the liberties of the evangelical party, "the Unitas Fratrum became a legally acknowledged church of the land, held as its own the Bethlehem Chapel at Prague, where John Hus, its forerunner, had proclaimed the Gospel, and had a bishop associated with the administrator of the Evangelical Consistory."

And then, when the Unitas Fratrum had reached a position of prosperity and widespread influence, there came a sudden and disastrous fall. The succession to the crown of Bohemia fell on Ferdinand of Tyrol, a bigoted Romanist; the evangelical party attempted to set him aside, and elected Frederick of the Palatinate, a Protestant, as their

THE MORAVIAN CHURCH

king. Obliged to defend their action on the field of battle, they met with a crushing defeat, and Ferdinand, with the Jesuits, set his heel upon Bohemia and Moravia. All Protestant churches and schools were forcibly closed, or given to the Jesuits, all the ministers of the Unitas Fratrum, Lutherans and Reformed, were ordered to leave the country in eight days. Then, after a cessation of pressure had lulled the people into a hope that the worst was over, suddenly and by craft a number of the most prominent members of the evangelical party were seized, tried, and condemned to imprisonment, torture, or death. On the 21st of June, 1621, — "the day of blood," — twenty-seven noblemen, many of whom belonged to the Unity of Brethren, met death on the scaffold; and by 1627 the Bohemian-Moravian branch of the Unitas Fratrum had apparently ceased to exist. The Polish branch continued longer, but was gradually absorbed by the Reformed Church of Poland.

The period which followed this blotting out of the Unity is often called the time of the "Hidden Seed." Here and there throughout the two kingdoms there were whole families, nominally yielding obedience to the Romish authorities, but secretly holding fast the faith and practice of the Brethren's Unity, and speaking to their children of a day which they believed was yet to come, when the Unitas Fratrum would again lift up its head among the churches. And for the preservation of the doctrine and rules of the Ancient Church, and the perpetuation of its organization, there was raised up a man, who not only made possible the resurrection of the Unitas Fratrum, but whose scholarly attainments and progressive spirit won him recognition as the foremost educator of his day, while later generations honor him as the originator of modern methods of teaching. John Amos Comenius was born March 28, 1592, in Moravia, the child of wealthy members of the Unitas Fratrum. Having finished his education, he entered into the service of that church as minister, and rector of the school at Prerau. When the downfall came, he joined the other exiles, and took up his abode in Lissa, Poland, where he was consecrated bishop in 1632. The publication of several works on education won him instant appreciation abroad, and he received numerous invitations to go to various countries, reorganize the schools, and establish colleges. Some of these invitations he accepted, others he declined, among the latter being the offer of the presidency of Harvard College in Massachusetts. But always and ever his church was his first consideration, and even when things looked utterly hopeless he prophesied its restoration. He republished the "Ratio Disciplinæ Ordinisque Ecclesiastici in Unitate Fratrum Bohemorum," by which the Renewed Church was modelled more than half a century later; and lest the episcopate be lost he took measures for the consecration of two new bishops, by whom the succession was carefully preserved until it was transferred to the Renewed Church at Herrnhut.

Fifty years after the eyes of Comenius were closed in death, the things for which he had longed and labored began to come to pass. And here again, as in the first founding of the Unitas Fratrum, there was no preconceived plan, no concerted action, but the agents were, so to speak, led blindfold to the task assigned them. On the estate of Hennersdorf, in Upper Lusatia, in Saxony, on the 26th of May, 1700, Nicholas Lewis, Count Zinzendorf, was born. Brought up by his pious grandmother, he early gave his heart to the Lord Jesus, and as he grew to manhood his one desire was to serve Him. On attaining his majority, the Count purchased the estate of Berthelsdorf, not far from Hennersdorf, installed Andrew Rothe, a devoted young Lutheran clergyman, as parish minister, and a few months later married Erdmuth Dorothea, Countess Reuss, who proved to be a consecrated and efficient helpmeet for him. About this time, through Rothe's suggestion, Zinzendorf had an interview with Christian David, a native of Moravia and a carpenter by trade, who had been born a Roman Catholic, but after much agony and long searching had found peace in the Protestant faith and had united with the Lutheran Church in Germany. Inspired with a longing to take back to his benighted countrymen the light that he had received, Christian David had made a number of visits to Moravia, and had formed an acquaintance with the Neissers, descendants of warm adherents of the ancient Unity of Brethren. The Neissers, and others with them, were very anxious to find a home in some Protestant country where they might have religious liberty, and Zinzendorf promised to try to find them a suitable place, meanwhile to receive them on his estate of Berthelsdorf.

Armed with this assurance Christian David returned to Moravia, and on the 27th of May, 1722, led the first body of emigrants across the border. Zinzendorf was not at home when they reached Berthelsdorf, but his steward allowed them to begin a little village a mile or so away. For some time the young nobleman paid little attention to them; but as their numbers increased by more arrivals from Moravia and Bohemia, and by Protestants from various other points, his notice was attracted to the pitiable religious tangle into which the settlement was growing, and with characteristic zeal he set to work to help them. Having established certain rules, according to the traditions brought by the Moravian descendants of the Unitas

Fratrum, harmony was gained, and soon after, to the great joy of the emigrants, the Count found a copy of the "Ratio Disciplinæ" published by Comenius, and the ancient discipline was fully restored. On August 13, 1727, in connection with the Lord's Supper, the Holy Spirit was poured out upon the communicants in an especial manner, the day being celebrated ever since as the birthday of the Renewed Church, now often called "Moravian," because so many members were from Moravia. For several years longer the settlement at Herrnhut remained nominally a part of the Lutheran Church, Zinzendorf himself accepting ordination as a Lutheran clergyman, that he might the better serve them. At last, however, he was forced to admit that the Lord intended the full restoration of the Unitas Fratrum as a separate church, and on March 13, 1735, David Nitchmann was consecrated the first bishop of the Renewed Church by the two surviving bishops of the ancient succession.

The history of the Renewed Church was not one of undimmed prosperity. Time and again the hand of opposition, even of persecution, was raised against it, but always with the effect of making it more widely and favorably known.

In 1732 the characteristic work of the Unitas Fratrum was undertaken — the work of foreign missions. While on a visit to Copenhagen, Zinzendorf became greatly impressed with the needs of the negroes in the West Indies, and the Esquimaux in Greenland. On his return he told the congregation of Herrnhut what he had heard, and their hearts, already fired with desire for some special service of God, rose in ready response. On the 8th of October two of them set sail for St. Thomas, ready to sell themselves as slaves if they could gain access to the slaves in no other way, and the next year missionaries to the Esquimaux were sent out.

In 1735 a settlement of Moravians was begun in Savannah, Georgia, being the first on the American continent. The intention was to establish a retreat in case of persecution in Germany, and a centre from which to reach the Indians. Owing to various causes the colony was broken up within a few years, but in 1741 a permanent organization was effected in Bethlehem, Pennsylvania, and from there missionaries were sent among the Indians; and in the course of years the church spread into other sections of the country. That the Moravian Church in America did not increase numerically as rapidly as might have been expected was owing to Zinzendorf's peculiar tenet that the business of the Unity was to preach Christ and convert the souls of men, but receive them into the Unitas Fratrum only when it could not well be avoided. This theory had good ground in Germany, where proselyting would have aroused a fierce antagonism from the State Church, but was a mistake in America, where the extension of a thoroughly organized church would have been a great boon to the scattered, un-shepherded members of many sects.

In 1742 the first British congregation was formally organized, though the church had been practically established in England for several years previously.

These three, the German, American, and English, now (1902) constitute the "Home Provinces" of the Unitas Fratrum or Moravian Church, with a membership respectively of 7734, 23,467, 5955. In America, within the past few years, the Moravian Church has radically changed its position as to Zinzendorf's theory of exclusiveness, and has recognized that, when properly guided, church extension is an essential of church life. In Germany, on the other hand, there is the peculiar service of the "Diaspora," whereby some 70,000 Lutherans, members of the State Church, are formed into "Societies" cared for by Moravian ministers, and giving the Moravian Church their interest and their pecuniary aid. It is largely owing to these Diaspora associates that the Unitas Fratrum has been able to carry on a mission work so out of all proportion to its size and means. Men and women willing to devote their lives to Christ's service the Unity has always had, but were it not for the liberality of these and other friends, it could never have gained or held its enviable position as the foremost missionary church in Christendom. To-day there are Moravian missions in Labrador and Alaska, among the North American Indians, in the West Indies, Central and South America, South and East Africa, Australia, and the Himalaya Mountains, with a membership of 96,877. Mission work has also been carried on for a number of years in the old home land of Bohemia and Moravia; and the Unity maintains a home for lepers at Jerusalem. Including all who belong to the Moravian Church or its "Societies," the Unitas Fratrum now numbers about 205,565 souls, representing all portions of the globe and races of men, differing each from each in every possible way except a common love for Christ, and the "unity of brethren."

BIOGRAPHICAL SKETCH OF THE PRINCIPALS OF SALEM FEMALE ACADEMY

BY MISS LEHMAN

Rev. Samuel Kramsch

As we look upon the portraits of the eleven principals who have guided Salem Female Academy and College, during one hundred years, we are struck by the strongly marked individuality of each face, each one in turn, to a certain extent, leaving the stamp of his individuality upon the school during his term of office; yet the Academy during all these years has formulated a character, an individuality, all her own, independent of what one man might do or not do. As one after the other passes from the scene of action, we realize more strongly than ever that "the Lord buries his workmen, but his work goes on."

On October 31, 1802, still celebrated as founder's day, a call was extended by the governing board of the Southern Province to Rev. Samuel Kramsch, then pastor of Hope, North Carolina, to take charge of Salem Female Academy, a new educational enterprise, the first in the South, and the third in America for the higher education of young women and girls. Rev. Mr. Kramsch was a native of Silesia, Prussia, born in 1758, the son of a Lutheran minister, who died leaving a large family, when this boy was still a child. He was sent to Gnadenberg, to a Moravian school, to be educated, where he was for seven years a diligent student, especially in the languages. Like his father he wished to become a minister, and later cheerfully accepted a call to America to become principal of a boys' school in Bethlehem, in Pennsylvania, landing at Philadelphia in 1783. He also taught at Nazareth Hall, being specially fitted for educational work. In 1792 he received a call to North Carolina, and married Susanna Elizabeth Langgaard, daughter of Rev. A. Langgaard, a professor in Bethlehem Seminary. His first charge was that of Hope, North Carolina, from which he was called to be the first principal of the Academy.

He was well educated, a fine linguist, an accomplished botanist and artist. His gifted wife, well acquainted with the internal economy of the best boarding-schools of the day, also brought all her talents to the work. Former pupils who have passed away often referred in their letters to the delightful walks of those early days, when rare wild flowers still abounded, and Mr. and Mrs. Kramsch strove to implant some of their botanical enthusiasm in the forming minds of their charges. On one of these walks, just beyond the Salem limits, where Winston now stands, the girls surprised two little fawns, caught one of them in an apron, brought it home, and took great pleasure in their pet until later, like most pets, it became unmanageable, and had to be killed. Both of Mr. Kramsch's daughters, talented women, became teachers in the Academy; the elder eventually became Mrs. Judge Blickensderfer, of Ohio, and the younger married Rev. Charles A. Van Vleck, of Salem. In 1806 Mr. Kramsch retired from the service of the Academy, and after a short residence in town returned to the pastorate of Hope. Here a great cross was laid upon him in approaching blindness, and though kept in abeyance by noted oculists, he at length

SKETCH OF PRINCIPALS OF ACADEMY

became totally blind. Returning to Salem, he died here in 1824, being a little over 67 years old, and lies buried in the Salem graveyard.

Rev. Abraham Steiner

The decade in the history of the Academy from 1806 to 1816 was a time of changes and improvements of different kinds. Bishop Reichel, the power behind the throne, administered the affairs in the interval between Mr. Kramsch's retirement, and the installation of Rev. Abraham Steiner, the Academy's second principal. Mr. Steiner lived at the corner of Academy and Main streets, north of the Widows' House, until a new house was built for him, the one at present occupied as Principal's House. The number of pupils increased so that a third room was opened in 1807, and a fourth in 1811. There was still not room enough in the Academy buildings, so a number of pupils lodged in private families in town, which arrangement continued some years until more house room was gained by additions to the old buildings.

Mr. Steiner was born in Bethlehem in 1758, and educated in Nazareth, where he spoke with great affection of the faithful teaching of Rev. Paul Tiersch, later the first minister of Salem. He went to Bethlehem, after he had attained his majority, and was soon employed as teacher in the Boys' Day School. Then he was called to Hope, New Jersey, to take charge of the church store for several years.

Mr. Steiner had from childhood been greatly interested in the Indians, so to his great joy he was allowed to accompany Rev. J. Heckewelder, the Moravian Apostle to the Indians, on a missionary tour along the Muskingum, in 1789. After this, Mr. Steiner was called to Bethabara, North Carolina, to take charge of the church store there. Arriving in Salem in 1789 he married his first wife, Christina Fisher, who died after a short married life of sixteen months; his second wife, Catherine Sehner, was also of Salem. They had four children, one son and three daughters. One of the daughters was one of the first pupils of the Academy, and later served as teacher before her marriage to Rev. C. F. Denke, and again did faithful service for twenty years in her widowhood, as teacher of the select class.

In 1799 a society was formed to reach the southern Indians, the Creeks and Cherokees, and Rev. Frederick Christian de Schweinitz visited the Cherokee country; after a second visit, a mission was established at Spring Place, the name being retained when the missionaries and their flock removed to the Indian Territory. Mr. Steiner's health gave way and he returned to Salem, leaving the work to other hands. In 1801 he was ordained by Bishop Reichel and took charge of the congregation of Hope, North Carolina, from which place he was called to be principal of the Academy, a position which he filled with ability for ten years. His clear insight, good sense, and practical knowledge made his term of office a prosperous one. He was a man of marked individuality, with a decided vein of humor in his composition, that tempered what would otherwise have been brusqueness. He laid out a fine large garden, some little distance below the Academy on Church Street, as a place where the recreation hours of the girls could be spent. Each room company had a large space assigned, and each girl had her separate little plot, where she could experiment at will.

Mr. Steiner's health declining, he resigned his position

SKETCH OF PRINCIPALS OF ACADEMY

in 1816, but he still assisted in various capacities. In 1822 he began to attend to the negro congregation of Salem, and held the first sermon for some sixty hearers. He was active in important duties in church and community, wherever friendly or social offices were required. In 1829 his wife died; his own health slowly declined, dropsy of the heart set in, and in 1833 his active, laborious life drew to a close. He was seventy-five years of age, and, like his predecessor, lies buried here in Salem, under the cedars in our graveyard.

Rev. Gotthold Benjamin Reichel

The third principal of the Academy was a gifted, scholarly man, who filled the position for seventeen years. The early part of his administration was a time of prosperity, but later, when his health greatly declined, and a severe money pressure affected the country, the number of pupils was considerably reduced. In 1824 an addition was made to the Academy building; some schoolrooms and a chapel were built: this last being consecrated September 24 gave rise to the well-known Chapel Festival, which was kept up many years.

Mr. Reichel was born in Nazareth, Pennsylvania, and there educated. His father, Bishop Reichel, then minister at Nazareth, and principal of the Boys' Boarding School, was appointed in 1802 to succeed Rev. J. D. Koehler as minister of Salem, North Carolina. The son accompanied his parents and sister south, two brothers being absent in Europe. It was largely owing to the influence and educational zeal of Bishop Reichel, the father, that the Academy was founded, and members of his family were identified with it for many years. When young Mr.

Reichel first came to Salem, he assisted Mr. Dalman in the Boys' School, but soon took the entire charge. In 1811 he was ordained by Bishop Herbst, and was soon after married to Frederika Henrietta Vierling. In 1816 he became principal of the Academy; he was an accomplished scholar, a zealous botanist, tall in person, dignified in manner. He introduced new studies, himself teaching and training teachers. From 1819 to 1829 he was assistant pastor of the congregation in Salem, and from 1829 to 1833 had sole charge in addition to his other duties. In 1829 his wife died almost suddenly, leaving him in declining health with a family of seven children. In 1830, while on a visit to Bethlehem, he married again, Mary Parsons, the accomplished sister of his brother's wife. In 1833 he died, at the early age of 48, and, like his two predecessors, rests in the quiet Salem God's Acre.

Rev. John Christian Jacobson

Upon Mr. Reichel's death, near the close of 1833, Rev. John Christian Jacobson was appointed the fourth principal of the Academy. He had been minister of Bethania seven years, and early in January, 1834, he assumed the duties of the new position with a characteristic zeal and energy, which were crowned with success. The financial depression throughout the South was over, and a period of general prosperity followed. The number of pupils, which had been very small, ran up to 77 the first year, to 137 the second, until in 1838 the school numbered 195 boarders, and 19 teachers. More room was urgently demanded, so in 1835 a new chapel was built, a frame building on the east side of South Hall. It became necessary to take possession of one room after the other in the old congre-

SKETCH OF PRINCIPALS OF ACADEMY

gation house for school uses. One room company lived for a time in the present Widows' House. Accordingly, in 1841, the school built a new chapel for the congregation, and also a minister's house, the brick building now occupied by the bishop.

Mr. Jacobson was born in 1795 at Burkall, near Tondern, in the duchy of Schleswig, in Denmark. His father was a missionary in the Diaspora service, and soon afterward removed to the village of Skiern, on the west coast of Jutland, where the boy spent the first six years of his life. He was then placed in the church boarding-school at Christiansfeld, and after eight years was transferred to the higher school at Niesky. Having finished his theological course, his whole future was changed by a call which came as a great surprise, to go to America. In 1816 he entered Nazareth Hall, where as teacher and professor he spent the next ten years of his life. In 1826 he was married to Lisetta Schnall, and at the close of the year they came to their first charge, Bethania, North Carolina. In 1834 he assumed the duties of principal of the Academy, where his ability and scholarly training found an appropriate sphere. His ten years of labor were marked by the most gratifying upbuilding of the school.

In 1844 his academic labors were continued by a call to Nazareth Hall in Pennsylvania. He had seven children, one of whom, Mrs. Edward Rondthaler, is living in the house built by her father sixty years ago. In 1849 Mr. Jacobson was called to Bethlehem as a member of the Provincial Elders' Conference, over which board he presided eighteen years. During this time his history was closely identified with that of the church. His patience in counsel, his energy in protracted journeys, and his habits of thorough and systematic work, gave him fitness and acceptance in his high office.

In 1854 he was ordained bishop at Lititz, and in 1867, under the weight of old age, he retired from the active work of the church, after a service of nearly fifty-one years. The last three years of his life were beautiful in their restfulness; it was the calm, cheerful tarrying of the pilgrim in the land of Beulah, almost within sight and hearing of the other shore. His strength gradually declined, and on Thanksgiving afternoon of 1870 he received the summons to come home at the ripe age of seventy-five years.

Rev. Charles Adolphus Bleck

Mr. Bleck was duly installed as the fifth principal in 1844. He was born near Lebanon, Pennsylvania, in 1804, and at seven years of age he went to Nazareth Hall. Later he entered the theological class, and from 1823 to 1831 served as teacher in the Hall, and professor in the Seminary.

During the summer of 1832, the dreadful cholera year, he assisted the Rev. W. H. Van Vleck in the church service in New York. He married Sophia Krause of Bethlehem Seminary, and soon after moved to Camden Valley, Washington County, New York, where he organized a Moravian congregation, himself securing funds with which to build a church and parsonage. During a part of his residence there he instructed a class of young men and boys, who were for the time members of his household. In the autumn of 1838 Mr. Bleck moved to New York City, where he served as pastor till 1842, when the call to Salem, North Carolina, reached him. Once more he assisted Bishop W. H. Van Vleck, his particular duties

SKETCH OF PRINCIPALS OF ACADEMY 325

being to conduct services at several outposts, and to visit members living out of town.

In 1844 he assumed the position of principal of the Academy, where his financial abilities were marked. He taught the Latin and French classes in the school, but in the natural sciences he was in his element, and succeeded in arousing enthusiastic interest where many teachers find simple indifference. In March, 1846, Mrs. Bleck died, leaving six children; her duties were then assumed by her sister-in-law, Miss Caroline Bleck, who was known and loved by many. In the autumn of 1848 Mr. Bleck's second marriage took place, in Alabama, to Mary Harrison. Mr. Bleck was then superseded by Rev. Emil A. de Schweinitz, and early in 1849 he removed to Bethlehem, Pennsylvania. In August he was appointed to take charge of the congregation of Gnadenhutten and Sharon, Ohio. He died suddenly in Gnadenhutten, on January 17, 1850, aged about forty-six years, and was buried in the Moravian graveyard in the town made memorable by the Indian massacre of 1782. About the time that Mr. Bleck's term of office closed in the Academy, important changes were being considered in the outward affairs of Salem itself, but they were not brought about till some years later.

Rt. Rev. Emil Adolphus de Schweinitz

The Academy pursued the even tenor of its way without any special occurrences during the next term of five years, that of Rev. Emil A. de Schweinitz. He was born in Salem in 1816, and spent a large portion of his life here, so that he was thoroughly identified with the best interests of the town. His family is directly descended from Count Zinzendorf; Mr. de Schweinitz was on his father's side the great-great-grandson and oldest lineal descendant of Zinzendorf. His father, Rev. Lewis David de Schweinitz, in 1816 filled the office of administrator of the church estates, and was a member of the Provincial Board. He was likewise known as one of the foremost botanists of the age, and his collections have greatly enriched botanical science. It is not often that we find such a family where father and four sons are regularly ordained ministers. Two of the sons, Emil and Edmund, were bishops, Robert the well-known principal of the Academy of years ago, and the fourth, Bernard, died while on a visit to Salem, in the first flush of a promising manhood.

Bishop de Schweinitz received his early education at Nazareth Hall, and in Gnadenfeld, Germany. Returning to America, he taught in the Hall and in the Seminary, was ordained by Bishop Benade, and married Sophia, eldest daughter of the late Bishop Herman. Five of his eight children are living at the present time. In 1848 he returned to his native place, Salem, and took charge of the Academy, but in 1853 he was appointed to the same office which his father had previously held, that of administrator of the church estates and member of the Provincial Board. His work lay largely in the financial interests of the Southern Province in which his clear insight and sound judgment added much to the prosperity of the Province. Through the troubled times of the late Civil War, he was able faithfully to hold the trust committed to him. His special work was not originally that of preacher or pastor, but in later years he entered upon both, from a desire to work more especially for Christ.

In 1874 he was consecrated bishop here in Salem, by

SKETCH OF PRINCIPALS OF ACADEMY

Bishops Shultz, Bigler, and his brother, Edmund de Schweinitz. Though holding the highest office in the Province he chose the service of a small congregation, that of New Philadelphia, and was one of the warmest friends of the mission work of the colored church. His failing health led among other things to a European voyage, but he came home to die, in November, 1879, at the age of sixty-three years, having served the church forty-two years. He was one of the strong, powerful figures in the church in Wachovia during the middle of the past century, — a faithful, judicious leader in the church he loved.

Rev. Robert William de Schweinitz

The name of the seventh principal of the Academy awakens tender recollections in the hearts of our alumnæ all over the country. His death in the latter part of 1901 came with the force of a personal bereavement to hundreds of our middle-aged alumnæ, and his name is a household word in numberless families in our Southland.

Mr. de Schweinitz was born in Salem, North Carolina, September 20, 1819; his father, Rev. Lewis de Schweinitz, in 1821 removed with his family to Bethlehem, where the father died thirteen years later. In 1830 Mr. de Schweinitz entered Nazareth Hall, and later the Theological Seminary. When his course was completed, he spent six years as teacher in the Hall, and then set out on a visit to Europe. Here he met his life companion, and in 1846 he was married to Marie Louise von Tschirschky, at Herrnhut, Saxony. In November of the same year he returned to America with his bride, after a most unpleasant, stormy voyage, lasting from September to November. In 1847 he became a professor in the Theological Seminary, and later was ordained by Bishop Benade. He was thence called to a pastorate in Graceham, Maryland, and to Lancaster, Pennsylvania. In February, 1853, he assumed the position of principal of the Academy, by which he is best known among us. He was at the helm at a time which required more than ordinary ability and good judgment, and his genial, kindly manner attracted all those who came in personal contact with him. During his term of thirteen years the school was numerically more prosperous than ever before. Many changes were introduced. The old congregation house, which had been used exclusively by the school, was torn down, and in 1854 the corner-stone of our present Main Hall was laid, and its walls arose on the old site. The present Academy Chapel, the third, was also erected. Our fine park, which goes by the unpretentious name "playgrounds," was laid out at the same time.

Then came the Civil War, when it was no light task to feed, clothe, and protect two hundred and more pupils, in this establishment, many of them refugees from more exposed sections. While other institutions of learning were compelled to close their doors, the Academy went on, never suspending its work one single day during those years of trouble. When at length Stoneman's raiders approached Salem in April, 1865, Mr. de Schweinitz, with the mayor of Salem, and other influential citizens, went out to meet them, to surrender the town, and ask protection for the Academy, which was granted. Sentinels were posted to protect us from the stragglers that are always found in the rear, and while neighboring towns were plundered of everything worth taking,

SKETCH OF PRINCIPALS OF ACADEMY

not a single act of lawlessness occurred about the Academy premises.

In July, 1866, Mr. de Schweinitz accepted the principalship of Nazareth Hall, but this service was cut short by his election in 1867 as president of the Provincial Elders' Conference, which position he retained eleven years. He then removed to West Bethlehem, and though entitled by his long service to a place among retired ministers, he accepted one position of trust after another. Failing health at length led to the resignation of his various duties in 1899. In 1881 his wife died. He had six children, three sons and three daughters, of whom one, Bertha, preceded him to the heavenly land.

The Academy always held a warm place in his affections, and at the commencement of 1886 he paid a visit to his relatives and warm friends in Salem. His presence seemed to be a magnetic force in the organization of the Alumnæ Association, and held the members together in closer union. The feebleness of advancing age grew upon him, bowing his tall, commanding figure, and he became totally blind. After much suffering he fell asleep in Jesus October 29, 1901, aged eighty-two years.

Rev. Maximilian Eugene Grunert

The Academy's eighth principal took the school at a time when the prospect was gloomy; the war was just well over, there was little or no money in the country, and universal bankruptcy and ruin overspread the South. Then came the reconstruction period, when a struggle for existence absorbed the minds of all, and educational interests received little attention. The faithfulness and economy of Mr. Grunert enabled the school to continue when almost every other institution had to suspend. When things began to brighten up somewhat, the financial depression of 1873 came on, and all those difficulties had to be met.

Mr. Grunert was a ripe European scholar and deep thinker, trained in our best German schools. He was born at Niesky, April 26, 1826, his father being a merchant. Coming to this country as a young man, he filled different positions, being teacher of the boys' school in Salem for a time. He then accepted the pastorate of Bethania in 1851, to which he came with his first wife, daughter of the Rev. S. T. Pfohl, warden of the Salem congregation. Of the five children of this marriage, one daughter, Anna, died in childhood. In 1858 he removed to Salem, where he served in many capacities, professor in the Academy, assistant pastor, and assistant principal from 1858 to 1866. When Mr. de Schweinitz resigned, he accepted the office of principal, which he held till 1877, being closely connected with the school for twenty years.

It was during his term in 1873 that South Hall was renovated, its height increased, the old steep roof replaced by a modern one, until it became a fair companion for its imposing sister, Main Hall. He was married three times, his second wife, Maria Butner, of Bethania, dying while he was principal; his third marriage, in 1871, was to Martha Smythe, a teacher in Bethlehem Seminary, who survived him fourteen years.

When he left Salem, in 1877, he served as pastor of Emmaus, Pennsylvania, then professor in the Theological Seminary in Bethlehem, filling different positions till, in 1886, he retired from the service. He lived in Nazareth, where he died suddenly of apoplexy June 4, 1887. His work was always characterized by the utmost faithfulness, thoroughness, and conscientiousness.

Rev. Joseph Theophilus Zorn

With the accession of Mr. Zorn, in 1877, it became evident that the old order of things must give place to the new. The South was recovering from its desolating war; good schools were springing up everywhere. It was a transition time in business, in education, in every interest in life, and prepared the way for the advancement we see at the opening of the twentieth century.

Mr. Zorn came to his new office from the mission field of the West Indies. He was born at Fairfield, Jamaica, in 1841, of noted missionary parentage. After passing through Nazareth Hall and the Theological Seminary, he taught for a time at the Hall, and thence entered upon the mission work in Jamaica. Taking charge of the Academy, he inaugurated many changes; a course of graduation was laid out, and the Senior Class of 1878 was the first to receive diplomas, at the close of the regular graduating exercises. A course of musical graduation was also arranged; Professor Agthe, and later Professor d'Anna, completely revolutionized former systems, both in vocal and instrumental music. Many necessary changes were likewise made in material things. He placed the art department on a more assured footing, and established a handsome studio, as well as a large and commodious reading room, which has become such an important factor in the academy work.

In 1884 Mr. Zorn resigned, and going North with his wife and family of one son and three daughters, he was for a time associate principal of Nazareth Hall, with his brother-in-law, Rev. Eugene Leibert. Thence Mr. Zorn took charge of a boys' school near Saratoga, New York; having left the Moravian Church, he took orders as an Episcopal minister, and is now living in Ticonderoga, New York.

Rt. Rev. Edward Rondthaler, D.D.

In September, 1884, Dr. Rondthaler, pastor of the congregation of Salem, took up the work as the tenth principal of the Academy, when Mr. Zorn left. A strong sense of duty and the urgent needs of the case caused him to assume this responsibility, in addition to his other work. At the same time Rev. John H. Clewell was called from Ohio to become assistant principal, and with his family moved into the principal's house.

Dr. Rondthaler went to his work with characteristic energy and whole-heartedness. Necessary changes were made; class and dwelling rooms were separated; the classes were relegated to South Hall and other localities, while the dwelling rooms became cosey, homelike study parlors with carpets, lace curtains, pictures, easy chairs, and the many little touches that go to make up an inviting whole.

The dormitory arrangements were revolutionized: Dr. Rondthaler introduced the system of alcoves, nicely curtained, and so arranged as to solve the problem of privacy without isolation. Many other improvements were introduced, and in May, 1888, he thought he might hand over the office entirely to Mr. Clewell, and devote himself exclusively to his special work, the ministry. He had infused new life into every department of the school. Visiting New England centres of learning, such as Wellesley, Holyoke, and Smith, he detected what was best suited to us in them, and returning, by his strong personal influence he engrafted them into our system ; he likewise visited friends and patrons, all over the South, leaving a cheery *entente cordiale* wherever he went.

In 1880 the degree of Doctor of Divinity was bestowed upon him by the University of North Carolina. In 1891 he was consecrated Bishop of the Unity, by Bishops Levering, Bachman, and Van Vleck. Dr. Rondthaler was born at Schoeneck, Pennsylvania, in 1842, while his father, Rev. Edward Ronthaler, Sr., was pastor there. Educated in our northern schools, his intellect has been further cultivated by study in European universities and by travel, visiting noted places in Europe, while in 1889 he journeyed to Egypt and Palestine, where the steps of the Master's career were reverently studied. He was pastor first in Brooklyn, and later in Philadelphia, when the call to Salem was accepted in 1877, and now for a quarter of a century his influence has pervaded and guided the work of the whole Southern Province. Though no longer principal of the Academy, he is still an integral part of its life, both as president of the Board of Trustees, and superintendent of the linguistic department.

Mrs. Rondthaler, as the daughter of Bishop Jacobson, a former noted principal of the Academy, has a double claim upon the affectionate regard of the school.

Rev. John Henry Clewell, Ph.D.

The present incumbent and the eleventh principal of the Academy is a native of Salem, born in 1855. After passing through the Theological Seminary in Bethlehem, he taught in the Salem Boys' School one year, and later took a further course of study in Union Theological Seminary, New York City. In 1900 the Moravian College at Bethlehem conferred on him the degree of Doctor of Philosophy. He has travelled extensively in the West and South, going also to Europe in 1899, at our last General Synod. He has been a regular contributor to a number of periodicals, and is especially interested in the line of historical research.

His first pastorate was that of Urichsville and Port Washington, Ohio, where he raised a large sum of money for these church buildings. From thence he came to Salem as assistant principal in 1884, and in 1888 took entire charge of the work.

Mrs. Clewell is on one side a member of the Wolle family, notably known in our church history, while on the other side she is connected with the Lineback family of Salem. Her position has been made increasingly responsible and active in the school, by the Board of Trustees, and she has entered into the work more intimately than was the case in former administrations. Her faithful service and good taste have been specially noticeable in the various social occasions of late years, in which our outside friends have been brought into closer sympathy with the Academy and its work.

Dr. Clewell's term has been one of improvement and advancement; numerous large buildings have been erected, and older ones remodelled and beautified. In 1888 the number of pupils seemed to demand more room, so August 28 work was begun east of the church, and though Annex Hall did not go up like the Temple of old without the "sound of hammer or of axe," it arose with astonishing celerity, and was finished November 17 of the same year, and occupied by the 9th and 10th room companies. The

SKETCH OF PRINCIPALS OF ACADEMY 335

space under the dining room was converted into a gymnasium, and first used for an informal entertainment of the Euterpean Society December 9, 1889.

The old parsonage north of the church was purchased by the school, and rolled back slowly, with many a creak and groan in its timbers, until it was drawn up alongside of Annex Hall, and connected therewith. It was fitted up in 1890 as Park Hall, primarily for the use of the domestic science department, senior class room, laboratory, etc. It has been renovated and improved in 1901, a piazza and various other attractions added, as the new infirmary, and it forms a handsome addition to our group of buildings.

The Academy buildings thus far have been South Hall, 1805; Main Hall, 1856; Annex Hall, 1888; Park Hall, 1890. To this handsome group Society Hall was added just in the rear of the chapel, and erected from August till November 4, 1892. Electric lights, improved modern plumbing, new furniture, beautified rooms and chapel, class memorials, are a few of the many desirable improvements of this administration.

The scholastic work has kept pace with these material changes: a commercial course has been established, and also a post graduate course. The elocution work has been systematized for graduation; the department of domestic science, a course in the care of the sick, or instruction in elementary trained nursing, and other departments have been established.

The erection of the proposed Alumnæ Centennial Memorial Building will be a fitting monument to signalize the completed hundred years of the school's history.

LISTS AND STATISTICS

BISHOPS OF THE UNITY

WHO HAVE SERVED IN THE SOUTHERN PROVINCE

1. John Michael Graff, consecrated 1773, died . . 1782
2. John Daniel Koehler, consecrated 1790, transferred . 1800
3. Charles G. Reichel, consecrated 1801, transferred to Pennsylvania 1811
4. John Herbst, consecrated 1811, died 1812
5. Jacob Van Vleck, consecrated 1815, retired . . 1822
6. Andrew Benade, consecrated 1822, transferred to Pennsylvania 1829
7. John C. Bechler, consecrated 1835, transferred to Europe 1836
8. William H. Van Vleck, consecrated 1836, transferred to Pennsylvania 1849
9. John G. Herman, consecrated 1846, died . . . 1854
10. George F. Bahnson, consecrated 1860, died . . 1869
11. Emil A. de Schweinitz, consecrated 1874, died . . 1879
12. Edward Rondthaler, consecrated 1891

MEMBERS OF THE PROVINCIAL ELDERS' CONFERENCE

1. Frederick William de Marshall, President . . . 1772–1802
2. John M. Graff 1772–1782
3. Paul Tiersch 1772–1774
4. Richard Utley 1772–1775
5. John Daniel Koehler 1785–1800
6. Gottfried Praezel 1785–1788
7. Christian Lewis Benzien 1785–1811
8. Charles G. Reichel, President 1802–1811
9. Simon Peter 1803–1819
10. John Herbst, President 1811–1812
11. Lewis David de Schweinitz 1812–1821
12. John Jacob Van Vleck, President 1812–1822
13. Christian Frederick Schaaf 1819–1841
14. Theodore Shultz 1821–1849
15. Andrew Benade, President 1822–1829
16. John C. Bechler, President 1829–1836
17. William H. Van Vleck, President 1836–1849
18. John C. Jacobson 1841–1844
19. Charles F. Kluge 1844–1853

LISTS AND STATISTICS 337

20. John G. Herman, President 1849-1854
21. George F. Bahnson, 1849, President 1858-1869
22. Emil A. de Schweinitz, 1853, President . . . 1869-1879
23. Levin T. Reichel, President 1854-1858
24. Robert de Schweinitz 1858-1865
25. C. Lewis Rights, 1865, President. 1880-1890
26. Samuel Thomas Pfohl 1869-1873
27. Max. Eugene Grunert 1874-1877
28. E. P. Greider 1877-1884
29. Edward Rondthaler, 1880, President 1890-
30. R. P. Leinbach 1884-1892
31. Dr. N. S. Siewers 1890-1899
32. James E. Hall 1892-
33. John W. Fries 1899-

MINISTERS OF THE SALEM CONGREGATION

1. Paul Tiersch 1771-1774
2. John M. Graff 1774-1782
3. John Frederick Peter 1782-1784
4. John Daniel Koehler 1784-1800
5. Christian Benzien 1800-1802
6. Charles G. Reichel 1802-1811
7. John Herbst 1811-1812
8. Simon Peter 1812-1812
9. Jacob Van Vleck 1812-1822
    G. Benjamin Reichel, assistant 1819-1829
10. Andrew Benade 1822-1829
11. G. Benjamin Reichel 1829-1833
12. John C. Bechler 1833-1836
13. William H. Van Vleck 1836-1849
    Henry A. Shultz, assistant 1839-1842
    Charles A. Bleck, assistant 1842-1844
    Samuel R. Huebner, assistant 1844-1849
    A. A. Reinke, assistant 1848-1849
14. George F. Bahnson 1849-1858, 1863-1869
15. Francis Holland 1858-1863
16. Albert Oerter 1870-1877
17. Edward Rondthaler 1877-
    John F. McCuiston 1886-1901
    Arthur D. Thaeler 1892-1901
    Howard E. Rondthaler 1894-
    Edward S. Crosland 1901-

MINISTERS OF THE BETHABARA CONGREGATION

During the Time of the Bethabara Economy

1. Bernard H. Grube 1753–1754
2. Jacob Lash, business manager 1753–1769
3. John Jacob Fries 1754–1755
4. Gottlob Hoffman 1755–1764
5. Christian Henry Rauch 1755–1756
6. David Bishop 1756–1760
7. Christian Seidel, German minister 1756–1759
8. J. M. Sauter 1757–1760
9. Jacob Rogers, English minister of Dobbs Parish . 1758–1762
10. John Ettwein, German minister 1759–1766
11. John Michael Graff 1762–1773
12. Abraham de Gammern 1762–1765
13. Lawrence Bagge 1764–1769
14. Matthew Schropp 1766–1767
15. Richard Utley, English minister of Dobbs Parish . 1766–1770
16. F. W. de Marshall . . . .

Bethabara after the Government was removed to Salem

1. Lawrence Bagge 1773–1784
2. John Jacob Ernst 1784–1791, 1800–1802
3. Abraham Hessler 1791–1800
4. C. D. Buchholz 1802–1802
5. Simon Peter 1802–1811
6. J. P. Kluge 1811–1813
7. J. L. Strohle 1813–1827
8. Gottlob Byhan 1832–1837
9. J. R. Schmidt 1839–1847
10. L. T. Oerter 1849–1854
11. M. E. Grunert 1854–1857
12. Jacob Siewers 1857–1865
13. C. L. Rights 1865–1873
14. E. P. Greider 1873–1875
15. J. B. Lineback 1875–1877
16. R. P. Leinbach 1877–1892
17. J. F. McCuiston 1892–1901
18. C. D. Crouch 1901–

MINISTERS OF THE BETHANIA CONGREGATION

1. David Bishop 1760–1763
2. L. G. Bachhof 1761–1770
3. John J. Ernst 1770–1784
4. Valentine Beck 1784–1791
5. Simon Peter 1791–1802
6. Christian Thomas Pfohl 1802–1823
7. J. P. Kluge, assistant 1813–1819
8. Peter Wolle, assistant 1819–1822
9. Charles A. Van Vleck 1822–1826
10. J. C. Jacobson 1820–1834
11. G. F. Bahnson 1834–1838
12. Julius T. Bechler 1838–1844
13. F. F. Hagen 1844–1851
14. M. E. Grunert 1851–1857
15. Jacob Siewers 1857–1865
16. C. L. Rights 1865–1873
17. E. P. Greider 1873–1877
18. R. P. Leinbach 1877–1892
19. Edward Crosland 1892–1901
20. F. Walter Grabs 1901–

MINISTERS OF THE FRIEDBERG CONGREGATION

1. L. G. Bachhof . 1770–1776
2. Valentine Beck . 1776–1784
3. Simon Peter . 1784–1791
4. Martin Schneider, 1791–1804
5. John Gambold . 1804–1805
6. C. D. Buchholz . 1805–1806
7. C. D. Ruede . 1807–1822
8. C. F. Denke . 1822–1832
9. H. A. Shultz . 1832–1839
10. S. R. Huebner . 1839–1844
11. E. T. Senseman . 1844–1851
12. F. F. Hagen . 1851–1854
13. Lewis Rights . 1854–1865
14. R. P. Leinbach . 1865–1872
15. A. Lichtenthaeler, 1872–1873
16. D. Z. Smith . 1873–1877
17. J. B. Lineback . 1877–1881
18. J. E. Hall . 1881–1901
19. J. F. McCuiston . 1901–

MINISTERS OF THE FRIEDLAND CONGREGATION

1. Toege Nissen 1775-1780
2. John Casper Heinzman 1780-1783
3. Peter Goetje 1785-1786
4. J. Martin Schneider 1786-1791
5. J. J. Ernst 1791-1800
6. J. J. Wohlfert 1801-1802, 1805-1806
7. C. D. Buchholz 1802-1805, 1807-1823
8. S. R. Huebner 1823-1827, 1843-1847
9. S. Thomas Pfohl 1827-1837
10. G. Byhan 1837-1841
11. Adam Haman 1841-1843
15. Lewis Rights 1846-1854, 1873-1889
16. J. C. Cook 1856-1859
17. Thomas Frye 1859-1859
18. R. P. Leinbach 1859-1865
19. Henry Cooper 1865-1868
20. J. A. Friebele 1868-1870
21. Isaac Prince 1870-1872
22. Samuel Woosley 1889-1896
23. F. W. Grabs 1896-1901
24. C. D. Crouch 1902-

MINISTERS OF THE HOPE CONGREGATION

1. J. C. Fritz 1780-1791
2. J. C. Wohlfert 1791-1792
3. Samuel Kramsch 1792-1802, 1813-1819
4. Abraham Steiner 1803-1806
5. J. L. Strohle 1808-1813
   Served from Friedberg 1820-1900
   Affiliated with Clemmonsville, August 13, 1900.
   There were three temporary pastorates as follows: —
   C. F. Denke 1820-1821
   H. G. Clauder 1838-1839
   Adam Haman 1839-1841

LISTS AND STATISTICS

MINISTERS OF THE NEW PHILADELPHIA CONGREGATION

1. S. R. Huebner 1846–1849
2. E. T. Senseman 1846–1849
3. Lawrence Oerter 1849–1852
4. Jacob Siewers 1852–1854
5. Lewis Rights 1854–1854, 1880–1889
   Served from Salem 1854–1858
6. Thomas Frye 1858–1864
7. E. A. de Schweinitz 1864–1873
8. A. Lichtenthaeler 1873–1877
9. D. Z. Smith 1877–1880
10. Samuel Woosley 1889–1896
11. F. W. Grabs 1896–

MINISTERS OF THE KERNERSVILLE CONGREGATION

1. Isaac Prince . . 1870–1872   2. C. L. Rights . . 1873–1889
3. Edward Crosland . . 1892–

MINISTERS OF THE PROVIDENCE CONGREGATION

1. C. L. Rights . . 1880–1889 | 3. F. Walter Grabs . 1896–1901
2. Samuel Woosley . 1889–1896 | 4. C. D. Crouch . . 1901.

MINISTERS OF THE OAK GROVE CONGREGATION

1. C. L. Rights . . 1887–1889   2. Samuel Woosley . 1889–1896
3. F. Walter Grabs . 1896–1901

MINISTER OF THE CLEMMONSVILLE CONGREGATION

1. James E. Hall 1899–

MINISTERS OF THE MAYODAN CONGREGATION

1. H. E. Rondthaler 1896–1901
2. W. E. Spaugh 1902–

MINISTERS OF THE AVALON CONGREGATION

1. H. E. Rondthaler . . . . , . . . 1901–1901
2. W. E. Spaugh 1902–

The Congregations, Chapels, and Sunday-schools, and the Ministers and Sunday-school Superintendents, and also the numerical strength of the Province, will be shown by the following two lists for January 1, 1902: —

CONGREGATIONS

Name	Number	Pastor
Alpha	31	F. W. Grabs
Bethabara	82	C. D. Crouch
Bethania	392	F. W. Grabs
Clemmonsville	140	J. E. Hall
Carmel	29	E. S. Crosland
Christ Church	176	H. E. Rondthaler
Calvary	180	E. S. Crosland
Colored Church	73	W. E. Spaugh
East Salem	85	E. S. Crosland
Eden	34	W. E. Spaugh
Friedberg	634	J. F. McCuiston
Friedland	243	C. D. Crouch
Fulp	61	
Kernersville	105	E. S. Crosland
Mizpah	77	F. W. Grabs
Macedonia	274	J. E. Hall
Mayodan	105	W. E. Spaugh
Moravia	54	H. E. Rondthaler
Mt. Bethel, Va.	270	C. D. Crouch
New Philadelphia	333	F. W. Grabs
Oak Grove	206	
Providence	187	
Salem Home Church	1319	Edward Rondthaler
South Side	173	C. D. Crouch
Wachovia Arbor	72	H. E. Rondthaler
Willow Hill, Va.	66	C. D. Crouch
Total, 26	5401	Ministers in the Province, 10

LISTS AND STATISTICS

SUNDAY-SCHOOLS

Name	Number	Superintendent
Alpha	67	E. T. Strupe
Advent	80	N. W. Shore
Academy	136	J. H. Clewell
Avalon	110	Edgar Hege
Bethabara	66	D. T. Hine
Bethania	59	Edgar Lineback
Bethesda	99	Julius Slater
Clemmonsville	62	J. E. Hall
Carmel	57	John Marshall
Christ Church	252	L. A. Brietz
Calvary	170	A. C. Hege
Colored Church	167	Emory Knause
Enterprise	186	D. A. Tesh
East Salem	97	H. E. Fries
Elm Street	283	E. A. Ebert
Eden	54	William Hege
Friedberg	217	J. F. McCuiston
Friedland	99	Noah Hine
Fulp	33	Mrs. E. E. Fulp
Fairview	139	H. W. Foltz
Hope	77	Frank Spaugh
Kernersville	64	J. P. Adkins
Mizpah	65	F. H. Lash
Macedonia	78	Walter Butner
Mayodan	195	S. P. Tesh
Moravia	70	Henry Sutton
Mt. Bethel, Va.	77	Mrs. John Clark
New Philadelphia	118	Columbus Reich
Olivet	75	E. A. Conrad
Oak Grove	99	Marion Smith
Providence	59	J. L. Walker
Salem Home Sunday-school	364	F. H. Fries
South Side	217	R. A. Spaugh
Union Cross	40	Daniel Hine
Wachovia Arbor	64	W. A. Walker
Willow Hill, Va.	66	Henry Woods
Cotton Mill School	135	C. E. Crist
Total, 37	4296	Total, 37

PROVINCIAL BOARDS.

Provincial Elders' Conference.

Edward Rondthaler, Chairman. James E. Hall, J. W. Fries.

Associate Financial Board.

C. T. Pfohl, E. F. Strickland, W. T. Vogler.

SALEM CONGREGATION BOARDS.

Board of Elders.

Edward Rondthaler, Chairman. C. T. Pfohl, H. W. Shore, F. H. Fries, J. H. Clewell.

Board of Trustees.

J. W. Fries, Chairman. H. F. Shaffner, W. A. Lemly, W. T. Vogler, H. A. Pfohl, W. C. Crist.

Boys' School Board.

Ex-officio members: Edward Rondthaler, J. W. Fries, J. T. Lineback. Elected members: C. E. Crist, F. H. Vogler, and B. J. Pfohl.

Centennial Board.

H. E. Fries, Chairman. W. S. Pfohl, Secretary and Treasurer. L. B. Brickenstein, Jacob Crouse, J. A. Vance, C. D. Ogburn, Charles S. Siewers, J. F. Shaffner, Jr.

TEACHERS IN SALEM BOYS' SCHOOL.

Edward Rondthaler, Principal. J. F. Brower, Head Master. K. B. Thigpen, Howard Rondthaler, W. S. Pfohl, Miss Nannie Sheets.

SALEM PRIMARY SCHOOLS.

Miss Amelia Steiner, Miss Sallie Vogler, Miss Donna Smith.

KINDERGARTEN SCHOOL.

Miss Lothman, Miss Alma Tise.

CLEMMONS SCHOOL TEACHERS.

J. K. Pfohl, Principal. Mrs. J. K. Pfohl, William Davis, Miss Nannie Bessent, Miss Clara Warner, J. E. Hall.

LISTS AND STATISTICS

SUPERINTENDENT WINSTON CITY SCHOOLS.

    Charles F. Tomlinson.

Total number of scholars in attendance in the Twin City of Winston-Salem, in 1902, including both races, nearly 3700. Teachers, 110.

MUNICIPAL GOVERNMENT.

Salem.

    J. A. Vance, Mayor. H. E. Fries, S. E. Butner, H. S. Crist, Charles Siewers, L. B. Brickenstein, H. F. Shaffner, G. H. Rights, Commissioners.

Winston.

    O. B. Eaton, Mayor. E. H. Wilson, Joe Jacobs, J. K. Norfleet, J. W. Byerly, W. G. Cranford, W. H. Marler, F. J. Liipfert, Frank C. Brown, J. W. Hill.

ALUMNÆ ASSOCIATION OFFICERS.

Former Presidents.

1. Mrs. J. D. Graham.
2. Miss M. E. Vogler.
3. Miss E. A. Lehman.
4. Mrs. Ellen Starbuck.

Present Officers.

    President,   Mrs. Lindsay Patterson.
    Vice-Presidents, Mrs. W. N. Reynolds.
                      Mrs. E. A. Ebert.
                      Mrs. H. Montague.
                      Mrs. Nelson Henry.
                      Mrs. Isaac Emerson.
    Secretary,   Miss Adelaide Fries.
    Treasurer,   Miss L. C. Shaffner.
    Executive Committee,

Mrs. F. H. Fries.	Miss Gertrude Siewers.
Mrs. J. H. Clewell.	Miss Kate Jones.
Mrs. P. H. Hanes.	Miss Bessie Pfohl.
Mrs. J. D. Laugenour.	Miss May Barber.
Mrs. Cicero Ogburn.	Miss Ida Miller.
Mrs. W. T. Brown.	Miss Bess Gray.
Miss Laura Lemly (deceased).	Miss Pamela Bynum.

SALEM FEMALE ACADEMY

PRINCIPALS

THE LIST WAS PREPARED BY MISS LOUISA SHAFFNER

1. Kramsch, Samuel G. 1802–1806
2. Steiner, Abraham G. 1806–1816
3. Reichel, G. Benjamin 1816–1834
4. Jacobson, John C. 1834–1844
5. Bleck, Charles A. 1844–1848
6. De Schweinitz, Emil A. 1848–1853
7. De Schweinitz, Robert 1853–1866
8. Grunert, Maximilian E. 1866–1877
9. Zorn, Theophilus 1877–1884
10. Rondthaler, Edward 1884–1888
11. Clewell, John H. 1888–

MUSIC PROFESSORS

WITH THE DATE WHEN THEY ENTERED UPON THEIR DUTIES

1. Grunert, Maximilian E. . 1853
2. Lineback, Edward W. . 1865
3. Meinung, Alexander . . 1865
4. Agthe, Frederick . . . 1878
5. D'Anna, Sig. Saverio . 1880
6. Markgraff, George . . . 1886
7. Schmolk, Paul 1891
8. Skilton, Charles . . . 1893
9. Shirley, H. A. 1896

THE FOLLOWING HAVE OCCUPIED THE POSITION OF SECRETARY OR BOOKKEEPER

1. Steiner, Abraham.
2. Boner, Joshua.
3. Lineback, James.
4. Wurreschke, L. B.
5. Pfohl, C. B.
6. Thaeler, Clarence.

LISTS AND STATISTICS 347

LIST OF TEACHERS AND PROFESSORS WHO HAVE SERVED IN SALEM ACADEMY FROM THE FOUNDING OF THE SCHOOL TILL THE PRESENT TIME

When two names are given, the second is the married name of the lady.

1. Meinung, Maria Saloma. Mrs. Ebbeke . . . 1804–1807
2. Praezel, Johanna Elizabeth. Mrs. F. C. Meinung . 1804–1808
3. Reichel, Sophia Dorothea. Mrs. Seidel . . . 1804–1809
4. Shober, Johanna Sophia. Mrs. Van Zevely . . 1805–1809
5. Praezel, Mrs. M. E. 1805–1813
6. Reuz, Johanna Elizabeth. Mrs. Oehmen . . . 1805–1814
7. Praezel, Agnes Susanna. Mrs. C. Peterson . . 1805–1816
8. Lineback, Barbara 1806–1807
9. Walk, Mary. Mrs. Curtis 1806–1809
10. Christman, Philpina. Mrs. Summers 1806–1820
11. Hartman, Rebecca 1806–1812
12. Danz, Elizabeth. Mrs. Winkler 1807–1808
13. Peter, Susanna Elizabeth. Mrs. Van Zevely . . 1807–1827
14. Nissen, Johanna Elizabeth. Mrs. Fries . . . 1808–1811
15. Fetter, Salome. Mrs. Friday 1809–1819
16. Vierling, Henrietta F. Mrs. Reichel 1811–1814
17. Steiner, Maria. Mrs. Denke 1811–1868
18. Shober, Anna Paulina. Mrs. J. G. Herman . . 1812–1820
19. Kummer, Maria Elizabeth 1814–1815
20. Transou, Elizabeth. Mrs. Senseman 1814–1816
21. Christman, Christina 1814–1820
22. Holder, Anna Rebecca. Mrs. Van Zevely . . 1814–1822
23. Kramsch, Charlotte Louisa. Mrs. Blickensderfer . 1814–1837
24. Christman, Johanna Salome. Mrs. Welfare . . 1816–1820
25. Fetter, Maria 1817–1818
26. Transou, Maria Catharine 1817–1818
27. Shober, Maria Theresa. Mrs. Wolle 1817–1819
28. Rhea, Ruth Montgomery. Mrs. Levering . . 1818–1820
29. Schneider, Christina C. Mrs. Benzien . . . 1818–1824
30. Lash, Susanna Elizabeth. Mrs. Crouse . . . 1819–1820
31. Kluge, Henrietta. Mrs. Moore 1819–1821
32. Belling, Maria 1820–1821
33. Towle, Mary. Mrs. Welfare 1820–1823
34. Boehler, Wilhelmina. Mrs. Lash 1820–1823
35. Gambold, Maria. Mrs. Copeland 1820–1824
36. Dull, Sibylla. Mrs. Philip Reich 1820–1824

348 HISTORY OF WACHOVIA

37. Towle, Sarah Louisa. Mrs. Vierling 1820-1825
38. Eberhard, Caroline. Mrs. Eder 1820-1828
39. Reich, Catharine. Mrs. D. Clewell 1821-1827
40. Shultz, Johanna Elizabeth 1822-1824
41. Shultz, Caroline. Mrs. Steiner 1822-1823
42. Bagge, Eliza 1824-1827
43. Lineback, Regina 1824-1842
44. Stauber, Lydia 1824-1870
45. Kitschelt, Sophia Christina 1825-1827
46. Benade, Mariam Ernestine 1825-1829
47. Belo, Henrietta. Mrs. Christman 1826-1827
48. Vierling, Eliza W. Mrs. C. Kremer 1826-1832
49. Pfohl, Charlotte F. 1826-1869
50. Lineback, Anna A. 1826-1859
51. Spach, Gertrude. Mrs. Mickey 1827-1829
52. Benade, Lucia T. 1827-1829
53. Byhan, Sophia D. Mrs. Van Boner 1827-1830
54. Crist, Anna E. Mrs. J. Boner 1827-1839
55. Ruede, Dorothea Sophia. Mrs. M. Vogler . . 1827-1839
56. Shultz, Lisetta 1828-1839
57. Reich, Louisa. Mrs. George Vogler 1829-1835
58. Blum, Martha. Mrs. Griffin 1830-1832
59. Meinung, Lisetta C. 1830-1844
60. Reichel, Clara. Mrs. Hagen 1833-1841
61. Belo, Theresa W. Mrs. Siddall 1834-1840
62. Shultz, Dorothea M. Mrs. Clewell 1835-1836
63. Blum, Maria Lavinia 1835-1841
64. Schnall, Henrietta 1835-1866
65. Hagen, Louisa. Mrs. Sussdorff 1836-1839
66. Shober, Henrietta 1837-1838
67. Ruede, Louisa. Mrs. Rogers 1837-1840
68. Belo, Louisa. Mrs. G. F. Bahnson 1837-1863
69. Byhan, Rachel. Mrs. L. Lineback 1838-1839
70. Peterson, Theresa 1838-1859
71. Blum, Lucinda. Mrs. A. Zevely 1839-1840
72. Reich, Henrietta. Mrs. Louis Belo 1839-1844
73. Rights, Susan. Mrs. T. Keehln 1839-1846
74. Senseman, Melinda. Mrs. Ragland 1839-1847
75. Zevely, Johanna Sophia. Mrs. A. Butner . . . 1839-1860
76. Herbst, Anna Aurelia. Mrs. E. Reich . . . 1840-1841
77. Keehln, Rosalie. Mrs. R. Crist 1840-1845
78. Hege, Theresa. Mrs. H. Meinung 1841-1841

LISTS AND STATISTICS 349

79. Bagge, Antoinette. Mrs. E. Brietz 1841–1842
80. Vogler, Louisa. Mrs. Senseman 1841–1844
81. Lineback, Sarah Ann. Mrs. Fulkerson . . . 1841–1845
82. Peterson, Henrietta. Mrs. Frebele 1842–1843
83. Senseman, Emma. Mrs. Stewart 1842–1852
84. Bagge, Lucinda 1842–1867
85. Blum, Julia. Mrs. Anthony 1843–1844
86. Levering, Caroline. Mrs. Henry Ruede . . . 1843–1845
87. Brietz, Lisetta 1843–1877
88. Vogler, Pauline 1844–1844
89. Smith, Charlotte. Mrs. E. Reinke 1844–1850
90. Burkhardt, Caroline. Mrs. Herman Ruede . . 1844–1845
91. Reichel, Angelica. Mrs. Warman 1844–1849
92. Warner, Olivia 1844–1856
93. Lineback, Emma 1844–1857
94. Hagen, Augusta 1845–1847
95. Haman, Maria. Mrs. T. Crist 1845–1848
96. Benzien, Francisca. Mrs. James Fisher . . . 1846–1854
97. Reichel, Amelia. Mrs. Kummer 1847–1848
98. Butner, Harriet. Mrs. E. Clemmons . . . 1847–1848
99. Pfohl, Clementine. Mrs. E. Meinung . . . 1847–1849
100. Hall, Augusta. Mrs. L. Winkler 1847–1852
101. Foltz, Sophia. Mrs. P. Leinbach 1847–1855
102. Senseman, Eliza. Mrs. Senseman 1847–1856
103. Reichel, Ernestine 1848–1870
104. Welfare, Ellen 1848–1849
105. Haines, Elizabeth. Mrs. C. Rights 1848–1852
106. Pfohl, Emma. Mrs. M. E. Grunert 1849–1851
107. Benzien, Hermina. Mrs. C. Hauser 1849–1857
108. Welfare, Jane 1849–1858
109. Herman, Louisa. Mrs. James Lineback . . . 1849–1860
110. Herman, Adelaide 1850–1869
111. Banner, Adelaide. Mrs. Everhardt 1851–1852
112. Kremer, Sophia. Mrs. Kernan 1851–1858
113. Morrow, Margaret. Mrs. C. Brietz 1852–1852
114. Van Vleck, Lisetta. Mrs. A. Meinung . . . 1852–1868
115. Welfare, Theophila 1852–1863
116. Van Vleck, Louisa 1851–
117. Blickensderfer, Ellen. Mrs. Starbuck . . . 1852–1855
118. Siewers, Caroline 1853–1860
119. Vogler, Maria 1853–1882
120. Demuth, Anna. Mrs. Regenas 1855–1856

350 HISTORY OF WACHOVIA

121. Siewers, Elizabeth. Mrs. A. F. Pfohl . . . 1855-1859
122. Fant, Gertrude. Mrs. H. Shepherd 1856-1858
123. Chitty, Elizabeth 1856-1878
124. Gibbons, Annie. Mrs. Lardner 1856-1858
125. Gibbons, Jennie 1856-1858
126. Gibbons, Kate 1856-1858
127. Peterson, Maria. Mrs. Transou 1857-1858
128. Stoltzenbach, Augusta. Mrs. C. Reinke . . . 1857-1859
129. Smith, Louisa. Mrs. Joseph Hall 1857-1859
130. Heisler, Maria 1858-1861
131. Fries, Caroline. Mrs. J. F. Shaffner 1858-1859
132. Chitty, Adelaide 1859-1860
133. Kremer, Catherine 1859-1862
134. Siewers, Margaret. Mrs. C. T. Pfohl . . . 1859-1865
135. Blum, Sarah A. Mrs. P. Leinbach 1859-1865
136. Van Vleck, Amelia 1859-
137. Steiner, Amelia 1857-1881
138. Shultz, Caroline. Mrs. Greer 1859-1860
139. Service, Caroline 1859-1860, 1869-1870
140. Siddall, Josephine. Mrs. J. W. Hunter . . . 1859-1867
141. Boner, Maria 1859-1879
142. Butner, Sophia 1860-1875
143. Clewell, Margaret. Mrs. R. Jenkins 1860-1863
144. Lange, Addie. Mrs. Cortelyou 1861-1862
145. Hege, Paulina. Mrs. S. Mickey 1861-1863
146. Kremer, Mary. Mrs. D. Headly 1862-1864
147. Zevely, Mary 1863-1865
148. Blum, Sophia 1863-1867
149. Sussdorff, Addie. Mrs. Wolle 1862-1865
150. Pfohl, Julia. Mrs. J. Stockton 1864-1865
151. Mack, Joanna. Mrs. W. T. Vogler 1864-1867
152. Pfohl, Mary. Mrs. J. Landquist 1864-1871
153. Lehman, Emma 1864-
154. Vogler, Mary 1866-1866
155. Brietz, Mary. Mrs. S. Mickey 1866-1867
156. Shaffner, Louisa 1866-
157. Clauder, Otelia. Mrs. Borheck 1866-1866
158. Siddall, Mary. Mrs. C. Stockton 1866-1875
159. Vogler, Martha. Mrs. E. Peterson 1866-1867
160. Vogler, Sarah 1866-1887, 1900-1901
161. Fogle, Mary A. 1866-1876, 1885-1894
162. Everhardt, Mary. Mrs. C. B. Pfohl 1867-1870
163. Sussdorff, Mary. Mrs. Prather 1867-1870

LISTS AND STATISTICS 351

164. Vogler, Mrs. S. D. 1867–1871
165. Shaffner, Sarah E. 1867–
166. Meinung, Mary E. 1867–
167. De Schweinitz, Adelaide. Mrs. H. Bahnson . . 1868–1870
168. Senseman, Mary. Mrs. S. Patterson . . . 1868–1873
169. Belo, Ellen. Mrs. Shelton 1869–1870
170. Boner, Lavinia. Mrs. Johnston 1869–1872
171. Chitty, Ella. Mrs. E. Strupe 1869–1872
172. Belo, Annie. Mrs. Holman 1869–1873
173. Crist, Annie. Mrs. Earnhardt 1869–1877
174. Bahnson, Carrie. Mrs. Norwood 1870–1876
175. Belo, Bertha. Mrs. W. Lemly 1870–1873
176. Blum, Hannah. Mrs. Anthony 1870–1873
177. Meinung, Adelaide 1870–1878
178. Chitty, Emma 1870–
179. Bahnson, Lizzie. Mrs. G. Pond 1871–1876
180. De Schweinitz, Eleanor. Mrs. N. T. Siewers . . 1872–1875
181. Belo, Agnes. Mrs. C. Buxton 1872–1879
182. Grunert, Louisa. Mrs. C. Smyth 1872–1879
183. Smith, Lizzie. Mrs. Benson 1873–1874
184. Smith, Emma 1873–1876
185. Heberhard, Mary 1873–1875
186. McOrn, Mary 1874–1878
187. Meller, Emma. Mrs. Thompson 1874–1875
188. Meinung, Cornelia. Mrs. Hilton 1874–1878
189. Patterson, Caroline. Mrs. Coble 1875–1881
190. Mack, Mary 1875–1884
191. Lott, Flora 1876–1877
192. Wurreschke, Mrs. Josephine 1878–1879
193. Greider, Emma. Mrs. E. Lehman 1880–1880
194. De Schweinitz, Anna. Mrs. F. Fries . . . 1880–1886
195. Vest, Sarah 1880–
196. Pittman, Annie L. Mrs. A. Vance 1880–1894
197. Rodgers, Ida. Mrs. Jones 1881–1881
198. Ward, Janie 1881–1884
199. Siewers, Gertrude 1881–
200. Erwin, Mattie 1882–1883
201. Pfohl, Constance 1882–1891
202. Parker, Ione. Mrs. O. Holt 1883–1884
203. Troeger, Edith 1883–1884
204. Jones, Carrie R. 1884–
205. Bernard, Mary 1884–1886
206. Lewis, Emma. Mrs. Hyde 1884–1887

352 HISTORY OF WACHOVIA

207. Carmichael, Alma. Mrs. Boozer 1884-1890
208. Heisler, Elizabeth 1884-
209. Shore, Ellen. Mrs. Seaber 1886-1891
210. Geitner, Mary 1887-1888
211. Pfohl, Elizabeth 1887-1888
212. Rondthaler, Alice J. Mrs. A. Chase . . . 1887-1895
213. Lineback, Elizabeth 1887-1890
214. Tate, Lula. Mrs. Jerome Stockard 1888-1889
215. Clark, Eliza 1888-1890
216. Winkler, Claudia 1888-1890
217. Evans, Katharine. Mrs. von Klenner . . . 1888-1891
218. Cooper, Emma. Mrs. McCalli 1888-1892
219. Baker, Helen 1889-1890
220. Bynum, Pamela 1889-1890
221. Laciar, Addie 1889-1891
222. Jenkins, Gertrude. Mrs. A. Howell . . . 1889-1891
223. Winkler, Mrs. A. 1890-1890
224. Jones, Annie. Mrs. Sprinkle 1890-1891
225. Chaffin, Lena. Mrs. Giles 1890-1891
226. Du Four, Margueritte 1890-1891
227. Meinung, Florence 1890-1895
228. Tietze, Lucy 1890-1894
229. Vest, Caroline 1890-
230. Smith, Mrs. A. L. 1890-1898
231. Settle, Florence 1890-1899
232. Fain, Lida 1891-1892
233. Matthewson, Susanna 1891-1892
234. Hege, Annie Louise. Mrs. R. Spaugh . . . 1891-1893
235. Mickey, Anna Caroline. Mrs. E. Crosland . . 1891-1893
236. Bessent, Margaret 1891-
237. Wolle, Grace 1891-1896
238. Scriber, Adelaide 1891-1900
239. Peterson, Henrietta 1891-1893
240. Siddall, Ella 1892-1894, 1901-1902
241. Barrow, Otelia 1892-
242. Brown, Ettie 1892-1898
243. Tracy, Antoinette 1892-1897
244. Gosling, Lillian. Mrs. W. G. Tyree . . . 1893-1895
245. McFadyen, Christiana 1893-1894
246. Query, Clara 1893-
247. Richardson, Jennie 1894-
248. Flake, Margie. Mrs. George Miller . . . 1894-1896
249. Morrison, Luda 1894-

LISTS AND STATISTICS 353

250. Scales, Nell. Mrs. Scott Fillman . . . 1894–1897
251. Lewis, Mamie 1895–
252. Siddall, Louisa 1895–
253. Brooke, Elizabeth 1896–1899
254. Harmon, Tilla 1896–1897
255. Strupe, Ella. Mrs. Harper 1896–1898
256. Wellborn, Lena. Mrs. Reeves 1897–1900
257. Shaffner, Etta 1897–1898
258. Porter, Hallie. Mrs. W. R. Crawford . . . 1897–1898
259. Richardson, Susie. Mrs. James Sloan . . . 1898–1900
260. Lineback, Emma 1898–1900
261. Lineback, Cornelia 1900–1901
262. La Porte, Mlle. Zoe 1900–
263. Mann, Mrs. Charlotte 1900–1901
264. Barber, Charlotte. Mrs. A. Walrath . . . 1900–1901
265. Miller, Dora 1901–1901
266. Lichtenthaeler, Annie 1901–1901
267. Stockton, Tilla 1901–1901
268. Butner, Mabel 1901–
269. Wright, Mary 1901–
270. Tuttle, Janet 1901–
271. Kerner, Mrs. Jennie 1901–
272. White, Blanche 1901–1902
273. Bonney, Emma 1901–
274. Jeter, Ethel 1901–
275. Greider, Mary 1902–

The following states and countries have sent pupils to Salem Academy and College: —

North Carolina	New York	District of Columbia
South Carolina	Kentucky	Ohio
Virginia	Pennsylvania	Brazil
Georgia	Missouri	New Mexico
Tennessee	Indian Territory	Rhode Island
Alabama	Massachusetts	Montana
Texas	Illinois	Iowa
Mississippi	West Indies	Washington
Florida	California	Colorado
Louisiana	Mexico	Alaska
Arkansas	Maryland	

NOTE. — The total list of boarding pupils since the opening of the school is nearly or quite seven thousand. The day pupils will increase this number to ten thousand or more.

INDEX

The following lists are not included in the index: —
Bishops who have served in the Southern Province, 336.
Boards and Officials, 344-345.
Congregations, Pastors, and Membership, 342.
First settlers and visitors to Wachovia, 1753-1762, 136 names, 56-58.
Members of the Provincial Elders' Conference, 1772-1902, 336.
Ministers of the Avalon Congregation, 341.
Ministers of the Bethabara Congregation, 338.
Ministers of the Bethania Congregation, 339.
Ministers of the Clemmonsville Congregation, 341.
Ministers of the Friedberg Congregation, 339.
Ministers of the Friedland Congregation, 340.
Ministers of the Hope Congregation, 340.
Ministers of the Kernersville Congregation, 341.
Ministers of the Mayodan Congregation, 341.
Ministers of the New Philadelphia Congregation, 341.
Ministers of the Oak Grove Congregation, 341.
Ministers of the Providence Congregation, 341.
Ministers of the Salem Congregation, 337.
Principals, Professors, &c., of Salem Female Academy, 346.
Soldiers in the Civil War from Salem, Winston, and neighbouring congregations alphabetically arranged, 246-249.
States and countries represented on register of Salem Female Academy, 353.
Sunday-schools, Superintendents, and Membership, 343.
Teachers of Salem Female Academy, 347-353.

Abbeville, 178.
Academy S.S., 281.
Academy, the, 290.
Adams, 131.
Advent, 281, 284.
Agthe, 331.
Alabama, 325.
Alamance, 73, 97, 102, 104, 105, 108, 110, 114, 120, 125.
Alaska, 316.
Alberti, 204.
Allen, 105.
Alpha, 283.
Alumnæ Association, 224, 293, 329.
America, 1, 2, 4, 45, 73, 91, 120, 129, 134, 136, 137, 138, 154, 161, 162, 163, 164, 165, 169, 177, 204, 216, 217, 260, 304, 315, 317, 318, 323, 326, 327.

Am. S.S. Union, 199, 278, 279, 282.
Ancient Church, 311.
Angel, 61.
Anglican Church, 301.
Annex Hall, 335.
Antes, 6, 9.
Appomattox, 242.
Armstrong, 106, 108, 123, 128, 134, 148; 149, 169.
Atlanta, 242.
Atlantic Ocean, 4.
Atwood, B., 238.
Augsburg Confession, 303.
Augusta, C. H., 15.
Aust, 92.
Australia, 316.
Austria, 9.
Avalon, 17, 275, 285.

Bachhof, 76.
Bachman, 181.
Bachman, Bishop, 333.
Bagge, 88, 92, 115, 128, 135, 141, 142, 143, 144, 146, 149, 151, 156, 176.
Bagge, Mrs., 105.
Bahnson, G. F., 87, 238, 239, 240, 280.
Bahnson, G. F., Jr., 287.
Bahnson, H. T., viii, 245.
Banner, 38.
Banner, H., 240.
Banton, 99.
Barrow, H. W., 238.
Basle, 209.
Battle, 144.
Beck, 93.
Beck, H., 201.
Belo, A. H., 238.
Belo, E., 218, 274.
Belo, H., 241.
Benade, Bishop, 326, 328.
Benbury, 155.
Benzien, 61, 62, 158, 170, 178, 182, 184, 185, 188, 189, 190, 196.
Beroth, J., 14, 67.
Berthelsdorf, 313.
Bessent, J. C., 245.
Bessent, N., 287.
Bethabara, N.C., 14, 24, 28, 32, 33, 34, 35, 37, 38, 39, 40, 41, 42, 44, 45, 46, 47, 48, 50, 51, 52, 54, 55, 58, 60, 61, 62, 63, 64, 65, 66, 67, 68, 72, 74, 76, 78, 82, 85, 87, 88, 91, 92, 93, 95, 97, 98, 100, 102, 103, 105, 108, 111, 114, 116, 118, 119, 120, 125, 126, 127, 128, 135, 142, 145, 151, 162, 166, 173, 174, 180, 181, 194, 200, 239, 283, 320.
Bethania, 27, 46, 47, 52, 53, 60, 63, 65, 66, 67, 68, 72, 91, 99, 100, 106, 112, 113, 120, 127, 128, 135, 145, 151, 163, 165, 198, 239, 250, 271, 283, 284, 322, 323, 330.
Bethesda, 285.
Bethlehem Chapel (Europe), 310.
Bethlehem, Pa., 2, 6, 28, 30, 36, 37, 40, 53, 91, 98, 100, 158, 178, 182, 186, 193, 315, 318, 319, 322, 325, 327, 329, 333.
Bethlehem Seminary, 318, 324, 330.
Biefel, 67, 71.
Bigler, Bishop, 327.
Bird, 52, 55.
Birkhead, 88.
Bishop, 200.
Bishops (list), 336.

"Black Boys," 112.
Black Walnut Bottom, 27, 64, 65.
Blantyre Hospital, 254.
Bleck, C. A., 324, 325.
Bleck, Miss, 325.
Bleck, Mrs., 325.
Blickensderfer, 318.
Blue Ridge, 205, 206, 285.
Bluff, 282.
Blum, 135, 141, 151.
Boards and Officials (list), 344, 345.
Boeckel, 77.
Boehler, F., 279.
Boehler, Peter, 28, 53, 55.
Bohemia, 3, 135, 191, 192, 302, 308, 310, 311, 313, 316.
Bohemian-Moravian Branch, 311.
Boner, J., 250, 251.
Bonn, 48, 60, 83, 93, 99, 105, 106, 111, 112, 119, 131, 170, 179.
Borg, 106, 107, 108.
Boston Harbour, 125.
Bowie, 178, 179.
Brietz, C., 218.
Brietz, E. A., 238.
British, 115, 136, 139, 159, 163, 164, 165, 166, 167, 169, 249.
Broad Bay, 78.
Broesing, 172, 173.
Brooklyn, 333.
Brooks, 143, 144, 148.
Brooks, C. B., 245.
Brunswick, 63, 98, 102, 103.
Brushy Fork, 85, 278.
Bryan, 144.
Burk, 159.
Burkhardt, 201.
Burkall, 323.
Burry, 62.
Butner, A., 218.
Butner, A. B., 238.
Butner, A. I., 165.
Butner, M., 330.
Button Engine, 272.
Byhan, 200.

Caanan, 202.
Calahan, 278.
Calixtines, 308, 309.
Calvary, 89, 90, 262, 284.
Calvary S.S., 281.
Cambridge, 178.
Camden, 161, 162, 170.
Camden Valley, N.Y., 324.

INDEX

Campbell, 169.
Cape Fear, 102, 125.
Carmel, 285.
Carmichael, F., 238.
Carr, 144, 147.
Carrol's Manor, 80.
Carter, 62.
Carter, R., 195.
Caruthers, 96, 97, 165.
Caswell, 142, 158, 195.
Catawba River, 5, 7.
Catawbas, 32, 51.
Catholic Church, 309, 313.
Cavalry, 10th Ohio, 251.
Cedar Ave., 251.
Centennial Mem. Building, 294, 335.
Centennial Society, 292.
Central America, 316.
Ceylon, 192.
Charleston, 81, 118, 178.
Charlotte, 97, 274, 275.
Cherokees, 32, 40, 45, 46, 50, 51, 52, 179, 186, 200, 201, 202, 280, 320.
Chitty, Mary, 80.
Chitty, R. L., 238, 264.
Christ Church, 281, 284.
Christendom, 316.
Christiansfeld, 323.
Christmas, 30, 31, 64.
Churton, 7, 157.
Civil War, 176, 219, 235, 249, 255, 256, 294, 326, 328.
Clarendon, Earl, 4.
Clauder, H. G., 200.
Clauder, C. J., 240.
Clemmons, E. T., 286, 287.
Clemmons Hill, 288.
Clemmonsville, 285, 286, 287, 288.
Clewell, A. A., 238.
Clewell, David, 239.
Clewell, M., 254.
Clewell, J. H., 287, 291, 332, 333, 334.
Clewell, Mrs., 334.
Clover Station, 243.
Colonial Records, 5.
Coloured S.S., 281.
Comenius, 135, 192, 294, 312, 314.
Committee of Safety, 123, 125, 126, 127, 128.
Conestoga, 73.
Confederate Troops, 252.
Confiscation, 133, 151, 156, 157.
Congregations, members, and pastors (list), 342.

Congregation House, 54.
Cool Spring, 281.
Cooper Run, 178.
Copenhagen, 314.
Corbin, F., 6.
Cornwallis, 123, 164, 165, 166, 167, 168, 169, 250.
Cossart, 157.
Cotton Mill S.S., 281, 284.
Cowpens (battle), 164.
Creeks, 32, 45, 201, 202, 320.
Cresson, 117.
Crist, J. R., 218.
Crosland, E. S., 284, 285.
Cross Creek, 142.
Crouch, C. D., 283, 284, 285.
Cunow, 158.

Dalman, 322.
Danish, 14.
Dan River, 15, 17, 18.
d'Anna, 331.
Danville, 243.
David, C., 313.
Delaware, 130, 136.
Denke, C. F., 320.
Denmark, 78.
de Rosette, 117.
de Schweinitz, B., 329.
de Schweinitz, Bernard, 326.
de Schweinitz, E. A., 87, 260, 325.
de Schweinitz, Edmund, 326, 327.
de Schweinitz, F. C., 178, 179, 320.
de Schweinitz, H. C., 178.
de Schweinitz, L. D., 75, 87, 158, 326, 327.
de Schweinitz, Robert, 226, 251, 253, 327, 328, 329, 330.
de Watteville, 75, 177, 181.
Diaspora, 1, 316.
Dickens, 167.
Dixon, 83.
Dobbs, Fort, 46.
Dobbs, Gov., 61, 63, 72, 83, 95, 98.
Dobbs Parish, 63, 127.
Dobson, 153, 154.
Dorothea Creek, 68.
Doub, 238.
Douthet, T. B., 238, 245.
Douthit, 79.
Dunkard, 33.

East Africa, 316.
Easter, 30, 70, 71, 90, 182, 250.
Easton, 130.

INDEX

East Salem S.S., 281, 284.
Eberhard, L. B., 238.
Eden, 284.
Edenton, 5, 6, 125.
Eder, 200.
Edward, Earl of Clar., 4.
Edwards, 114.
Egypt, 333.
Elbe, 87.
Elm St. S.S., 281, 284.
Elrod, 79, 80.
Emma Moore Mem., 294.
Emmaus, 130, 330.
"Enge Conferenz," 55.
English (England), 10, 32, 33, 80, 83, 102, 122, 125, 137, 139, 160, 161, 167, 172, 193, 218, 262, 315.
Episcopal Church, 135, 137.
Esquimaux in Greenland, 314, 315.
Ettwein, 79, 186.
Europe, 1, 2, 3, 4, 91, 140, 172, 173, 177, 181, 193, 204, 216, 321, 327, 333, 334.
Euterpean Society, 335.

Fairview S.S., 281, 284.
Fanning, 96, 99, 104, 112.
Farmville, 243.
Fayetteville, 28, 60, 126, 161, 195.
Federal, 249, 250, 256.
Feldhausen, H., 14.
Ferdinand of Tyrol, 310, 311.
Fiedler, 79.
Fish, 48, 49.
Fisher, C., 320.
Florida, 4, 83, 136, 204, 236.
Fogle, A., 203, 250, 255.
Fogle Bros., 276.
Fogle, C. H., 265.
Fogle, Chas., 265.
Foltz's kitchen, 272.
Forkland, 7.
"Forsyth County," viii, 92, 151, 176, 209, 211, 215, 241, 277.
Fort, 32, 39, 40.
France, 32, 33, 40, 44, 177.
France, La, engine, 272.
Freeholders, 62.
Frederick of Palatinate, 310.
Fredericksburg, 239, 240.
Frey (list), 77.
Freydeck, 7.
Friebele, 205.
Friedberg, 26, 28, 72, 75, 76, 77, 79, 80, 86, 198, 281, 282, 284.

Friedrich, 111, 112.
Friends, 74.
Fries, Adelaide, viii, 92, 151, 209, 308.
Fries engine, 271.
Fries, F., 218, 226.
Fries, F. H., 265, 275, 276, 281.
Fries, H. E., viii, 275.
Fries, H. W., 287.
Fries, J. W., viii, 288.
Fries mills, 254.
Fries (minister), 28, 54.
Fries (post-office), 275.
Fries power plant, 276.
Fries store, 89.
Fritz, 80, 181.
Frohok, 55, 99.
Frommel, 86.
Fulp, 282, 285.

Gambold, 200.
Gamewell, 272.
Gammon, 83, 98.
Gammon, Mrs., 83.
Gates, 161.
Gates Co., 195.
Geneva, 302.
George III, 112, 115, 122, 130, 131, 134, 137, 138, 139.
Georgia, 135, 136, 162, 167, 172, 190, 201, 202, 250.
German, 10, 14, 76, 78, 80, 218, 262.
German Reformed, 78.
Germanton, 211.
Germany, 1, 3, 53, 172, 193, 271, 313, 315, 316.
Gervais, J. L., 178.
Gilbert, 148.
Gnadenberg, 317.
Gnadenfeld, 326.
Gnadenhutten, Ohio, 325.
Gnadenhutten, Pa., 36.
Grabs, 66, 67, 68.
Grabs, F. W., 284, 285.
Graceham, Md., 328.
Graeter, 77.
Graff, 77, 82, 91, 92, 93, 99, 100, 115, 117, 128.
Granville, Lord, 2, 4, 6, 12, 13, 92, 153, 156.
Gray, R., 209.
Gray, Wiley, 241.
Grays, Forsyth, 238.
Great Britain, 138, 145, 154, 170.
Great Lakes, 32.

INDEX

Green Co., 202.
Greene, 123, 159, 163, 164, 165, 166, 167, 168.
Greenland, missions, 98, 180, 192.
Greensboro, 168, 243, 259.
Gregor, 75, 91.
Grube, 14, 73, 186.
Grunert, M. E., 260, 329, 330.
Guilford, 105, 141, 168, 170, 242, 285.

Haberland, J., 14, 28.
Hagan, 206.
Hahn, 79.
Halifax, 152, 153.
Hall, 106.
Hall, J. E., 285, 286, 287, 288, 291.
Hall, S. G., 238.
Hall, Wm., 180.
"Hals Krankheit," 180.
Haltem, 34, 62.
Hamilton, 36, 73, 130.
Hampton's store, 88, 89.
Hancock, 131.
Handely, 62.
Harrison, M., 325.
Hartman, 77.
Harvard College, 312.
Hauser, 41, 67.
Hauser, A., 240.
Hawkins, 143, 144, 148, 202.
Haw River, 34.
Heckewelder, 153, 319.
Hege, 67.
Hege, C. A., 276.
Hehl, 53, 55.
Heidelberg, 76.
Heintzman, 166.
Hennersdorf, 312, 313.
Herbst, 93, 322.
Herman, Bishop, 201, 202, 203, 326.
Herrnhut, 216, 312, 314, 327.
Hessians, 130.
Hickory, 5, 7.
Hicks, 201.
Hidden Seed, 311.
Hillsboro, 98, 99, 100, 104, 110, 112, 134, 141, 168, 195.
Hillsboro, Lord, 104.
Himalaya Mountains, 316.
Hine, 79.
Hinshaw, G. W., 265, 266.
Historical Society, 25, 110, 181, 193, 271.
"History of Wachovia," 293, 295.
Holder, 67, 83, 88, 92, 93, 112, 119.

Holder, R., 207.
Holland, 12, 193.
Holstein, 14.
Holyoke, 332.
Home Church, 284.
Home Guard, 242.
Hooper, 149.
Hope, 72, 76, 79, 80.
Hope, N. C., 317, 318, 320.
Hope, N. J., 319.
Horsefield, T., 6.
Hortus medicus (list), 21.
Hortus medicus (map), 22.
Howard, 104.
Hughes, 38, 46, 62, 63, 105.
Hunter, 106, 107, 108.
Hunter, J. W., 251.
Hus, 308, 310.
Husbands, H., 96, 97, 106, 108, 100, 111.
Hussite War, 309.
Hutberg, 69.
Hutton, 12, 156, 157, 158.

Independence, War of, 72.
Indian Territory, 202, 320.
Indian War, 2, 40, 44, 53, 58, 69, 72, 76, 79.
Ingebretsen, E., 14, 69, 71.
Irish, 10.

Jackson, 182.
Jacobson, J. C., 322, 323, 333.
Jamaica, 331.
James River, 15.
James, S. C., 238.
Jarvis, 105, 108.
Jefferson, 194.
Jerusalem, 316.
Jesuits, 311.
Johanna Creek, 82.
John Samuel, 90.
Jones, S., 113.

Kalberlahn, 14, 28, 29, 60, 69, 71.
Kapp, 67.
Keehln, F. E., 238.
Keehln, T. F., 218.
Kernersville, 203, 285.
King's highway, 60.
King's Mountain, 163.
Kinney-Bradshaw, 286.
Kirkland, 195.
Klan, J., 117.

360 INDEX

Klein, 83.
Kluge, 158.
Knoxboro, 172.
Knoxville, 179.
Koehler, 177, 178, 181, 182, 184, 321.
Koenigsderfer, 14, 28.
Koenigstein, 87.
Kralitz Bible, 310.
Kramsch, Samuel, 189, 193, 195, 317, 318, 319.
Kramsch, S. & E., 207.
Krause, Anna J., 61.
Krause, S., 324.
Kremer, 67.
Kremer, Mrs. E., 254.
Kremser, 182.
Kroehn, 79.
Kuenzel, 79.

Labrador, 192, 316.
Lancaster, Pa., 74, 328.
Land Office, 5, 24.
Langgaard, 318.
Lanier, 106, 108, 123, 129, 134, 149.
Lanius. 79.
Lash, A., 240.
Lash, Anna, 71.
Laugenour, 86.
Laurens, 131, 178, 179.
Leather Stocking Tales, 49.
Lebanon, Pa., 324.
Lech, 85, 86.
Lee, General, 251, 252.
Lehman, E., viii, 317.
Leibert, E., 332.
Leinbach, R. P., 260.
Lentzner, 71.
Leslie, 49.
Levering, Bishop, 333.
Lewis, 179.
Lewis, N., 240.
Lexington, 15.
Lincoln, 256.
Lindsay House, 4.
Lindsey, 141.
Lineback, B., 201.
Lineback, J. A., 90.
Lineback, J. T., viii, 281, 282.
Lisher, J., 14, 28.
Lissa Folios, 309.
List, settlers and visitors 1753-62, 136 names, 56.
Lititz, in Europe, 308.
Lititz, Pa., 2, 91, 181, 324.

Little Carpenter, 51, 74.
Loesch Creek, 7.
Loesch (Lash), H., 6, 14, 15, 48, 61.
Loesch (Lash), J., 14, 15, 28, 37, 38, 52, 61, 62, 63, 65, 66, 67, 68, 83, 86, 99, 102, 112.
London, 4, 12, 156, 158.
Long Cane Creek, 178.
Lorez, 91.
Lung, J., 14.
Lusatia, Upper, 312.
Luther, 302.
Lutheran Church, 1, 78, 301, 311, 313, 314, 317.

Macedonia, 199, 286.
Mahoni, 36, 48.
Main Hall, 226, 228, 231, 238, 250, 294, 328, 330, 335.
Maine, 78.
Makefy, 50.
Manassas, 239.
Maps, 11, 19, 22, 39, 94.
Marshall, 75, 81, 85, 86, 87, 90, 92, 98, 110, 111, 112, 113, 115, 116, 117, 156, 157, 158, 172, 178, 182, 183, 184, 186.
Martin, 72, 120, 143, 144, 147, 155, 158, 159, 183, 185.
Maryland, 15, 80, 137, 140.
Massachusetts, 312.
Mayo River, 15.
Mayodan, 15, 17, 275, 285.
McBride, 211, 213.
McCuiston, 207, 284, 286.
McCullah's Farm, 202.
McGruder, J. O., 266.
McKellock, 99.
Mecklenburg, 125, 167.
Medical Garden, 22.
Meinung, 272.
Meinung, S., 195.
Merk, J., 6, 7.
Merkfield, 7.
Merkley, C., 14.
Merrill, 111.
Metcalf, 151.
Meteor, 82.
Methodist, 55, 238, 287.
Meyer, 93, 108.
Micklejohn, 99.
Mickey, S., 218.
Miksch, 93.
Miller, 6, 7, 79, 111, 112, 172, 173.
Miller, Capt., 239.

INDEX

Ministers of the Congregation in Wachovia, 337, 338, 339, 340, 341.
Missions in Greenland, 100.
Mississippi River, 202.
Missouri, 202, 203.
Mizpah, 283.
Mock, 200.
Monk's Corner, 178.
Montfort, 7.
Moore, 97.
Moore's Creek, 126.
Mooresville, 275.
Moravia, 3, 136, 191, 192, 302, 309, 310, 311, 312, 313, 314, 316.
Moravia (cong.), 285.
Moravian, 1, 2, 3, 4, 12, 17, 27, 29, 36, 37, 55, 59, 64, 73, 74, 75, 76, 77, 79, 87, 100, 104, 105, 108, 110, 111, 121, 122, 123, 125, 129, 130, 133, 134, 135, 136, 140, 141, 142, 143, 144, 145, 146, 149, 150, 151, 152, 153, 154, 155, 156, 159, 160, 162, 167, 170, 172, 177, 178, 192, 193, 200, 204, 207, 208, 209, 216, 217, 235, 245, 246, 260, 261, 277, 281, 293, 296, 297, 301, 302, 303, 304, 308, 313, 314, 315, 316.
Moravian Campe, 116.
Moravian College, Beth., 334.
Moravian Falls, 5.
"Moravians in North Carolina," viii, 76.
Morgan, 164.
Morganton, 5, 7.
Mt. Airy, 206.
Mt. Bethel, 206, 207, 285.
Muddy Creek, 6, 9, 25, 28, 80, 211.
Mueller, 77.
Mulberry Fields, 82.
Murchison, D., 238.
Muscongus River, 78.
Mushback, 112.
Muskingum, 319.

Nagel, 71.
Napoleonic power, 177.
Nash, A., 144, 154.
Nazareth Hall, 318, 323, 324, 326, 327, 329, 331.
Nazareth, Pa., 2, 319, 321, 330.
Neissers, 313.
Neuwied, 177.
Newbern, 61, 62, 63, 81, 95, 98, 109, 154.
New England, 3, 47, 332.
New Hope, 7.
New Jersey, 140.

New Philadelphia, 285, 327.
New River, 33.
New World, 303.
New Year's Day, 58.
New York, 10, 14, 32, 74, 120, 137, 158, 177, 324.
Nicholas of Prague, 309.
Nickolites, 143.
Niesky, 323, 330.
Ninety-six, 178.
Nissen, 79.
Nissen works, 276.
Nitchmann, D., 314.
Nitschman, 55.
Norfleet, A., 195.
North, 220, 235, 236, 241, 331.
North America, 127, 134.
North American Indians, 316.
North Carolina, 1, 2, 3, 4, 5, 6, 8, 9, 10, 13, 15, 16, 17, 18, 23, 24, 26, 31, 32, 35, 43, 45, 47, 52, 53, 54, 74, 75, 78, 95, 98, 115, 119, 120, 121, 125, 132, 133, 135, 136, 137, 138, 139, 140, 145, 147, 151, 152, 157, 161, 167, 168, 173, 178, 194, 201, 205, 206, 211, 220, 236, 257, 304, 317, 318.
Northern Province, 203, 260.
Norway, 14.
N. W. N. C. Railway, 274.
N. & W. Railway, 274, 275, 285.

Oak Grove, 282, 285.
Oak Ridge, 285.
Ohio, 43, 55, 211, 318, 332.
Old Town, 283.
Old World, 303.
Oli, 7.
Olivet, 283.
Oo-yu-ge-lo-gee, 200, 202.
Opiz, A. M., 61, 67.
Orange Co., 96, 108, 157.
Organ, 58.
Owens, 9, 34, 37.

Pacific Ocean, 4.
Padget, 80.
Page, W. H., viii.
Palatinate, 78.
Palestine, 333.
Palmer, Gen., 250, 251.
Paper Mill, 85.
Park Hall, 335.
Paris, 170, 178.

INDEX

Parsons, 143, 144, 148.
Parsons, M., 322.
Patterson, 142.
Paxton, 74.
Peace Jubilee, 160, 170, 171.
Penn, Gov., 73.
Pennsylvania, 1, 2, 6, 7, 10, 13, 14, 18, 28, 32, 36, 43, 53, 73, 76, 83, 86, 91, 130, 136, 137, 140, 193, 218, 268, 288.
Perth Amboy, 74.
Petersbach, 85.
Petersburg, 240, 242, 244.
Peters Creek, 85.
Peterson, H., 14, 29, 40, 66, 68, 88.
Peterson, 201.
Peterson, S., 207.
Pettycord, 80.
Pfeil, J., 14.
Pfohl, C. B., viii, 245.
Pfohl, C. T., 288.
Pfohl, J. K., 286, 287, 288.
Pfohl, S. T., 281, 330.
Pfohl, W. J., 238, 241.
Pfohl, W. S., viii, 267.
Philadelphia, N.C., 199.
Philadelphia, Pa., 6, 55, 74, 122, 125, 131, 177, 218, 318, 333.
Philips, M., 195.
Pickens, 162, 163, 167.
Pilgrim, 47.
Pilot Mountain, 15.
Pine Tree store, 103, 112.
Pleasant Fork, 278.
Poland, 192, 310, 311, 312.
Potomac River, 15.
Port Washington, O., 334.
Postal Tel. Co., 276.
Pough, 111.
Powell, J., 80.
Praezel, 88, 153, 178.
Praezel, J. E., 195.
Prague, 308, 310.
Prerau, 312.
Presbyterian, 104.
Priest, Wm., 51.
Principals of S. F. A., 346.
Professors of Music, etc., S. F. A., 346.
Proprietors, 4.
Proske, 200.
Protestant, 78, 301, 313.
Provincial Elders' Conference, 336.
Providence, 282, 285.
Province Island, 74.
Prussia, 310, 317.

Quakers, 97, 121.

Raleigh, 97.
Ranke, 67.
Rasp, 88.
Rauch, 40, 61, 62, 63.
Reading, 74.
Reedy Branch, 178.
Reedy Creek, 112.
Reformation, German, 308.
Reformed Church, 301, 303, 311.
Regulators, 72, 81, 96, 97, 103, 104, 105, 106, 107, 108, 109, 110, 112, 113, 118, 120, 125.
Reich, F., 240.
Reich, J. A., 238.
Reich, J. H., 238.
Reichel, viii, 76, 87, 95, 151, 179, 194, 195, 196, 197, 200, 279, 319, 321.
Reichel, G. B., 321, 322.
Reichel, J. F., 174.
Reichmont, 7.
Renewed Church, 312, 314.
Reuss, Countess, 313.
Reuter, 66, 88, 93.
Revolution, 26, 60, 72, 73, 91, 93, 95, 120, 121, 123, 161, 164, 165, 172, 176, 182, 211, 236, 249, 256.
Reynolds Spring, 264, 265.
Rhein, 177.
Rice, A., 51.
Richenau, 301.
Richmond, 239, 242.
R. & S. Railway, 275.
Ried, 79.
Rifles, Forsyth, 238.
Rights, A., 238.
Rights, C. L., 203, 206, 260.
Rights, Theo., 201.
Roanoke River, 15, 16.
Robinson, 49.
Rogers, 63, 79.
Rogers, Mrs., 68, 69, 70, 71.
Rome, 308, 309.
Rominger, 79.
Romish Church, 301.
Rondthaler, Bishop, viii, 87, 261, 284, 286, 287, 288, 291, 301, 332, 333.
Rondthaler, E., Sr., 333.
Rondthaler, H. E., 284, 285, 291.
Rondthaler, Mrs. E., 323, 333.
Roth, 73.
Rothe, 313.
Rough and Ready, engine, 271.

INDEX 363

Rowan, 141, 157.
Rudolf II, 310.
Ruede, 206.
Russian, 177.
Rutherford, 119, 123, 144, 145, 146, 147.

St. Thomas, 314.
Salem, 13, 49, 72, 73, 76, 78, 84, 85, 86, 87, 88, 90, 91, 92, 93, 94, 95, 100, 108, 112, 113, 119, 120, 123, 127, 128, 129, 132, 134, 135, 145, 151, 156, 158, 159, 163, 166, 167, 168, 170, 171, 172, 173, 174, 177, 180, 181, 182, 186, 187, 194, 195, 198, 200, 202, 203, 204, 205, 206, 207, 209, 211, 217, 218, 219, 220, 222, 224, 231, 235, 237, 238, 239, 241, 242, 245, 246, 249, 254, 255, 257, 259, 261, 262, 264, 265, 266, 272, 275, 278, 279, 281, 282, 284, 285, 286, 292, 295, 318, 319, 321, 322, 324, 325, 326, 327, 328, 329, 330, 333.
Salem Boys' School, 292, 333.
Salem Female Academy, 186, 191, 194, 199, 220, 231, 233, 238, 243, 250, 257, 258, 278, 292, 293, 295, 317, 318, 319, 320, 321, 322, 323, 325, 326, 327, 328, 329, 330, 331, 332, 333, 334, 335.
Salem Fire Department, 266, 267.
Salem Home S.S., 251, 281.
Salem Square, 90.
Salem Water Supply Company, 264, 265.
Salisbury, 38, 46, 61, 62, 102, 104, 108, 126, 129, 156, 182.
Santa Cruz, 142.
Santee River, 179.
Saratoga, N.Y., 332.
Savannah, Ga., 179, 315.
Saxony, 216, 312.
Schaff, 279.
Schleswig, Denmark, 323.
Schmick, 73.
Schmidt, 67, 88, 200.
Schnall, L., 323.
Schneider, 79, 179.
Schnepf, 92.
Schoeneck, Pa., 288.
Schoenthal, 7.
Schropp, 83.
Scotland Neck, 195.
Sehner, C., 320.
Seidel, Mrs., 69, 71.
Seidel, N., 14, 28, 65, 66, 68, 69, 71.
Seiz, 79.
Sennet, 6.

Serepta, 177.
Shaffner, H. F., 265.
Shaffner, J. F., viii, 88, 211, 238, 245, 264, 265.
Shaffner, L. C., viii, 346.
Shaffner's house, 272.
Sharon, O., 325.
Shaub, 71.
Shaub, L., 254.
Sheets, 286.
Shenandoah, 15.
Shepherd, 147.
Sheppard, J., 240.
Shober, 182.
Shober, P. & H., 195, 207, 279.
Shore, 68.
Shore, Henry, 239.
Shultz, C. A., 238.
Shultz, H. A., 281, 327.
Shultz, J. E., 238.
Shultz, P. T., 238.
Shuman, 202.
Siewers, Charles S., 276.
Siewers, J., 204, 205, 206.
Siewers' shop, 272.
Silesia, 317.
Silkhope, 172.
Skiern, Jutland, 323.
Smith, A., 71.
Smith College, 333.
Smith, D. Z., 200.
Smythe, M., 330.
Society Hall, 335.
Soelle, 75, 78, 80, 204.
South, 220, 233, 235, 236, 241, 256, 260, 317, 322, 331, 333, 334.
South Africa, 192, 316.
South America, 316.
South Carolina, 10, 51, 60, 161, 162, 164, 178, 179, 190, 220, 236.
Southern Province, 175, 178, 260, 333.
Southern Railway, 274, 275.
Southern States, 183, 191.
South Fork, 113.
South Hall, 197, 258, 322, 330, 332, 335.
South Sea, 4.
Southside factories, 276.
South Side S.S., 281, 284.
Spach, Adam, 28, 76, 77.
Spach's works, 276.
Spangenberg, 4, 6, 9, 12, 28, 53, 55, 65, 67, 68, 70, 87, 178, 304.
Spangenberg papers, 5, 10.
Spaniards, 136.

Spanish War, 236.
Spaugh, W., 201.
Spaugh, W. E., 284, 285.
Spring Place, 202, 320.
Spring Place, new, 202.
Stach, 180.
Stafford, 86.
Staiert, A., 195.
States represented in Academy, 353.
Stauber, 61, 77.
Staunton, 15.
Steiner, 67, 88, 93, 179, 200, 319, 320.
Steiner, M. & S., 195, 207.
Steward, 159.
Stewart, L., 254.
Stockberger, 93.
Stokes County, 209, 278, 281, 282.
Stoneman, Gen., 328.
Storehouse, 52.
Strasburg, 302.
Strickland, E. F., 288.
Strudwick, 141, 146.
Strudwick, E., 195.
Strupe, 68.
Strupe, 286.
Sunday-school statistics, etc., 343.
Surry Co., 108, 128, 149, 150, 156, 157.
Susquehanna, 15.
Sussdorff, G., 238.
Swiss, 82.
Switzerland, 193.

Taborites, 308, 309.
Tarboro, 195.
Tarleton, 164.
Tayhill, chief, 179.
Taylor, 159.
Teachers, S. F. A., 347, 348, 349, 350, 351, 352, 353.
Tellico Blockhouse, 179.
Tennessee, 201, 202, 220, 250.
Tennessee River, 179.
Thaeler, A., 291.
Theological Seminary, 326, 327, 328, 330, 331, 333.
Thomas, 49.
Ticonderoga, N.Y., 332.
Tiersch, 91, 92, 172, 319.
Time of sorrow, 53.
Tondern, 323.
Tories, 125, 126, 129, 130, 162, 166, 167, 168.
Town Fork, 49.
Trombones, 82.

Tryon, 72, 73, 75, 87, 95, 96, 97, 98, 102, 103, 104, 105, 109, 110, 111, 112, 113, 115, 116, 118, 119, 120, 123, 142, 162.
Tryon, Mrs., 99, 100, 101.
Tschirschky, M. L., 327.
Turner, 213.
Tuscarawas River, 55.
Twin City, 266, 274, 276, 281.

Union Army, 250.
Union Cross, 285.
Union Theological Seminary, N.Y., 334.
Unitas Fratrum, 1, 139, 145, 152, 156, 301, 302, 308, 309, 310, 311, 312, 314, 315, 316.
United Brethren, 110, 116, 117, 144, 145, 184, 185, 194, 205, 313.
United States, 138, 139, 147, 148, 160, 170, 176, 183, 184, 191, 194, 214, 220.
Unity, 5, 91, 136, 173, 198, 216, 217, 257, 284, 309, 310, 311, 315, 316.
University of N.C., 333.
Urichsville, O., 334.
Utley, 75, 77, 80, 91, 92, 93, 113, 115, 116, 172, 204.

Van, J. & M., 201.
Van Laer, 12.
Van Vleck, 87, 158, 206, 324.
Van Vleck, H. J., 333.
Vance, Gov., 253, 294.
Vance, J. A., 276.
Vierling, F. H., 322.
Vigilant, engine, 271.
Virginia, 13, 17, 33, 52, 132, 159, 162, 169, 205, 206, 207, 213, 220, 237, 239, 250, 285.
Vogler, C., 79.
Vogler, J., 206, 281.
Vogler, J. R., 238.
Vogler, L., 254.
Vogler, Miles, 200.
Vogler, W. T., 288.
Volts, 77.
Von der Merk, 119.

Wach, 85, 86.
Wachau, 7, 9.
Wachovia, 1, 2, 3, 5, 7, 9, 10, 11, 13, 14, 15, 18, 20, 24, 26, 27, 28, 29, 32, 34, 35, 40, 42, 44, 45, 47, 52, 53, 54, 55, 61, 63, 64, 65, 72, 73, 76, 78, 79, 80, 83, 84, 85, 87, 90, 91, 95, 97, 98, 100, 102, 103,

INDEX

104, 108, 110, 112, 115, 116, 117, 119, 121, 122, 126, 128, 129, 130, 131, 133, 134, 135, 137, 138, 141, 143, 145, 151, 152, 154, 156, 157, 158, 159, 160, 161, 162, 163, 164, 165, 166, 167, 169, 170, 172, 173, 174, 176, 177, 178, 182, 185, 186, 187, 189, 190, 198, 199, 200, 203, 204, 209, 216, 218, 235, 236, 249, 256, 257, 260, 277, 283, 288, 296, 297, 304, 327.
Wachovia Arbour, 282, 284.
Wachovia Moravian, 90, 180, 181, 290, 291, 292.
Waddell, 97, 108, 112, 118, 123.
Wagner, 172.
Wagner, 26, 53, 60, 82.
Waldensians, 309.
Waldo, G., 78.
Waldoboro, 78.
Walk, 77.
Walker, 119.
Wallon, 128.
Walnut Cove, 15, 49.
Ward, 201, 202.
Ward's Gap, 206.
Warner, 200.
Washington, 32, 123, 130, 131, 140, 182, 183, 185.
Washington City, 200.
Washington, W., 164.
Webster, 169.
Weidell, 62.
Welfare, 200.
Wellesley, 332.
Wesley, John, 55.
West, 220, 241, 334.
West Indies, 177, 314, 316.
Wharton, 238.
Whigs, 168.
Whiteaker, 143, 144.

White House, 222.
White, W. H., 245.
Whittington, B., 287.
Wiley, 97.
Wilkes, 167, 169.
Wilkesboro, 5, 274, 275.
Williams, 123, 148.
Willow Hill, 207, 285.
Wilmington, 28, 78, 82, 169.
Wilson, T. J., 209.
Winston, 84, 209, 211, 213, 214, 219, 237, 245, 246, 259, 264, 266, 272, 275, 277, 284, 318.
Winston Fire Department, 272.
Winston, Maj., 211.
Winston-Salem, 207, 214, 245, 259, 275, 276, 281, 293.
Winston Water Supply Co., 265.
Wohlfert, 200.
Wolf, Great, 75.
Wood, 287.
Woodman, 50.
Woodstock, 204.
Wright, G., 108, 109, 110.
Wurreschke, Mrs., viii.
Würtemberg, 78.
W. U. Tel. Co., 276.
Wutke, 63, 71.

Yadkin River, 48, 112, 276, 286.
Yadkin Valley, 9, 28, 34, 86, 113.
York, 76.

Zeisberger, 53, 55, 73, 303.
Zeist, 177.
Zevely, Van, 205, 206.
Zigler, 88.
Zinzendorf, 3, 9, 86, 87, 101, 302, 303, 312, 313, 314, 315, 325, 326.
Zorn, J. T., 331, 332.

www.ingramcontent.com/pod-product-compliance
Lightning Source LLC
Chambersburg PA
CBHW050833230426
43667CB00012B/1978